What You See is Not What You Get

What You See is Not What You Get

Developing Financial Skills

A. John Thomas

Viva Books

New Delhi | Mumbai | Chennai | Kolkata | Bengaluru | Hyderabad | Kochi | Guwahati

Publisher's note

Every possible effort has been made to ensure that the information contained in this book is accurate at the time of going to press, and the publisher and author cannot accept responsibility for any errors or omissions, however caused. No responsibility for loss or damage occasioned to any person acting, or refraining from action, as a result of the material in this publication can be accepted by the editor, the publisher or the author.

Every effort has been made to trace the owners of copyright material used in this book. The author and the publisher will be grateful for any omission brought to their notice for acknowledgment in the future editions of the book.

First Published 2014

Viva Books Private Limited

- 4737/23, Ansari Road, Daryaganj, New Delhi 110 002
  Tel. 42242200, 23258325, 23283121, Email: vivadelhi@vivagroupindia.net
- 76, Service Industries, Shirvane, Sector 1, Nerul, Navi Mumbai 400 706
  Tel. 27721273, 27721274, Email: vivamumbai@vivagroupindia.net
- Megh Tower, Old No. 307, New No. 165, Poonamallee High Road, Maduravoyal, Chennai 600 095
  Tel. 044-23780991, 23780992, Email: vivachennai@vivagroupindia.net
- B-103, Jindal Towers, 21/1A/3 Darga Road, Kolkata 700 017
  Tel. 22816713, Email: vivakolkata@vivagroupindia.net
- 7, GF, Sovereign Park Aptts., 56-58, K. R. Road, Basavanagudi, Bengaluru 560 004
  Tel. 26607409, Email: vivabangalore@vivagroupindia.net
- 101-102, Moghal Marc Apartments, 3-4-637 to 641, Narayanguda, Hyderabad 500 029
  Tel. 27564481, Email: vivahyderabad@vivagroupindia.net
- First Floor, Beevi Towers, SRM Road, Kaloor, Kochi 682 018
  Tel. 0484-2403055, 2403056, Email: vivakochi@vivagroupindia.net
- 232, GNB Road, Beside UCO Bank, Silpukhuri, Guwahati 781 003
  Tel. 0361-2666386, Email: vivaguwahati@vivagroupindia.net

www.vivagroupindia.com

ISBN: 978-81-309-2432-8

Published by Vinod Vasishtha for Viva Books Private Limited, 4737/23, Ansari Road, Daryaganj, New Delhi 110 002.

Printed and bound by Raj Press, R-3, Inderpuri, New Delhi 110 012.

SUB-0026/SSUB-0033

Contents

Part Three : Financial Skills at Work

Preface

All champions are excellent sports persons. But all sports persons are not champions in every sport. A rock-climber needs to develop special skills to excel in the difficult art of rock-climbing. He would not perhaps be able to utilize the same skills and expertise if he wants to be a champion cricketer. The two sporting activities are quite different. The same analogy could hold good when it relates to management expertise in a particular profession. Every Industry has its own peculiar idioms and nuances of operations. While Finance management has its own well established traditions and practice, adapting it to various Industry-needs calls for specialized skills. Key monitoring parameters used in manufacturing or mining sectors cannot be straightaway applied to Telecommunications. No one ventures to play a game before learning the basic rules.

We have worked with thousands of executives, top-and-middle management level teaching them the basic rules of the game and the financial side of business. We have realized over the years that the level of financial intelligence, within the organizations among executives of all hues needs improvement. The greater the understanding of the financial issues, the more it helps people to get involved. They begin to understand what part of the organization they belong to and how they fit in with the overall company objectives, and how they can contribute to the results. It is not only the non-financial managers like engineers, HR professionals, legal and so on, but managers of every stripe can appreciate the specific 'location' they find themselves within the organization and how they relate to a particular 'line-item' in one of the financial statements that the company produces annually.

What are Financial Skills?

It isn't some innate ability that you are born with. It is no more than a set of skills that can be learned and used. Accountants use specialized language that sounds like 'Martian' to the non-accountants. They are into 'accounting' which is a highly technical way of producing the numbers that go into financial statements. We are not talking about that here. You need not be accountants to be financially savvy. But you will need to understand their tricks only so much as to know what the numbers really mean and how they hang together. Most senior executives are expected to pick up these skills as they go up the ladder. Because it is tough to manage a business without it and if you try you are sure to make some drastically wrong decisions.

Financial intelligence boils down to at least four distinct skills. When you finish reading this book you should be competent in all of them.

They are:

1. **Understanding the Accounting Process**: You will need to know how accounting is in fact, for the most part, a set of estimates, assumptions and opinions rather than hardcore mechanical recording of numbers. You must appreciate that it is an art as much as a science. Applying assumptions differently in different situations leads to a different set of numbers in the three statements mentioned above.
2. **Developing the Basic Skills**: How to read and understand a full set of financial statements, The balance sheet, the

profit and loss account and the cash flow statement. You need to understand the basics of financial measurement and presentation. You need to know what the numbers in each of these statements really say about the financial situation of the organization it pertains to. You need to know the difference between profit and cash. You need to know why the balance sheet balances.

3. **Applying the Skills**: When you have acquired the foundational skills and the ability to appreciate the numbers that appear in the reports, you can utilize these skills to analyze any company's statements in depth. Financially savvy executives play around with return on investment analysis, profitability ratios and credit-worthiness of the business. You can spot disaster before it strikes and identify growth stalls and liquidity problems of your own company.
4. **Connecting the 'Inside' with the 'Outside'**: The first three skills teach you how to look inside the contours of your own company. But that is not enough. The financial results of a company are just that. It can be understood only by understanding the External context in which your company is operating. That is the 'Big Picture'. The top executive's primary job is to connect the internal processes of the company with its external context. True Financial intelligence demands a clear understanding of the regulatory, economic, and competitive outside environment, to cater to the changing customer expectations and technological paradigm shifts that affect the number results of your company to manage it for long term growth and sustainability.

How to Read this Book

This book is organized into four parts. One for each skill set. If you are confident in the foundation-skills, you can start with the part that interests you most. However, since the flow of the topic starts with the foundation chapters progressively advancing to the top-level skills, it is recommended that you begin at the beginning. At the end of each part we have a set of concepts-based problems entitles 'Find the Needle in the Haystack'. These are designed to challenge your understanding of the concepts. They also demonstrate that theoretical concepts sometimes do not fully explain the real world entirely. You can attempt to discover the answers to some of these issues on your own. Each chapter ends with a brief summary preceded by 'quipping' heads. Ignore them!

Any new concept is defined immediately within the same page you encounter it, in a little box of its own. Don't worry if you miss something. A complete list of definitions is provided at the end of the book.

You can't learn swimming by subscribing to a website, online. The consequences may turn out to be quite a tiny disaster. I have provided exercise worksheets in the Appendix. These may be already familiar to you. Nevertheless, you need to try them out. Don't worry about getting the wrong answers, because they are already provided. Keep in mind that financial skill doesn't end with this book. This could be a first step in an interesting, exciting journey where you gain both professionally and personally. I think it will open up a whole new aspect of the concepts and curiosities you are already concerned with.

This book is completely free of jargons.

I promise not to use the words 'debit' and 'credit'.

Introduction

This book is not another 'teach-yourself-accounting' book. Nor does it not presuppose any accounting knowledge. It is not an elementary textbook for would-be accountants either. This book does not contain any accounting jargon like 'debit', 'credit', 'Ledger', 'Trial Balance' and so on. Then why is it worth reading? This book is about 'Financial Skills', or the skills needed to make the financial numbers talk to you. Or more precisely about the basic skills that can be employed to search for the 'real stuff' behind the mass of financial data that hits you every day in the form of company reports, newspaper comments, magazine articles about business organizations, and so on. It is meant for every one with a curiosity about finance and its exotic world to simplify, elaborate and what appears to be inscrutable. These skills in an executive or employee help to make a meaningful contribution to the organization he or she is working for.

Why You Need Financial Skills

This basic skill-set is the Financial Intelligence that managers everywhere use to measure, assess and gauge the performance level of the business they are managing. Business management is ultimately a game of numbers. The really good players understand what the numbers mean. If you want to be a strategic player who can impact the course of your organization, you must first learn to crack the code that produces these numbers on which so many day to day decisions are made. Some executives think that they have reached this far without it and they are no worse for it. But think again. If your well thought out brilliant idea gets rejected at the approval stage, because the 'finance people' won't have it, you probably missed to connect with the criteria used for evaluation of projects used in your company. You will be puzzled if your company just declared a dividend but did not have the cash to pay out and had to borrow the money to pay that dividend. You might even be shocked if your CFO friend insisted that 'loss' is an *asset and not a liability*.

How It Benefits You

Here is a probable list of benefits you will gain if you have the basic financial skills.

1. Three financial statements (balance sheet, profit and loss account and the cash flow statement) are like a map of your company's financial layout. Tourist maps generally have a red balloon 'YOU ARE HERE'. In this case, can you find out where you fit in? In the organizational chart you may be a Divisional Maintenance Engineer. Your actions impact a line 'Selling, General and Administrative Expenses (SG&A)' in the profit and loss account. The higher you move up in the organization, the more number of lines your actions will impact. Every move you make on a day-to-day basis affects the resultant number in all these statements. You will learn that they are in fact so interconnected, that any change in one affects one or both of the others.
2. You can move from a status-quo manager to a strategic manager. Without an appreciation of where you fit in, you

will merely try to maintain the status-quo. This is true in a large organization with many levels of reporting. But the moment you have a clear idea about the impact of your decisions on the financial results of your company, you will try to strategically manage your resources to align your goals with company objectives.

3. You can critically evaluate your own company and its actions weighing them against the ground realities. I am not arguing that after reading this book you will be able to spot financial frauds in the making. But you will certainly be able to watch trends in growth and creeping costs of operations. You will be better placed to understand the stories, reports and comments in the financial papers about your company or other businesses and how far they merit credibility. Even if you don't know all the answers, you will certainly have many questions to ask.

4. No matter what your position is in a business organization, you are a businessman. If you are a telecommunications executive, you must know how your company makes money. What is your company's business model? What is your company's strategy? What is the nature of the products your company is trying to sell? How much margin does it make on each sale? How does your competitor do the same business? What does your company do with the money it makes? Is it investing in the right equipments for future growth or is it just putting all that extra cash in the bank?

   A look at the balance sheets of Bharat Sanchar Nigam Limited (BSNL) will reveal that it was accumulating cash at the rate of about ₹10,000 crs every year from 2005 to 2008. It did not invest this money in building mobile networks, while there was a huge demand for mobile connections in India during 2005-07. Since the money was not used for investing, after merely three years, BSNL were facing liquidity problems. Strange, and yet true. How can you be effective unless you behave like a businessman with basic necessary financial skills? If your current employer is to succeed, you need to.

Cash

Many executives and top-managers sometimes get confused between 'cash' and 'profits'. When we talk about cash, as it appears in the balance sheet, we are talking about the real stuff. It is hard currency in the Bank. 'Profit'/'Loss' is simply a figure that balances revenues and expenses. You will understand this in Part 1 and 2.

5. Ability to spot the biases built into the accounting numbers. In part 1 of this book we will discuss the problem of biases in detail. For the present, it may surprise you that accounting results and reports are a matter of opinion of the accountant. You will understand why this is so and that they try their best to be objective. For example, your company owns land for its operations. In the balance sheet these properties will be shown at the value they had when it was actually acquired. The 'value' shown in the balance sheet will be the same even after twenty years of its purchase, even though it may be worth several times that price. Accountants know that if they show the *market price every year*, it is likely to cause more confusion. So as a matter of convention they use the acquisition price (except when the company actually sells the land or the company itself is sold to another).
6. Another example is Depreciation. You will learn about this important concept in the part where we explain the accounting process. Let me gently caution you, that till you have acquired a fair amount of Financial Intelligence, all that appears in the accounting statements, is not what that really looks like.

Depreciation

It is a method used by accountants to match revenues of a period with its costs. Since the capital assets and other machinery used for producing the goods and services can be used for more than one year (*a typical accounting period*) only a part of the cost of equipments used during the year is considered as cost of production for that year. That portion of the cost of the equipment is called depreciation.

7. The willingness to analyze and examine data before making a decision. Although this book mentions the workplace and the skills needed to successfully contribute towards the organization you work for, it can help you in your personal life as well. Consider your decision to invest in shares or bonds of a company. You can get fooled by the broker recommendations or by tips from some glossy business magazine or even by the mere hype surrounding an issue of shares. Let us look at the 'Face book Issue' itself. Let us ask the basic questions we asked before. What is its business model? What does it sell? How does it sell it and what is the strategy used? What is its net worth as a business? You will find that the answers are not so difficult if you have the basic financial skills needed to arrive at the key facts. It is amazing how investors fail to ask questions about its revenue projections and are prepared to part with cash without having even a preliminary understanding of these basic metrics. At the time of writing Face Book share is quoting 16% below issue price.

How It Benefits Your Company

Finance is like the proverbial invisible chord that binds the business together in quest for results. We know that, what really matters in your organization are not the processes you have or your products, but the people working in it. Their actions and reactions to situations and people within the organization and outside it actually impact the numbers that appear in the annual reports of companies. The strength of the organization depends on the ability of the workplace culture to align the varied actions of its employees towards a common goal. Financial intelligence motivates the executives to try out different methods of improving the processes they control. Awareness of the financial aspect of day-to-day transactions makes them look at the bigger picture. These combined impacts actually show up in various ways. Here is a small list.

1. Better Decisions. Decision makers often incorporate what they understand about the competition, consumer behavior and technological aspects of the product into their routine decisions. But ignoring the financial aspects cannot only be downright foolish but sometimes disastrous. It may look innocuous if some executives ignore financial prudence in a very large organization, but the cumulative effect of such ignorance could be substantial. Making decisions solely based on numbers is neither desirable nor wise as you will understand later in this book, but financial intelligence makes the actors smarter and more informed in their choices.
2. Goals Alignment. Employees in a company like tiny iron filings fall in all directions, loosely directing their efforts as considered suitable. But financial intelligence acts like a magnet that makes all these individual filings face in the same direction. Everyone looks towards profitability and cash flow, thereby trying to fit in and contribute.

....he has now become incomprehensible.. there was confusion enough when he was quite healthy.. you see, he is an author...

The Obstacles

The description given above looks great, on paper. However, our experience in teaching the topic of financial skills to executives in other streams have shown two types of road-blocks towards the path of the salvation. Firstly, there are personal attitudes and concerns. Secondly, there are organizational issues.

First are the organizational issues. Your company's accountants may keep a tight leash on the way they go about producing these numbers. They may expect to control and instruct, but not disclose their intentions. But you still can get the information if you understand their methods in general. Accountants need your inputs to arrive at their conclusion about what numbers are to be shown where and how much. For instance, they need the date of purchase of your equipments and their purchase price to arrive at the amount of depreciation to be shown as expenses for the current period. They want to know whether you have paid full or in instalments, and for how long that will continue. If you cannot appreciate this, you might imagine that they are poking their noses into what is rightfully your territory. Again if they ask, how much of the stock already issued to you, is still left over, they need it to calculate the average cost of inventory at the period closing. Failure to understand this might lead you to think that they are questioning your efficiency in project implementation. Such organizational knowledge gap is neither desirable, nor does it lead to healthy workplace relationships. If such a situation persists within your organization, you can help. A clear understanding of the accounting process will empower you, and won't let the accountants get the better of you.

Secondly, non-accountants have always viewed accounting as something exotic. Jargons fly about in the accountant's language repertoire like fruit-flies around jack-fruits. They will explain away 'impossible' as though they care less. For example, they insist that loss is an asset to the company! (*By the way, it is true*). Well, welcome to the party. The other misconception is that accounting involves a lot of Math. This is certainly not true. I wish to repeat here that to be financially intelligent you don't need to become accountants at all. You just need to understand the process, especially the assumptions, estimations and allocations that cause biases in the numbers produced by them.

You might think that you don't have the time! This is merely an excuse. The chapters in this book are on purpose very short. It takes just a reading of these four sections, and you will be much more knowledgeable about finance. The numbers and financial statements won't scare you. As your career advances, you have to learn finance, eventually. Ignoring this fact is like avoiding a visit to the dentist, because of the imagined pain that his drill might cause you. Over the period of your career as an executive or investor, your tooth-problem only gets worse. It would be far easier to attend to that niggling little tooth straight away.

PART ONE

FOUNDATION SKILLS

1

Understanding the Accounting Process

What is the Purpose of Financial Reporting?

'THE PRIMARY GOAL OF FINANCIAL ACCOUNTING IS THE DISSEMINATION *of financial information that accurately measures the profitability and financial condition of the company*'. That is what any standard textbook on accounting will tell you. But regularly you read in the papers, about the wonderfully innovative ways in which companies try to avoid doing precisely this. They show phantom sales, hide expenses, and sometimes show 'cash in the bank' where none exists. You can read a shockingly revealing tale of this in the 'Satyam Computers Scandal'.[1]

You might think that it is not possible for the management to show anything less than the candid picture. Legal and other regulatory compliances make it extremely hazardous for managers to indulge in this practice. Even if managers fail, highly trained auditors, who are impartial and professional, have to certify the accounts after a thorough scrutiny. These arguments hardly explain, as in other matters, the gap between theory and practice.

Managers and CEOs typically have a short life span at the helm. They need to show performance upfront. Long term company goals and the trust of the investors and outside agencies are important, but may fall outside the planning span of the top-executives. When bonuses and career path are on the line, short term results become priority. There is a great temptation to manipulate results, declare dividends and show growth which may not be based on hard reality on the ground. In other words, the intents of the company and its managers may not be consistent with the goal of financial reporting as stated in standard textbooks. You might now imagine that in a public sector company, where the salaries and perks are fixed, and promotions are based largely on seniority; such manipulation of accounts is not necessary or beneficial to the CEO in anyway. Think again. In MTNL, a public sector company, the CEO tinkered with the depreciation rates, to show profits and to earn a second term in office. In recent months, the new Chairman of the 'The State Bank of India' on assuming charge stated that some of the numbers stated during the previous periods had to be written back as they were not acceptable as consistent with facts. In highly regulated sectors like the telecommunications industry in India, leading operators are alleged to have understated revenues to avoid paying taxes. Yet another problem is that investors are impatient to have their returns in the stock market. They hold the shares for 12-18 months and keenly watch quarterly results of companies. Managements are under pressure to put out attractive numbers, and are not prepared for volatility of their companies valuations.

Right at the outset of this book I have stated a word of caution in your journey towards gaining financial skills. This is because, awareness of this aspect is fundamental to a meaningful evaluation of financial reports. There is an elaborate system of standards and conventions in the accounting profession. Compliance to legal provisions and regulatory guidelines are mandatory in disclosure of the financial position of a company.

Accounting Standards

'Generally Accepted Accounting Principles' (GAAP) in India, called the Indian GAAP refers to the set of standards approved by National Advisory Council on Accounting Standards (NACAS) for recording of transactions in the company's books of accounts. Indian Company's Act 1956 makes it mandatory for all registered companies to comply with GAAP. The Auditor certifies that the accounts as presented to them by the management are GAAP compliant.

Yet, there are perfectly legal methods of injecting a color into these statements that suit the purpose of the management. If nothing else, awareness that the management may have something up its sleeve, encourage you to be skeptical, and trust your commonsense instincts when something in the financial statements does not ring quite so true.

Assumptions and Estimates and Biases

The fact is that accounting is an art as much as it is a science. Every practitioner knows this. But it is not so widely understood by the users of financial statements. They tend to believe that every number that shows up in these reports is based on reality. In fact, it is neither true nor possible. We will explain why.

The accountants have no way of knowing some reality even though they wish for it. For example they have no way of knowing how long a telephone exchange will continue to function properly after installation. It may breakdown due to over usage (*electromechanical exchanges*) or may become useless due to technological obsolescence (*invasion of mobile switching systems*). Since the lifespan is unknown, they won't know how much costs of the original exchange system should be allocated to the current year. Again, in a phone company, there are engineers working in operations and new projects simultaneously. How much of his salary is capital expenditure and how much is for operations? If the accountant allots say 70% to capital, then he can show lower expenses and higher gross profit than if he allots 50% each.

Capital Expenditure and Operating Expenses

Capital Expenditure is the purchase of equipment or assets that last more than a year. Since equipments work only with human supervision, part of the salary of the engineers managing it also constitutes capital expenditure. These items appear on the Balance Sheet. Only a portion of these expenditures (depreciation) appear in the income statement, thus affecting profits. Operating expenses are needed to run the business day-to-day. These items like wages, salaries, appear on the income statement, as deductions from total revenues, fully impacting profits.

Thus accounting is approximation of reality. The assumptions and estimates on which the accountants base their judgment is the key to understanding how close the numbers represent the reality. These judgments actually constitute a bias in the numbers. Bias is not in the racist sense, that all accountants wear colored glasses. Certainly not! *Bias* here means that the numbers are skewed in one direction or other. It is the job of the accountants to do this on a daily basis and that's the way they can finally put the financial statements together. Financial intelligence calls for an appreciation of this fundamental truth. That is why it is possible to pin-point certain extreme biases in the numbers, and financially savvy analysts are able to call the bluff. The line between innovative accounting practices and financial fraud is rather wavy.

What the Numbers Really Mean

Let us make an honest attempt to look at the way some of these numbers finally come to appear on the three financial statements that accountants present.

Judgmental Biases

You would not have thought it possible or necessary for judgments regarding some of the following items. But, I can tell you with confidence that almost all the numbers do have a certain amount of judgment lurking behind them. For example:

1. Revenue

You would perhaps imagine that there is no need to estimate revenue. After all, revenue is what your company gets when a service is *sold* to the customer. But when does a 'sale' take place?

- When the agreement to purchase is signed?
- When the service is actually delivered?
- When the bill is sent to the customer?
- When the customer pays the bill?

Imagine a builder of housing complexes. He signs the agreement for purchase and regularly collects money from you for the house to be delivered two years from now. After you have made the final instalment, he registers the sale-deed, and hands over the key. You are the happy and proud owner of a brand new house. Now, look at it from the builder's point of view. During these two years, he has no revenue whatsoever! You might say that, part of your instalments goes towards his share of the profit. But when does he actually make the sale to you so that he can recognize that portion of the instalment as his revenue?

Too complicated for you to find a satisfactory answer? Yes, the accountant is a lot less smart than you. Imagine his predicament.

You can see the answer to this one in the notes to this chapter at the end of the book.[2]

Such issues crop up in other industries like mining, road construction, turnkey projects as well. Even in the Telecom industry. For example, when a customer buys a pre-paid recharge coupon, he pays the cash immediately. But he will use the charge-value over a period of time. In some cases, usage stretches over several months. How much of the money paid by the subscriber actually becomes the revenue of the Operator? BSNL takes the entire money of the customer as revenue in the first instance. BHARTI and IDEA take only that portion of the money which the customer has actually used up, as revenue.[3]

The Income Statement

Also called the profit and loss account, or, statement of earnings, or consolidated statement of operations. By whatever name, it is still an income statement, *for a period* showing total income, total expenses, and Gross profit. Net profit is what is left over after all other expenses and taxes are deducted.

Some people talk about the **Top-Line** (*Sales/ Revenue*), **Bottom-Line** (*net result of operations*) and **Middle-Line** (*Expenses*). After all we need some journalese in the dry world of accounting too!

The issue gets further complicated in the case of sales of services or products bundled with annual maintenance contract as a package deal. This is a common practice for photocopier machines. How much of the sale-price (inclusive of a twelve month service contract) should be called revenue if a machine is sold in November? The proper thing to logically do is to take the value of service-contract for the remaining five months (*November to March of next year, if the company's accounts are closed in March every year*) only as revenue.

Xerox Corporation sold copiers on four year leases including service maintenance. Xerox executives decided to recognize a percentage of the service contract as revenue. Faced with falling sales and fear of its stock plummeting in the stock market, they started recognizing ever increasing percentages as revenue. Imagine yourself as an executive in the Xerox Corporation. You would have paid incentives to your sales people for good performance, and bonuses to the entire staff, thinking that the company is doing fine. Telecommunications industry has also innovative strategies like bundled handset sales. It is important to know how revenues are recorded in such cases.

If, on the other hand, we wait for the customers to pay the bill, in order to count the revenue and the customer in fact defaults, did not the company actually make a sale? There has been a sale, because *the services were actually delivered*. Therefore accountants always record a 'sale' when the services are delivered, whether cash payment is received or not. Thus we can appreciate that the total sales figure that your company shows as the first line in the income statement, in fact merely represents the amount of cash that is due to be received from the customers. That is one of the reasons why total sales figure does not represent total cash received.

2. Operating Expenses

This is called the 'middle-line'. It consists four major items at least. They are (1) Labor Expenses or Employee Benefits (2) Selling General and Administrative Expenses, (3) Depreciation and Amortization, (4) Interest Expenses. Some companies use more nomenclatures as they may wish to classify expenses in more detail. Telecom operators in India have shown costs specific to the industry like Access Charges, Network Operating Costs, Spectrum Charges, License Fee Costs etc. If you wish to have a complete list of such classifications you may refer to notes to this chapter.[4] By whatever names these are called you must need to appreciate that these are deductions from the top-line or the total income generated during the period of report. What remains is the Gross Profit. It will be immediately clear to you that you can increase the profit by decreasing the costs or by increasing revenues or by a combined action on both these lines.

> **Amortization**
>
> In financial literature you might find the words amortization and depreciation being used interchangeably. This is not correct. Depreciation refers to the expensing of Physical assets like buildings, machinery. Amortization is the expensing of intangible assets like patents and copyright.

A reading of the previous section showed that managers in companies can shore up the top-line by aggressive revenue recognition methods. Perhaps it made you wonder whether they can do the opposite by aggressive refusal to recognize expenses. If you did, you are right, they actually do.

IBM's turnaround story is well told in a famous book, by its then Chairman Louis Gerstner 'Who Says Elephants Can't Dance?'[5] He claimed in 1999 that the 'strong expense management' was the key to recent improvements in the company. The story is so interesting, that it is worth telling in some detail. In the annual report of 1999, in the Management discussion and analysis, one sentence stated that 'Selling General and Administrative Expenses (SG&A)' (*refer to earlier sections: SG&A is a line item in the expense side of the Income Statement*), included benefits associated with the sale of one of the company's divisions. There was no explanation as to how a gain was treated as an expense! Now here is the interesting part of how miracles can be worked with creativity. IBM had a policy of putting all one-time charges and gains into the 'General' portion of SG&A. This practice had great advantages from IBM's point of view. It not only boosts income, but avoids paying tax. Gerstner's claim to have improved performance by strong expense management methods sounded somewhat sour.

Here is another story. This time a company operating in the telecommunications sector classified all its advertising and customer acquisition methods through the direct mail system as capital expenses, since the rules permitted it. It then recognized the depreciation costs associated with such capital expenditure over a period of 12-18 months. It then reported a net profit of $6.2 million instead of a loss of $6 million.

You will go wrong if you jump to the conclusion, that all companies manipulate their expenses and that it is a rather easy thing to do. There are clear rules and standards laid down for recording expenses, as already stated. Consequent on the revelation of the practices by IBM, regulatory authorities have ruled that occasional gains are to be recorded as 'other income' immediately after the line showing income from operations. But as a financially intelligent user of these reports, you must understand that judgments regarding the classification of expenses and income affect the profitability of the company and its share price. You must have a 'nose' for understanding where the numbers are actually 'hard' (i.e. well supported by reasonable assumptions and is uncontroversial), and where they are 'soft' (i.e. relatively dependent on judgmental calls). While reading each line in the income statement, critically ask yourself at least the following questions:

1. What are the assumptions behind this number?
2. Is it an estimate or is it the actual figure?
3. What biases are there in these assumptions and estimates?
4. What and where does it impact in the statements?

You may be surprised to know that the answers to most of these questions are all tucked away in the annual report itself. In the IBM example above, the management had revealed how it treated the occasional gains. Well, not fully but partially, in various parts of the report itself. When you don't find the answers anywhere in the report, it is the time to question the validity of the numbers.

Let us elaborate. Kochi Shipyard is the largest public sector shipbuilding and Ship repairing yard in India. The Ministry of shipping was considering a possible disinvestment of the fully owned company. We refer to the annual report for the period ending March 2009. In its middle line, the company showed nothing unusual. In fact, the net earnings after tax increased a whopping 70% over previous period. The earnings per share rose to a healthy ₹14.13 paisa. You would be fooled into thinking that the Shipping Company was cruising at full steam ahead. The balance sheet of the company had in fact shrunk by half its size and destroying the net worth of the company by nearly 3/4th of what it was. On raising the issue with the CFO, he claimed that there was 'nothing swept under the carpet'. He was speaking the truth. The notes to the accounts stated clearly that hedging operations of the company and loss on derivatives in foreign currency were placed under the shareholder's funds at their fair value. The relevant Accounting standards allowed this treatment.

The fact still remains that even though the company was claiming to have made a net profit and declared a dividend, the owners of the company lost nearly 3/4th of the total value of investments during the year.

3. Capital Expenditure

You already know that classifying expenditure as capital expenses brings in the advantage of reducing operational expenses in the income statement. This is because operating expenses reduce gross profit immediately, but capital expenditure affects gross profit over several accounting periods through the mechanics of depreciation. A forward looking company will always spend its available cash to increase revenues in future. A healthy growth of business is possible only if newer and more efficient productive assets are deployed. This is especially true for companies that operate in highly competitive environment or in markets where disruptive technological shifts can completely destroy existing revenue streams. This has happened to incumbent telecom operators during the tectonic shift of customer preferences from fixed services to wireless services. If you are working in such environments you will be able to see the trend of expenditures within your company as you learn to observe the accounting numbers. You need some understanding of the figures to decipher the total expenditures within you company. This becomes clear in part 3 of this book.

In the present section, we are concerned with the assumptions and biases which are introduced into the accounting for capital expenditure. The policy with regard to recognition of an expenditure as capital is generally stated in the annual reports of companies. BSNL is the largest Telecom operator in India, in terms of the size of its physical network for telecom operations. It has a policy of adding to the cost of its equipment purchases, all other costs associated with readying the equipment for connecting to the network. Expenses like transportation, part of the salary of staff, expenditure connected with obtaining clearances and so on. Replacement of network elements is capitalized only if it adds to revenue generating capabilities. The astute reader would have already identified the judgmental and estimation biases involved. Just to recap: how much salary and benefits of staff should be part of the equipment cost? How do we estimate the additional revenue generating capacity of the replaced equipment? These and other questions are necessarily to be answered before the total expenditure on capital can be assessed. As you can see it is not a perfect world. But we try.

4. Depreciation

As compared to any other item in the income statement, the concept of depreciation and its usage by accountants hold the potential for the highest levels of judgmental issues. This is because of two reasons. Firstly, the initial costs of the equipments that a business acquires, needs to be spread over the entire life of such assets. Secondly, the act of spreading the costs is based on the *useful life* of the assets themselves. The critical assumptions and estimations about the useful life, and how much cost is to be allotted to a particular period, rest in the hands of the accounting management. In industries like telecommunications, the network costs are considerable. The useful life of the equipments is not known clearly as the rate of advancement in technology is very fast. It is easy to make a wrong call on the quantum of depreciation in such situations.

The way this expense is shown in the income statement, affects profitability, as it forms a large chunk of the total costs. You will learn about this aspect in more detail in our discussion of the income statement in our next chapter. The purpose of introducing this subject here is to convey the idea that judgment and opinion of the accountant impact some items more than others.

There are two other aspects about depreciation that you must understand. You already know now, that depreciation appears as a cost in the income statement and that more of it has the effect of reducing the profits, and vice versa. But what generally readers fail to grasp is that this cost is not a cash outflow for the company. In other words, it does not affect the amount of cash you have in the bank, no matter how much depreciation is shown as expense in the statement. Depreciation is a non-cash expense. This is the first of the two aspects.

Non-Cash Expense

A non-cash expense is an item shown as cost in the income statement for which no cash has been paid out. This is because; it is merely an accounting trick to spread out the cost that is already incurred in some earlier occasion. Depreciation is a portion of the total cost, shown this year; similarly provision is an anticipated cost for which no cash is paid now.

The second aspect you must understand is that the economic reduction in value of an asset and the accounting depreciation are two different concepts. Indeed an asset like, say a delivery truck, loses its value as it gets older. But the accounting for depreciation of the truck is all about allocation of the total costs of purchase of the truck over its useful life, and not about its value. A patent which your company obtained after prolonged research and development may lose its entire value if a new type of technology comes into the market, regardless of what the amortized cost the accountant shows in the books. Similarly some assets your company owns may appreciate in value, even though the accountant may write-down its depreciated value every year. Here in lies the difference between 'book' value and the 'market value' of the company. We will devote a full section to the concept of value at the end of this chapter.

5. Accruals & Allocations

Let us get to the definition straightaway:

> **Accruals & Allocations**
>
> The purpose of accruals is to count the chickens before they hatch. In other words, to calculate a payment obligation, before it becomes payable. Good examples are interest payments due by the year end, or rent for premises that is already paid up in for the full year. By using accruals, a company can measure what it owes looking forward and what cash revenue it expects to receive.

Allocations are apportionments of overhead costs to different departments or products or geographical areas within the company. This is mainly used for reporting of segmental results.

Just as with purchase of machinery or other physical assets, a company can purchase non physical assets, which are to be used for more than one accounting period. Example, prepaid expenses like rental of premises and salaries which are not disbursed to the staff. Another example could be the developmental costs incurred for the new product launch. This would reveal the profitability of the development effort as it tries to match the revenues with the costs. A decision to continue with the product or abandon it can then be easily arrived at. Stories of well-meaning products that were launched, that couldn't make sustainable profits are all too common. DuPont's pilot venture, from 2006-08 in Andhra Pradesh to solve malnutrition problems by getting rural mothers to cook with soya protein as a routine practice failed when accountants matched costs and sales revenues. The story is the same for ITC's famous *E-chaupal* initiative. Expenditures associated with such businesses are invariably found to be higher per unit of output, and therefore could be justified only at a higher price, which the intended customers did not accept. (*Erik Simanis, Reality Check at the Bottom of the Pyramid. HBR June 2012*)[6]

You are most likely to come across allocations when you try to understand the reports about the products and segments of a company. This is technically called segment reporting. All the expenses and revenues of the company as a whole are apportioned between the major product segments. Some companies call it verticals, others demarcate operations geographically. Major telecom operators in India use the product-wise segmentations; Vodafone prefers to report its country-wise results.

You might initially think that it is not such a complicated matter at all. Well, logically you may be right. But in practice, it involves a huge amount of judgmental exercise by the accountant. For example, how do we allocate the costs of training imparted by the company's own training centers to the various products and services? How much of the revenue earnings of the company are due to the training imparted? There are administrative offices and other establishments like the store depots whose expenses are to be allocated to various products. The corporate Headquarters which has a large staff to monitor, plan and ideate does not seem to produce any revenue. But they do incur heavy expenditures. The criteria adopted by the accountant to apportion the total of such expenses can make or break the profitability or otherwise of some products. It is therefore important to understand that reasonableness based on clear data inputs should be the basis of such decisions. Nevertheless the human element of judgment will always play a crucial part in allocations accounting.

The judgmental aspect of accruals can creep in here and can affect the profitability, as shown in the income statement. Our intention here is to demonstrate that accounting for what the company owes and what it owns can be more complicated than meets the eyes. The processes associated with it somewhat colors the statements that finally appear.

6. The Concept of Value

The most important statement that the account has to show at the end of his arduous labors is called the balance sheet. We define the balance sheet as follows:

> **The Balance Sheet**
>
> The balance sheet of a company is like your wedding Photograph taken on a particular day. It shows what the company looks like on that day. It lists all that the company OWNS and all that IT OWES, and what it is worth on that day which is called NET WORTH. Yes, you will try to put in your best appearance on your wedding day!

The essentiality of the balance sheet is the concept of the net worth of the company. The whole point in preparing a balance sheet is to project what a business ultimately is worth. Having said that, we should perhaps ask the other question in the same breath: Does the balance sheet then achieve its purpose? Let us examine.

If we deduct all that the company owes from all that it owns, what remains will be value of what is left over. Net value of the business as on a particular day therefore is the value of what remains after all obligations have been paid out. Here we run into at least two basic problems. First, what the company OWNS is actually an estimate of its real value. Similarly what it OWES. Therefore what remains is itself an estimate of its actual value. This we are convinced from a reading of the earlier sections.

There are people who argue that this type of accounting, which ultimately leaves you still unsure of the value of the exercise itself, is quirky. The problem is not new. But let us examine the other side of the picture. Historically several groups of people have attempted to arrive at a 'fair price' (*read value*) for parties to exchange goods and services. There are the philosophers, economists, tax collectors, and judiciary. Economists tried to define value as the units of labor embedded into the product. Some people tried to say that the value of a property is the value of rent that could be obtained from it; others said that it depended on the 'next-best use it could be put to'. Judiciary often found it extremely difficult to assess the value of bankrupt companies for settlement of creditor's claims.

The problem with these approaches is that they assume that there exists a 'true value'. In that case, accountancy is best left to philosophers and metaphysics. The truth is that in the business world, value is determined by independent parties, transacting with each other, each trying to protect his own self interest. Accountants have remarkable insight into this fact and have with commendable clarity, adopted the price so arrived at as the basis of their system. This has the greatest advantage of being verifiable and establishing a benchmark for all future references. The reader of the balance sheet therefore has to bear this in mind, that historically recorded cost of what a company OWNS and what it OWES forms the basis for estimating the value that one considers fair if he is thinking of buying or selling ownership of the company. All other alternatives suggested though appear to have tremendous conceptual value are of little practical application in the business world.

...well, you see, to be absolutely honest with you, everybody lies...
But it does not matter since nobody notices..........

Summary of Chapter One

In this chapter, we have taken you through some of the key features of the practice of accounting and elements of caution that the intelligent reader must exercise while trying to understand the numbers. They are: (1) The concept of historical cost as opposed to the philosophical concept of value, (2) the general notion that all numbers have some wisp of judgmental bias built into them, (3) even with all these weaknesses the system of accounting and the results obtained through it represent a foundational starting point for arriving at the fair value of a business, (4) even if the concept of 'net worth' might appear to be elusive, it can be arrived at in practice if one is skilful enough to make the numbers speak.

The true purpose of financial statements is to present a clear and impartial picture of the financial position of the company. However, the modern corporation is run by professional managers who are paid employees of the company. They may sometimes wish to present a picture that suits them. Therefore the financially savvy reader of these statements must carefully look for signs and tell-tale symptoms that hide motives of the management.

To enable you to do this at least partially, we have taken you through the processes that lie behind the art of accounting. We gently pointed out that accountants are, by the very nature of the process, constrained to use estimates and assumptions, while trying to record these figures that make up the financial statements. This sometimes introduces biases into the process. There are clear norms, conventions and regulatory guidelines for doing this. Financial skill involves an in-depth assessment of the reasonableness of these assumptions enabling you to see whether the reports reflect the true financial position.

Finally we talked about the most important concept of valuation of a company. The important thing about valuation is that in business value means the price two parties are willing to pay. Thus, it cannot be assessed by the accountants or anyone other than the parties themselves. We will return to the practical meanings of this statement in subsequent chapters.

2
Understanding Balance Sheet Concepts

YOUR CHILDREN GENERALLY BRING HOME THE PROGRESS CARD from school to show you. Children, whose class marks for the term are good, happily show it, others with some trepidation. But you would generally glance at the previous term results and the ones before, trying to compare it with the current ones. You know the kind of progress your child is making. However, these term results are only pointers to the capabilities and talents your child really possesses. You can mentally estimate whether she is putting up the performances that match her talents. The term-results refer to the profit and loss account that the company produces every quarter. But the summation of the results is contained in the results of the final exams. This is the balance sheet. It is the cumulative impact on the financial results of the company since its inception. We have defined the balance sheet as a statement of what the company owns and what it owes and what remains with the owners on a particular date. While the profit and loss statement is the result of a *period* of operations, balance sheet is overall impact of these results on the state of finances of the company over the several years shown on a *particular* day. These are interrelated. You cannot understand the balance sheet without the profit and loss account and vice-versa. In this chapter we explore the many aspects of the balance sheet.

Book Value and Market Value

The balance sheet is a remarkable invention. It is certainly useful to talk about a summary of things owned and owed. But it has two major shortcomings. First, the values of things as they are shown in the balance sheet very rarely match the values in practice. We have encountered this value problem in the previous section. Secondly, some of the most valuable things that a modern corporation has do not appear in the balance sheet at all. For example, everyone recognizes that it is not the machines or computers by themselves that produce goods and services which are of use to the customers. It is the talent, creativity and human effort that does these things. So far no accountant or financial expert has devised a satisfactory method of showing this valuable asset in the balance sheet.

The two shortcomings of the balance sheet brings us the important aspects of book value and market value. The value of all things owned by the company as recorded in the balance sheet is called the book value. However, since all things of value of the company are not recorded, the total actual value of the company is different. This value is called the market value. Roughly this is the price that can be obtained if all the things of value (*both recorded and not recorded*) are sold in the market. Financially, it is the price of a share of the company in the stock market multiplied by the number of shares of the company. This is the market capitalization of the company and represents the total value of the company.

The Stock Market

Also known as the equity market, in which shares are issued and traded. A SHARE is a slice/unit of ownership in a company. This market has two main sections: the primary and secondary market. The primary market is where new issues called Initial Public Offering (IPO) are made. These shares are subsequently traded in the secondary market.

The price of a share is arrived at by two unrelated parties willingly transacting. This price is therefore considered the 'fair-value' of the share. The value of a company is the total price of all its shares put together. It is called the 'market capitalization' of the company or its 'market value'.

Accountants have not completely ignored all things invisible. They show the value of intangibles where it can be measured with some reasonable yardstick. Telecommunications operators show a major asset called the 'Entry License' fee paid as an asset in the balance sheet at the price paid for it to the Government. This is so because without a license you cannot operate the business legally. The most interesting development in the 1990s and thereafter is the balance sheet item called 'software' which is recognized as a valuable asset. But it can be priced. The important thing to understand here is that balance sheet will not carry an item, if it has no historical price. Something will appear in the balance sheet only if it has been involved in a transaction (*purchase or sale*).

This last sentence brings us to the elusive concept of Goodwill.

The Concept of Goodwill

Accountants are conservative to the extent of showing only historical costs in the balance she`et. They ignore most intangibles that have no accepted yardstick for measurement. In fact, even the beginning student of accounting will understand that a corporation has valuable assets like employees, customer database, proprietary knowledge, patents, brand-value reputation, strategic location and other advantages etc which do not appear in the balance sheet. Some enthusiasts have pushed the scale in the opposite direction. During the Dotcom era in the 1990's, valuations of companies reached unimaginable limits. These companies had little or no physical assets whatsoever. All they had, in many instances, was the 'eyeballs' on their websites. Yet investors somehow believed that the corporation of the future was based on innovative business model inhabiting the rarified cyberspace somewhere on the world-wide-web. They believed that the earning-power of the companies depended on inspired software and innovative methods. Value was not created in ordinary bricks-and-mortar workplaces.

In financial parlance, this means that investors were willing to pay prices that took into account intangibles. They were adding to the assets all sorts of items that had no historical prices and no measurable yardstick for estimating it. When a buyer is willing to pay more than the value of all the items in the balance sheet the difference between the price paid and the value on the book is a premium. When one company buys out another company, at a price more than the net worth (*what is owned minus what is owed*), the difference is called Goodwill.

Goodwill

Goodwill comes into play when one company buys another company. It is the difference between net assets bought and the price actually paid. The buying company pays a premium over the stated net worth because it sees values in intangibles like brand-image, human talents, customer base and so on.

The concept of goodwill is closely tied to the value problem. When one company buys another company, cash (*in the balance sheet, the real stuff*) goes out. What comes into the buyer's hands is the new set of physical assets and the assets called goodwill, to compensate for cash. The value of all these assets is in fact subjective. That of goodwill is even more so. The most important thing to understand here is that the value of all that is owned must exceed the value of all that is owed. Otherwise, the company will not be able to meet all its obligations to all its creditors. Again, since goodwill is not a physical asset, cannot be sold off for cash. Therefore the financially savvy will always look for physical assets and compare to liabilities. It will be prudent to ignore goodwill in such cases.

Net Worth

Now we come to the most important concept in the whole of finance. True equity or owner's capital refers to the present value of all future cash flows likely to be received by the owner. Let me warn you. This is not easy to spot in the accountants' figures. This is because as always the accountant is concerned with only what can be measured.

In accounting terms equity is always the net worth of the business. We will use these words interchangeably in this book. It is simply the difference between what is owned and what is owed.

Owner's Equity

EQUITY is the shareholder's present stake in the company. It is represented by the book-value as in the balance sheet of the company. It is calculated by deducting all outside payments from what is owned by the company. Another way to see it is, to think of it as the cumulative impact of the results of doing business over several accounting periods. (*The share capital initially given to the company and its accumulations through profits or deductions through losses over several years*). True equity is elusive because it requires the assessment of future earnings potential. The accountant's measure is merely a guide and acts as pointer to arrive at this value.

This is the best measure of the financial performance of a business.

This concept is at the very core of finance. We will go into some detail. At the very start of this chapter we alluded to grades at school. Consider the grade you got for your semester-end exams. You spend the entire semester working hard, expending your efforts at studies and other activities, balancing out work and play and taking exams. The instructor gives you an A, or B+ or whatever. This is your profits. (*Result of your efforts for a certain quarter*). The balance sheet is more like your overall grade obtained in the final exams. You can see the relationship straightaway. Annual results are the cumulative performance results of your years in college. Any one particular semester result does not determine it but, certainly affects your cumulative average.

Employees and executives, who are unaware of this aspect, sometimes get alarmed when their company reports a loss during some quarters. Unions and associations get worked up and the blame-game starts. But when you, as a financially intelligent executive, look at the balance sheet of the company over several years, you may notice that the accumulated surpluses and reserves far exceed the liabilities that a company owes. If your company makes a profit in one quarter, the owner's equity (*read net worth*) will increase, and will decrease when there is a loss during any quarter. But the overall position (*net earnings retained over the years*) may have actually increased.

Now, we come to a key aspect of the concept of owner's equity. Intuitively, you may have guessed, that the above paragraph is true. But what is not easily apparent is the fact that owner's have invested in the business, to get a satisfactory return in the long-run for their money. In other words, investors are forward looking. Future returns are important to them. If a business has potential to earn more money, no matter what it is earning at present, they would like to stay invested. Consider for a minute the situation in a business which is on the verge of developing a product (*a new drug to cure diabetes, perhaps*). Its current performance may be very average. But investors are willing to pay a large premium to its net worth because of its future earnings capacity.

How Can We Measure Net Worth?

Insurmountable difficulties await you if you try to measure owner's equity through conventional accounting statements. This is because the accounts profession prefers to deal with only those items that are measurable objectively. The true definition of equity is stated to be the present value of all future cash flows that can be expected to accumulate from the business to the owner's of capital.

Present Value and Future Value

In its most basic form present value principle states that a rupee *now* is worth more than a rupee *tomorrow*. That is because today is real and tomorrow is uncertain. The future is both uncertain and risky. Finance people therefore, *disallow a portion* of the future cash to make it worth as much as today. This portion that remains after disallowing is called discounted cash flow or the present value of future cash flows.

This is notoriously elusive in practice. There are at least two practical difficulties: 1) How to estimate future cash flows? 2) How to estimate present value of the cash flow? Even if you can divine the future cash flows, how much of it do we discount? This involves an estimation of the risk and uncertainty attached to the future. Finance professionals are not all agreed on how to estimate risk and uncertainty. But the principle that these two aspects have to be factored in while estimating future returns, lies at the core of financial decision making process. We will return to this all important concept in later chapters.[1]

Don't lose heart. There is light at the end of the tunnel. Relying on the stock market valuation of the share of a company is the more practical way in which accountants and finance professionals arrive at the elusive concept of net worth. This is the consensus of a large number of investors' estimation of future values. Investors have only a single minded aim to get a reasonably satisfactory return on their investment. They keenly follow the company's activities and discount the good news and bad news about the company. A massive strike by employees, sudden increase in rate of interest by the Reserve bank (affecting debt obligations of companies), a new and attractive product offer from a competitor and so on, have impact on share prices.

Now the smart reader, you may ask: What about companies whose shares are not traded in the stock market? Yes, there is a problem. Financially skilled folks have attempted to solve this problem through comparison with peer-group companies. They have attempted to compare the earning level of similar companies operating in the same industry, and apply the same price multiple to arrive at the value of its net worth.

There is yet another more vexing issue. The very fact that this book is in your hands tells me that you have more than cursory interest in the subject. You might certainly have wondered, whether the total value of a company, as reflected in its share prices in the market can vary so much from day to day. For example, the day the supreme court announced that the licenses issued by the government of India to some telecom firms were invalid the share prices of those companies collapsed overnight. There is a tendency for the share-prices to fluctuate violently even by the hour. Does that imply that companies lose or gain total value by the hour?

Part of the answer must lie in the phenomenon called 'sentiment'. Behavioral scientists have shown that human beings react to news disproportionately. Share prices are driven partly by the sentimental reactions of the traders to news about the company. It can be, therefore, reasonably concluded that stock market is far more volatile than the actual factors influencing it would warrant. The moral of the story is that the valuations as reflected by the equity market are not to be taken blindly. The valuation of the net worth of a company arrived at by all these methods, cannot be expected to be equal to the price that a sale of its assets would fetch. This price may be more than the historical costs as recorded in the balance sheet. It is, therefore, important to understand that the true value of the owner's capital is known only when two parties, transacting at arm's-length arrive at a mutually agreed price.

How to Read a Balance Sheet

In the previous chapter, you have seen the little box defining balance sheet. We compared it to a wedding photograph. Looking at the balance sheet is rather like admiring your own wedding photograph. Well, almost. The wedding day is special, in more ways than one. Different cultures have different meanings to the ceremonies and symbolism used. Though the international accounting standards board (IASB)[2] is constantly trying to bring in practices that make comparisons easy between companies and companies located in different regions of the world, these differences will persist. Each country has its own regulations to prescribe how the accounting statements are to be presented. The US GAAP is, therefore, quite different from the Indian GAAP. The wedding photograph will, therefore, look rather different here in India and in the USA. But essentially it is still a wedding. The balance sheet is intended to display the financial position of a company, but the little trappings and decorations may have slightly different meanings. A second aspect you need to remember is that appearances are put on deliberately as it is meant to be a public display. Just like a wedding. It is the skill of the financially savvy executive to look behind all these display and get to the facts. To do this we need to look at the photograph and what is behind the scenes.

1. What You Need to See

Most people read the income statement first. It is rather easier to understand. It is straight forward and intuitive. What is received, what is spent and what is left.

The balance sheet is not so direct. There are several ways to look at it. Firstly, it tells you what the company owns and owes. Secondly, it tells you where the money has come from, so that the company could own those things. It further tells you what all things the company did with the money it has. For example it tells you how much of physical assets it purchased over the years, how much of cash has been paid to buy intangible assets (software, licenses, goodwill etc) and how much money is put into production of the goods it is doing business in. You can see how much cash is left in the bank after all this, and how much cash is yet to be paid by the company's customers and others. This is quite a lot as it is. But there is more. The true beauty of the balance is in the eye of the beholder. (*Rather like the bride standing by your side in that photograph!*).

When looking at a balance sheet, among the most important things you want to get a feel for is a company's liquidity. Liquidity is a company's ability to meet its short-term obligations, such as its working capital needs. You can find the working capital by deducting the total of payment obligations due within the year (current liabilities) from the total of cash that is due within the year (liquid and semi-liquid assets or current assets). It is common sense to decipher that you should always be having more cash coming in than going out at any point in time. In other words, your net figure for working capital (*current assets minus current liabilities*) should be a positive figure. If not, you will have trouble meeting your suppliers, and paying your salaries on time. These are tell-tale signs that the company is having working capital difficulties. Employees within BSNL which was flush with funds accumulated over the surpluses from previous years have suddenly found that part of their allowances is being pruned. A financially savvy executive working in BSNL would have anticipated this right at the beginning of the financial year 2011-12 when the balance sheet of the company showed a negative net working capital figure as on 31st March of 2011.

Next up is solvency. Here, the financially skilled reader wants to look at the level of total debt relative to the equity used to run a business by its owners. Solvency is a measure of the company's ability to sustain its activities over a longer period of time. You can get a rough idea of this aspect by looking at the proportion of physical assets that are financed by borrowing. You must also look at the surpluses being generated by the business. Observe the change in surpluses from the previous period, is it increasing or decreasing? If the company is not accumulating reserves how can it finance its expansion and replace its old or outdated machinery? Will the business then be sustainable and survive in the long run? You will learn to answer these and other questions when you complete reading the chapter seven, dealing with diagnostic tools for the balance sheet.

2. How to Look Behind the Scenes

Though a balance sheet is intended to be a gateway to understanding a company's financial position, there are many dark corners. The balance sheet is always as on a particular date. A company can use any twelve month period as its accounting year. Many companies use the calendar year. In India as a convention, companies use 1st April to 31st March as the fiscal year, in order to coincide with the government of India's financial year. The income statement is the report for the fiscal year. The balance sheet is the final score dated as at 31st March. This is because the Government of India uses it as their Financial Year.

Balance sheets used to come in format, called the 'T-shape' with left-hand column (*showing liabilities*) and a right-hand column (*showing assets*). They don't any more. It now comes in a 'vertical-format' showing what is owed (*liabilities at the top*) and what is owned (*assets at the bottom*).

Make sure you update the knowledge of your company's balance sheet on a regular basis. You need to read the entire annual report, starting with the management discussion and analysis. Very often the company uses it as a vehicle for advertising its potential rather than telling the actual problems. Do not forget to read the notes to accounts and its accompanying schedules forming part of the balance sheet. This is where all the assumptions, biases and estimates regarding all the numbers appearing in the balance sheet are explained. If any item in the balance sheet is not explained by its appropriate schedule, raise a yellow flag. Something is hidden. Most companies don't hide information. They bury it. (For example, Reliance Communications has more than 14 pages of notes in its annual report for 2010-11. Bharti Airtel has 32 pages of notes to accounts. Both companies have separate schedules and statement of significant accounting policies in addition to this.) The numbers listed on a balance sheet provide you with data that can help you make smarter decisions. These numbers will also give you a head's up when trouble is brewing. Don't be intimidated. Use the tool to make informed conclusions about your own company.

3. Asking the Right Questions

You will come across changes in the figures shown in the balance sheet from year to year. Ask yourself whether these changes represent an increase in the net worth or erosion in the total value. The easiest way for companies to lose value is to write off some items shown in the previous period. I have already referred to Kochi Shipyard case, where a huge loss of value occurred in the balance sheet, without affecting the profit and loss account. Telecommunications major Nortel Networks wrote down $12 billion after the euphoria over internet and telecom. Other companies lose value slowly and steadily over a longer period due to eroding profits, mismanagement, failure to invest in modernization of plant and networks. The creeping nature of such reduction in net worth often leaves the employees and management with a strong sense of belief 'that things will be alright next year'. However this attitude results in the gross failure to use the information available in the financial statements to unearth the real cause of the creeping decline in values.

Financial intelligence has to serve only one purpose. It must be used to improve financial position, either your own or of the organization you work for. Asking the right questions to unearth the basic nature of the operations you are involved with is the first step. The next is to connect the knowledge gained to improve the processes within your company. Waiting for a good next year may turn out to be a long time to wait.

The specific questions to be asked while reading a balance sheet will be discussed in part three.[3]

What the Company Owns

Assets are what your company owns. You will find two types of assets listed in the balance sheet – fixed assets and current assets. The former refers to all items that are used for more than a year. The latter refers to all items to be used up within a year. You will notice that both these are assets and how they are called is just matter of time involved of their useful life. Examples of fixed assets are land, buildings, machinery and other equipments and even software and patents. The special item called goodwill is already dealt with earlier. Just remember that it is also a fixed asset like land or buildings. All revenues come because of these items and their productivity.

Current assets are generally cash and near cash items like securities, stocks and bonds, which can be turned into cash easily. Accounts receivable are payments due from customers and others which are likely to be received within a year. Inventory refers to finished goods and raw materials that could be turned into cash by the year end. Service companies do not carry much inventory. But manufacturing ones do.

Different companies use various names for these assets, depending on the convention in their industry.

When companies claim to have assets in their books they mean the real thing. Companies, like normal people also can tell a lie. When an oil exploration company claims to have millions of tons of crude available beneath the ground under their allocated area, no one has really gone below to verify it. Ok, their claim has been verified by geological survey experts and satellite imagery. Yet, these reserves may not be exploitable due to economic reasons. Satyam Infotech Hyderabad claimed to have millions of rupees as fixed deposit in the bank. It actually lied.

What the Company Owes

These are what the company owes. You will be able to grasp this when you think of the company as an artificial person, who is different from its own members. Any transaction that this artificial person engages in, affects the record books of accounts. Liabilities, therefore, are all those payments the company must pay back to the people who gave it. Another way to understand liabilities is to think of it as the methods by which the company has obtained its financial resources. Thus the company gets money from individuals who take a share (share capital), or from people who lend money to the company.

Just like assets, liabilities can also be classified according to the time period involved. It can be for more than a year (long term) or for within a year (short term). Long term liabilities are: owner's capital and long-term borrowings (loans). Short-term liabilities include things like accounts payable, overdrafts from banks and accruals of payments.

A special mention is needed regarding retained earnings or sometimes called accumulated surpluses and reserves. This is an item which the company owes to its shareholders. This is the portion of the profits that have not been paid as dividends, but plowed back into the business. Some readers may imagine here that retained earnings are real cash accumulated. This may or may not be true. The figure represents the source of money that has been used up in the business in previous periods. This would have been used for buying fixed assets or current assets or meeting obligations. It could even have been kept in the bank as cash. Microsoft is one large corporation in the habit of preserving large portion of profits in the form of cash. Again, until 2009, BSNL, a telecom operator in India, had accumulated cash to the tune of ₹381 billion in its current assets. At the time of writing, there is a debate among financial journalists as to why Infosys, a software services major, has accumulated cash reserves similar to BSNL and yet is not deploying it in acquiring other companies.

Of course, you may see a negative figure in this line. It would then be called accumulated losses. It represents the erosion of the shareholders' capital over the years.

Why the Balance Sheet Balances

Luca Pacioli is perhaps the greatest link between the middle ages and the modern world. He is one of the least known heroes of the renaissance period. He had among his students, Leonardo da Vinci, who drew illustrations for his book. A humble Franciscan monk, Pacioli, perhaps deserves a place in history of all times as the inventor of the balance sheet, and the system of accounting based on it. It affects modern business like the internet impacts our lives in the present day. The brilliance of the balance sheet is that it balances. We need to understand why.

The business and its owner are two different entities. When we separate out the business and its owner as two individual persons, it is easy to see that at any point in time, what the business owns must be always equal to what belongs to the owner plus what is owed to the others. Luca Pacioli formalized this concept thus:

What the business owned he called *assets*. What it had to pay to the others he called *liabilities*. What it owed to the owner of the business he named *equity*.

He then arrived at a simple statement:

Assets = Liabilities + equity

This roughly translates as:

What is owned (by the business) = what is owed (by the business) + what is left over (for the owner)

This is intuitively true. If a business made a profit, it belonged to the owner. If it made a loss, the owner got less at the end of the period. This must be true for all businesses and at all times. That is why today accountants call this the 'Balance Sheet', because it is always in balance.

So long as you remember that every transaction made by the artificial person called the company affects both sides of the balance sheet, you will be ok. Luca Pacioli used to tell his students, who worked for Venetian merchants, not to go to bed until the balance sheet is in balance at the end of the day. This is because to make the balance sheet balance, the accountant must record every transaction faithfully, reflecting what it looks like from the company's side and what it means to the party transacting with the company. If done correctly, the balance sheet must always balance. Otherwise the accountant will have a sleepless night. Understanding this is a basic requirement for building the foundations of your financial skill.

For several years now, you have been telling me that the numbers speak...well now they have finally spoken. You're fired!!!

Summary of Chapter Two

The Concept of the balance sheet is at the very foundation of a modern accounting system. It is the single most important statement that the accountant produces. All other statements are related to it. It brings us closest to the value of the business at a particular point in time. However, it has its limitations and serious shortcomings, if used blindly. The reason is that a lot of assumptions and estimates go into its preparation. This is because of the fundamental practicalities involved in the accounting process. Just because the balance sheet has its weaknesses it would not be advisable to throw the baby out with the bath water. It is a most practical way of recording business transactions. Here value means the recorded historical value realized when two parties are dealing at arms' length. There are really no alternatives to this. That is the reason why it is used so widely and used as the starting point for the valuation of the net worth of a business. So long as we understand the difference between book value and market value, and appreciate the process of understanding the mechanism of numbers, we can use the balance sheet intelligently.

3

The Income Statement

THE ESSENTIAL PURPOSE OF AN INCOME STATEMENT IS TO TELL the story of the business during a period. The period generally is a quarter or a year. It tells you whether the story is good, bad or indifferent. Unlike the balance sheet, the profit and loss account (P&L) as it is called by accountants, is not difficult to understand. It shows total income, total costs and what remains, which is either a surplus or a loss. But there really is a little problem here. Like many things in life, the numbers are not what they appear to be.

The total income, total expenses and therefore what remains are in fact all best estimates and not the reality.[1] This makes profit merely an estimate and an approximation to reality. So what is real? Well, cash in the bank is real. Adding to the net worth of the company is real. Increasing the price of the shares of your company in the stock market is real. Addition to the bonuses and medical benefits of the employees is real. Improving the lives of the community where your company is located by producing and selling services and goods that improve the standard of living of the general public is real.

Deciphering real profitability needs basic financial skills.[2]

The Statement for All Seasons

Most corporations publish their quarterly results. We have seen in the previous sections, that accounting uses estimates and assumptions to arrive at the numbers. We also know that these practices do not invalidate these statements, but is an attempt to synchronize the revenues and costs. Financial skills involve grasping this basic truth. Once you grasp this, you will be active enough to contribute to the organization's target of managing itself to profitability.

Profit is Not All Cash

First, let us see why accounting profits is not really cash profits. Income statement starts with total revenue or sales as the top line. As you have understood in the first chapter, revenue refers to the expected cash that is due to be received from the customers who bought services. Telecommunications operators allow their customers to make calls on their network and at the end of a certain period (usually a month) they dispatch invoices. Customers are allowed another fortnight or 21 days to pay the money for the calls they made during the previous month. This would mean that a customer who made the calls on say January 1st, gets an invoice on 1st February and is allowed time up to 21st of February to pay for that call with grace period of seven days to pay with a small penalty. The telecom company receives no cash even on 1st of March, even if the customer has already paid by check or by credit card. In many cases, customers need reminding. The experience of Telecom operators show that only about 34% of the customers pay up in time. Some customers don't pay up at all. Accountants call them bad debts.

Bad Debts Provision

When a business provides a service in good-faith to a customer on the promise of future payment, it is considered income of the business. The amount receivable from such customers is kept in the balance sheet as something which the company owns. However, some customers fail to keep their promise and default. These amounts are deducted from revenue in the profit and loss account. Such deductions make up the provision for bad debts.

The accountant records revenue when the services are delivered: i.e., on January 1st, and deducts all expenses to arrive at the profit figure. There is absolutely no cash in the bank, but there is profit in the income statement! A telecom operator typically bills millions of customers in a month. The profit figure and the cash figure can differ significantly. It is true that the same applies to the costs as well. But you can see how far away from reality we are when we talk about profit and cash numbers.

Do Profits Add to Net Worth?

Do profits in the income statement add to the net worth? This is the question we raised in our sermon about reality. Well, to answer this, we need to understand the mechanics of the income statement itself. Profit is a surplus that will get added to the owners' capital in the balance sheet. However, the management may choose to distribute the surplus in the form of dividend to the shareholders. In that case, it will not get added up in the balance sheet. But the very declaration of dividend may have the effect of increasing the share price in the stock market. If so, it will certainly increase the market value of the firm, even though the book value remains the same as before. When the market value increases, the owners' equity increases.

However, if the shareholders believe that the company management distributed the dividend because it is not capable of identifying investment opportunities, such dividend distribution may have the opposite impact. Infosys Technologies Limited, the leading software power house in India, is known to hoard cash surpluses, year after year. The price-earnings multiple in Bombay Stock Exchange for Infosys appear to have stuck a plateau. Shareholders are perhaps expecting the company to deploy cash more aggressively in future growth.

Earnings Multiple

It is the price in the stock market for a company's share expressed as times the net profit of the company. Another form of the multiple is the ratio of price to the earnings of the company called P/E ratio. Some analysts consider this multiple as the expectation investors have on the company's future performance.

There can be instances where the company loses value despite having a profitable surplus. This classic case is that of a company writing down its goodwill in the balance sheet. This action does not appear in the income statement, but directly affects total company value in the balance sheet. We have referred to the case of Kochi Shipyard's write-off of substantial balance sheet figure of ₹440 crores in 2009. This may have been the cumulative impact of the company's hedging account losses over several years, but brought to the books in a particularly good year when the company performed well. Incomes during 2008-09 had risen nearly 70%. Investors and executives who failed to understand the concept of cumulative value creation as exhibited in the balance sheet of Kochi Shipyard would be fooled into thinking that the company's performance is above par.

At the time of writing this book, India is in a phase of meltdown. The economy has taken a beating in terms of inflationary pressures and slowdown in manufacturing consequent on falling demand.

The country's leadership is perceived as helpless in the reality of the political economy in trying to push through much needed innovative reforms in many sectors. Due to the combined effect of the European crisis and the underperforming current account balance of trade for India, the Rupee is falling in value. The, situation though unattractive in the general way, benefits some individual companies. Surprised? Imagine a company like Tata Consultancy Services or Infosys. A significant proportion of the income of these companies is from the dollar countries.[3] A falling rupee against the dollar immediately boosts their top-line in terms of rupee values. On 12th July 2012 Infosys declared its Q1 results. In rupee terms the earnings jumped 32.92% from previous period. (In dollar terms the increase was a mere 4.8%). Investors and readers who only look at the numbers, without understanding what they really mean in terms of addition to the worth of the company will arrive at the wrong bus-station. On the same day the stock-price multiple on the National Stock Exchange for Infosys Ltd. fell to 14.8 from 17.3 on the previous day.

Smoothening Out the Earnings

We return once more to the standard textbook on accounting. It states that the objective of preparing financial statements is the dissemination of the accurate financial position of the company. We have somehow qualified this statement implying that accounting involves a large dose of estimations. But this does not take away their intrinsic value so long as you know what the assumptions are. It is the hidden aspects of these biases that are really worrisome. Financial intelligence is a skill that will enable you to uncover or at least partially question some of the numbers that appear in financial statements. But this exercise may not be as easy as said in every case.

Harvard researcher Richard Zeckhauser[4] has found, for instance that companies have a tendency to report small increases in earnings, even if the actual profitability is higher. This technique is called smoothing the earnings that are reported from period to period. You may wonder how a company can hide incomes. It is not difficult. You have learned in the previous section that there are things called provisions. A provision is just that, it is a discretionary item. It provides for future eventualities that may or may not materialize. By increasing the amount under provisions, (*which behaves like a cost and has the effect of reducing the net income*), the accountant can report lower profits than there actually is.

Discretionary Items

There are some items in the profit and loss account, which is purely based on the discretionary judgment of the accountant. Provisions, contingent liabilities, contingent incomes, which become cost or income depending on events that are likely to happen or not happen. The accountant is expected to be conservative in estimating these. That means: hesitate to show it as income, but be eager to show it as a loss if there is any doubt.

Now, you may ponder, why on earth he should want to do that. There are two explanations. One: the stock market reacts sharply to the income statement and is wary of abnormal increases. Two: tax considerations. The higher the income reported the higher taxes that are to be paid. It is better to write back the provisions, when the business is not so good in subsequent years. You keep the tax man away and the stock market happy.

The take away from this sections' discussion is that, financial reporting is influenced by many distortions of reality. As a financially savvy person, you must have this basic understanding to gain a clearer perspective of what you are actually dealing with.

What is Profit?

Profit is the engine driving the business train. It is the result of the efforts of a whole host of people working in the organization at various levels. It drives innovations, demands discipline, encourages frugality, and prevents inefficiency and wastage. Profit-motive drives people to take risks, households save money to invest. The ultimate result of profit-making is the growth of the economy and better life for people.

Despite all this glorification of profit, a clear definition of profit is difficult. Economists theorize that profits make the entity 'better off' at the end of the period. But what does 'better off' actually mean? Others use profit in different contexts meaning different things at the same time. For the accountant:

Profit = Revenue − costs

Countless issues can quickly crop up. What is revenue? What costs? When to count revenue? When to show costs and how much? And so on. For the financially skilled person, these questions are not important. What really matters to him is the difference between accounting profits and bona fide profits.

The Correct Definition of Profit

No matter how meticulously costs have been deducted from revenues, no calculation of profit can be correct in the real sense unless:

The owners of the business have more than what they owned beforehand

There can be no profit without increase in net worth. Net worth is what remains with the owner after all that the company owes to the outsiders are paid off.

Accounting profit is what the accountants say it is. The Accounting standards and guidelines prescribe the method of calculation of revenues and expenditures. The accounting profit is what remains in the statement, after deducting from income all relevant expenses in accordance with all these rules. Any accounting profit that does not increase the net worth of the owners may satisfy most readers of the financial statements. But to you as a financially skilled reader, this is not true profit unless it can be ensured by a clear appraisal of the statement that it has in fact resulted in an increase in the net worth of the owner. At this stage the reader is strongly advised to return to our section on whether profits add to net worth. This is the litmus test for judging real profits, no matter what the accounting figures may claim.

The Many Forms of Profit

Profit is the sun around which the managerial planets revolve. In this circumvolution, there is a 360° view of the managerial aspects of the issue. Depending on his angle of view, the manager calls profit by various names. Though it adds no value to the essentiality of the concept, it has certain practical aspects in management.

The milestones in arriving at the net addition to the wealth of the company after a period of operations are generally three: (1) the gross profit, (2) the operating profit and (3) the net profit. Before we get to the details a little clarification is in order. The period of operations of a company is called the accounting year. In India, the fiscal year is from 1st April to 31st March. Under the Income tax law in India, companies are required to file tax returns for the fiscal year. Therefore the enterprises that use the fiscal year as the accounting year need to prepare only one set of accounts. Others must prepare two financial statements, one for the shareholders and another one for the tax authorities.

Accounting Period and Fiscal Year

More than 87% of the companies listed in the National Stock Exchange in India use the fiscal year for their accounting year. But some companies do use other periods. Sugar companies like to coincide their accounting period with the crushing season. Hindu businessmen use the Diwali festival as the beginning of their accounting year. Some Indian companies owned by foreign companies must follow the accounting year of their parent.

Different forms of profit in effect refer to the different types of operations and Industries. Manufacturing companies deduct the cost of manufacturing to arrive at the gross profit. It tells the manager about the basic surplus that is available in the product. (*Gross profit = revenue – cost of goods sold*). It is apparent that if this part of the business is not profitable, it is not probably wise to continue in business. Perhaps the basic processes, or technology or materials have to be altered. Managers focus attention depending on where the gross figures are headed.

It is interesting to note that some industries like the services sector do not have this concept at all. For these businesses the operating profit is more relevant. This is fashionably and frequently called, EBITDA or earnings before interest, taxes, depreciation and amortization. By now, you have met all these little-fellows in our earlier sections. The EBITDA figure is a good indicator of how well a company is being managed.

This last statement needs to be qualified. In theory EBITDA represents the true performance parameter of the operations of a company. However, it has two major shortcomings. Firstly, it does not reflect the total of all recurring and operational expenses. Very often organization show non-recurring costs as part of operations. Examples include restructuring costs, like retrenchment of employees. Secondly major investments into the future, which are essential part of a company's growth and survival strategy, are not reflected. Considering these two aspects, we recommend that you would rather look at EBIT (Earnings before Interest and Tax) as a better measure of the operational performance from a managerial perspective. Earnings before Taxes and Interest avoid the above two issues and at the same time has the advantage of ignoring the distortions introduced by the use of borrowings in operating a business.

As always the numbers are affected by the biases. It is important to know if there are any one time charges. The accountant's use of depreciation is to be carefully understood before depending on the EBITDA in its published form.

An important word of caution is in order. The tendency to ignore depreciation while analyzing operating profit, because of an inherent lack of faith in the depreciation numbers is widespread. However, let us look at the telecommunications operator whose main assets in the era of mobile communications consist of radio spectrum which becomes more valuable as it becomes scarcer and more applications develop. But through successive income statements, the telecom service provider may show perennial loses year after. But eventually he can sell the business at a handsome price, when he finally decides to exit the business altogether. This scene is very likely to be enacted in the Indian telecom space, if some of the operators who have lost their licenses decide to exit the country. In such cases the financially intelligent executive will be much wiser to use a better measure of operating profit called the operating cash flow.

Ignoring depreciation from the income statement altogether is a discretion that the financially savvy reader must exercise carefully. When a business has assets in the balance sheet that mainly consist of machinery and plant that wear out with usage and time, applying the depreciation in the most appropriate manner yields a better view of the addition to net worth by way of surpluses. In other cases, we must be alert to distinguish between accounting profits and real profits.

Net profit is a concept that has relevance to the shareholders as a group. Managers are concerned with it because very often, though not justifiably, the market reactions are based on this single number. It is the net surplus after all deductions are made from the operating profit. There are three groups of claimants on the operating profit pie. The first is the government, next the business itself and third the shareholder.

Managers sometimes use techniques of tax-planning and analyze tax implications of purchase and sales to minimize the impact on the net profit. Regulatory environment and the annual budgeting exercise of the government are keenly watched. Tax avoidance as a practice is not one of recent origin. However, investors do not take kindly to certain avoidance tricks that border on illegality, when discovered. Tax planners exploit the differences in tax rates within the tax framework of a country or those between two or more countries. The tax planner takes advantage of this tax differential – from highly taxed to lesser-taxed and non-taxed situations. It would be near-impossible to eliminate the variation of tax rates within an income tax act or between the rates imposed by other fiscal statutes in a single country. When international income is considered it is clear that such differentials between nations can never be eliminated. Our purpose in this section is merely to point out that tax avoidance will exist in some form or other in the foreseeable future. When attempting to assess real profits of operations tax considerations can play an important role. It must be understood that corporations which use devious means to appear legal in achieving reduction in income tax, may increase their chances of being caught up in judicial tangle. This drags them into costly litigation that eventually undoes matching gains in taxes and net profits.

Plowing back profits into future income generating investments is something the shareholders welcome instead of divided declarations.

Dividend, though desirable, is not a deciding factor in staying invested in the company as far as a majority of the shareholders are concerned. They interpret dividend more as a signal. The companies themselves use this to advertise their performance levels. Savvy investors are able to see through the games of dividend and its timing, especially when the company in question is under pressure to show results. The scene in the corporate world is rather fuzzy and various companies send out mixed signals to counter the impact. In general the dividend declaring company is more often than not right in their abilities to maintain market capitalization levels.

The Dividend Signal

Interpretation	Increase dividend	No dividend or Decrease dividend
good news	prosperity	directors are on to something new/big
bad news	running out of investment ideas	company has cash flow problems

The financially intelligent approach to the dividend policy should be to consider several key factors. For example:

- What are the current investment opportunities available to the business?
- Are they likely to change in the next few years?
- What is the current cash position?
- Does it have sufficient cash for its needs in the foreseeable future?
- Is it holding too much cash?
- Legally, are there any restraints on paying out a dividend this year?

The Issue is Recognition

No matter how many times this aspect has been emphasized, the issue about the income statement shrinks down to the issue of revenue recognition. Repeated instances of companies trying to boost up their share prices, or managers attempting to put up great performances, have their basics in this aspect. But you will find that sooner than later, such methods implode on the companies themselves. It is amazing that many people don't critically examine revenue reporting practices, assuming that auditors have done their certification.

A reading of the 2010 annual report of Reebok India Ltd would have raised at least one red flag. But the issue was missed by the auditor. In 2010, there was a sharp increase in the money due to Reebok from distributors and retailers. In fact this figure was about 90% of the total sales revenue figure. This had risen from about 42% of sales in the previous year. (This is a *red flag, an abnormal increase in customers who owed monies to the company*). The progress of the sales during the year would have shown that the 84% of the sales of the company took place during July to December 2009. In other words, the company was pushing goods to the distributors, to show higher sales. The end customer never bought the goods, no money came in. But accounting showed higher sales and higher profits. The intelligent reader would have immediately cross checked for the actual operating cash received during the same period. Net profit is net increase in wealth, not phantom sales figures in some income statement.

Some of the commonest methods used in boosting revenues through innovative recognition methods are also some of the easiest to detect. Loading distribution channels as demonstrated in practice by Reebok India Ltd. cannot be sustained over long periods of time. Sooner or later, distributors will refuse to take on extra inventory, due to additional costs involved. They will refuse to pay the company until genuine customers buy. Some companies just simply make up the figures to meet targets. In the telecommunications industry, 'bragging rights' belong to the operators with the highest subscription numbers. Though it does nothing to boost revenue or profits, but somehow this has come to be accepted as normal. Monthly subscription figures are brandied about by the numerous journalists in the print and visual media regularly. This then forms the basis for the governments of India's figures for penetration levels, and ARPU (Average Revenue Per User) calculations. The reality is somewhat different. Estimation of active subscribers in the system is as low as 70%. A large number of these subscribers have multiple SIM cards that are seldom used. The rate of disconnections in the network is not disclosed by any operator. Policy making and financial allocations, based on such reporting of figures, can go wrong. It is recommended here that the cross-checking of reported figures with cash generation, would yield sufficient evidence to make a realistic assessment on many issues.

One might think it naïve or silly of the managers to do this. The reason why this happens is not naiveté but overconfidence. Managers sometimes believe, like motivational speakers, that sincerely hoping for something will make it happen. They estimate that, future earnings and sales will rise to cover the estimates they have actually built in into the statements. But reality sometimes hits these positive attitudes hard. Things don't work out as planned. Then the game begins and the cover up starts. The key point about such a course of action for the manager is that he cannot get off the ride whenever things go wrong. Because getting off is getting caught. Ramalinga Raju, CMD of Satyam Computer Services, who had manipulated the company's financials for several years, stated: 'It is like riding a tiger, not knowing how to get off without being eaten.'

those are the accounting standards...
if you don't like them, I have others....

Summary of Chapter Three

The income statement is to tell the story of the company's performance during the past one year, to which the statement relates. We had to clearly understand the mechanics of its preparation. We saw that it is easy to equate profits with cash and that could be wrong. But we now understand that profits without a matching cash generation are lot of smoke. If so, what is the essentiality of the profit concept? Any action that does not lead to a genuine addition to the wealth of the owners cannot be real. It is surprising that many companies in fact try very hard to mask the real or indifferent performance in wealth creation by stretching the concept. But they are easy to detect, if we follow the simple rule and apply the litmus test. A company's operations should have benefitted some of its stakeholders in real terms. They are the owners, employees, customers and the community in general.

At several instance we have pointed outside the income statement to get a clearer picture of the performance of the company. The reported profits can be verified to a large extent by cross-references to the balance sheet and the cash flow statements. The stated dividends are in fact a signal emanating from the company boards to investors and general public and needs to be interpreted on its own merits. In most cases, the financially savvy reader needs to understand the external environment in which the company is operating. Financial statements alone cannot capture a company's ability to respond to its environment or its corporate culture that drives its internal processes.

4 The Statement of Cash Flows

IN THE PREVIOUS TWO CHAPTERS, WE LOOKED AT THE BALANCE Sheet and the Income Statement. We now know that the balance sheet just presents a picture, although somewhat subjective, of what a company owns and how it managed to get the finances to own it. It is a completely still photograph, not an action video. We do not know what happened before or after. So we looked at the profit and loss account or the income statement. We could see some of the operations the company carried out and what the net result was. But unfortunately, this statement was based on the matching principle. It did not tell us the actual position of anything. Not even that of its final result, the net profit. They all turned out to be estimates. Looking at either the balance sheet or the income statement raised many questions instead.

Why Cash Matters

The cash flow statement is now a standard feature of financial reporting. Companies listed on the Indian stock exchanges have to publish such reports along with its balance sheet and profit and loss accounts. There are important considerations why this is necessary. Here is a small list.

Firstly, there is a difference between the earnings as reported in the income statement and the real cash generated from the business operations. We have seen this and understand why. Secondly, income is a matter of opinion of the accountant. Numerous occasions where the assumptions and estimates were used to meet management's needs has made it an unfair basis for comparison of performances between companies. The publicly owned company is under pressure to report profits. It will make use of every trick in the book to report higher incomes and lower expenses. The privately owned company, on the other hand, will attempt to report diminished earnings to avoid paying extra tax to the government. Thirdly, the system is open to unscrupulous people to manipulate figures, under an elaborate web of deals within deals, sometimes going on for many years that investors and users have a diminished faith in its utility. Fourthly, financial statements prepared under the concept of historical costs, do not reflect the very real problem of inflation. The ability of an enterprise to meet its obligations, continue operations or expand capacity cannot be assessed merely by reading the balance sheet and P&L statements. Finally, there is indeed a difference between income and cash. While income is an opinion, cash is a fact.

Profit and Cash Go Together

By now you have a pretty good idea, as to why profit does not automatically mean cash in the bank. We know that all sales do not immediately result in cash receipts for the company. Then again all expenses shown in the income statement do not mean a cash outflow either. Some expenses are merely accounting entries to match revenues and expenses during the period of reporting. Further, long-term expenses on addition to equipments and factories appear in the income statement but partially only in the form of depreciation.

There is another aspect to this. All cash receipts are not income and all outflows are not expenses. A company may receive cash from borrowings or from new issues of its shares. This does not constitute revenues. The same is true if the company issues bonds and debentures. The money received as a result does not appear in the income statement as revenue. Because these receipts are not the result of the operations of the company, but money has merely travelled from the owners of the company to the company's books. This, in fact, is the same cash in another pair of artificial hands. The differences between cash and profits will persist.

How Profitable Companies Go Out of Business

Sweetie's Dream Dolls is a new venture selling stuffed dolls. They look soft and fluffy attracting lots of children, with mothers in tow. The founder has innovative styles based on her unique training background, and starts the venture with ₹10,000 cash in the bank. Let's assume that she has monthly operating expenses of ₹10,000, and the costs of goods sold (COGS) are 60%. The income statement for SDD for three months looks like this:

Month (in ₹)	January	February	March
Sales	20,000	30,000	45,000
COGS (Cost of Goods Sold)	12,000	18,000	27,000
Gross Profit	8,000	12,000	18,000
Expenses	10,000	10,000	10,000
Net Profit	**(2,000)**	**2,000**	**8,000**

The business looks good, on paper. But is it really a good business? The cash flow tells a different story. The owner employs two girls, who are to be paid monthly salaries. The suppliers of felt and stuffing also have to be paid in 30 days. Sweetie's Dream Dolls has arrangement with specialized shops that display these dolls. They say that, the dolls are good, but slow moving. They will pay the owner of SDD in 60 days only.

By end January, the owner has paid out all the money in her bank. But no cash has been received from the shops. Her bank balance is zero. End February, SDD still gets no cash, even though she has ₹50,000 in receivables. But salary and materials have to be paid out. A total of (₹10,000 + ₹12,000) ₹22,000 is deficit. Surely March will turn the situation around? Not really. In fact it is worse off in March because it has to pay the salary of February (₹10, 000) plus expenses (₹18, 000), a total of ₹28, 000. Oh yes, another ₹2,000 for the balance of January payments. Owner of Sweet Dream Dolls gets a grand sum of ₹20,000 from the shops as payment for January sales and has now a total deficit of ₹10,000.

This is how profitable companies go out of business. They run out of cash.

How Cash Rich Companies Go Out of Business

Biggest Telecommunications Company Ltd (BTC) is a giant telecom operator entering the mobile telecommunications segment. Experts believe that the future of telecom is radio and wireless technology. Its cost of goods sold (COGS) is a high 90% of sales and rising fast because of its legacy system, as a previous wire line operator. Its yearly operating expenses are in the region of ₹350 billion. The sales for the first five years are given below:

Period (₹ billions)	**2008**	**2009**	**2010**	**2011**	**2012**
Total Sales	380	360	320	300	290
Operating Expenses	330	340	340	360	370
Gross Profit	50	20	(20)	(60)	(80)

Let us assume that BTC Ltd starts its new venture with a cash balance of ₹80 billion in the bank, because that is what it had after operating profitably for several years in the landline segment. What does its cash flow look like? Unlike other companies, being a retailer, let us assume for the sake of simplicity that BTC receives its cash almost immediately because it has a good collection practices. During 2008, company piles up a cash balance of ₹130 billion. The next year cash balance is ₹150 billion. During 2010, though it sustains an operating loss of ₹20 billion its cash balance remains ₹130 billion. During the subsequent year 2011, the company has further losses, but it still has cash flow of ₹70 billion.

Cash based businesses can get a totally wrong picture of what is going on. In this case BTC's cash balances look healthy, even though the company has turned unprofitable in the new venture. But this cannot go on forever, by the year 2012 the company has totally run out of cash with ₹10 billion in deficits. The fate of BTC is inevitable because subsequent periods are loss-making and does not add to the cash flow of the company. If it fails to regain profitability it will face serious cash problems. The only reasonable path for the company is to cut down operating expenses to match revenues, until it can come up with a plan to find new revenue generation possibilities.

BTC Ltd story is not purely imaginary. It has parallels in the real world. For a time the piling up of cash balances give the impression of health to the unwary manager who has not yet come to grips with the reality of the accounting system. But ultimately the company must become profitable by the standards of the financial statements. In the BTC case, book-loses eventually led to using up of cash and the negative cash flow in a very short period of three years. This is how cash rich companies go out of business.

Understanding the difference between cash and profits and their respective roles in the business is a key level of financial acumen for the executives. It is one which the managers have not had opportunity to grasp fully. However, this aspect of the business should engage a great deal of time to the financially aware executives, because the future course of action depends on it. Let us see how these concepts apply in real business world. Let us suppose that your company is caught in the situation where lack of operating cash is ruining its prospects of survival. What you need to recognize here is the very important aspect of raising money in the cheapest possible way to manage your operations without adding to the costs substantially. This is in fact a fundamental job of financial management. You will also look for ways to speed up your collections, so that too much cash is not locked up in your sales receivable. The art of working capital management is what we are talking about here. This is finance at its best.

Imagine again the case of BTC Ltd narrated above. What BTC urgently needs is managerial ability to bring operational costs down to the barest minimum without affecting ongoing revenue potential. This will call for skills in identifying and eliminating waste of cash resources in current practices. It is necessary to explore additional revenue generation opportunities, without adding to costs of operations. Borrowing funds for short-term working capital requirements or for paying salaries will only lead the company further down the slippery slope. It could look at cutting down its scale of operations by getting rid of unprofitable business segments. The key point here is that once the cash flow turns negative, outcomes look bleak for the owners.

Timing of actions is the other take away from a clear understanding of cash flow situation. Chasing customers who tend to pay late, offering appropriate incentives to collections agents and managing bad-debts policy etc keep cash flowing in. Locking up precious cash in inventory should be discouraged. The lessons boil down to two. Both profits and cash are important. Though they are different, managers need to keep an eye on both. This basic level of understanding leads to better actions and better performance. Looking at the cash flow statement is a most useful way of understanding the financial situation of a company. Merely showing the earnings in the accounting statement has its value, but needs to be understood by the context of its ability to maintain operations as well.

This brings us to an important concept. The life-cycle of business units is not unlike the human experience of the various stages of one's life.

Cash-Flow and the Business Life Cycle

It would be hazardous to draw conclusions from a mere reading of the cash flow statements without first understanding the stage of growth of the company in question. It also matters whether it is operating in a mature industry or a new one.

Start-up companies have voracious need for cash during the initial years. Our imaginary company Sweetie's Dream Dolls would fall in this category. With very little cash coming in, new start-ups struggle to stay in business unless it can find willing investors and lenders quickly. That is perhaps the reason why start-up ventures are generally funded by venture capitalists and angel investors. They are not mature enough to approach the public for funds.

Venture Capitalists and Angel Investors

Venture capital may include money, managerial and technical expertise. This form of raising capital is popular among new companies or ventures with limited operating history, which cannot raise funds by borrowing. The venture capitalists usually get a say in company decisions, and are partial owners in the business.

Angel investors are from friends and family, give more favorable terms than other lenders, as they are usually investing in the person rather than the viability of the business. They are focused on helping the business succeed, rather than reaping a huge profit from their investment. Angel investor is essentially the exact opposite of a venture capitalist.

Emerging growth companies survive the initial start-up phase and have established a certain reputation as a company with growth potential. However, they are not established well enough to reap benefits from past investments and are also in need of cash to service a growing customer base and need further investments in equipments and infrastructure. A typical example would be the telecommunications companies operating in the mobile services segment in India. Bharti Airtel is the largest private telecom services provider in India. During 2011 it has a total revenue of ₹380 billion and net profits after tax of ₹77 billion. However, cash balances during the year were a mere ₹1.2 billion. The large scale of its operations and tremendous expansion programs took a heavy toll on its cash requirements. It has operating cash flow to the tune of ₹132 billion but its growth required funding to the tune of ₹191 billion. The gap was covered through long-term borrowings and liquidation of investments.

Heavy reliance on eternal borrowings increases the vulnerability of companies in the emerging growth phase. Its ability to finance further expansions through raising funds will become more restricted. The banking sector in India is already overexposed to the telecom sector because of its heavy lending for the 3G auctions during 2010. Bharti Airtel has been experiencing a secular decline in its net profits for all the quarters ending Q410 to Q312. This is typical of a company that has a high debt burden to service, increasing revenues every quarter, with interest costs pulling down its net income.

Established growth companies, on the other hand, exhibit slightly different characteristics. They have a higher level of investments in fixed assets than the level of depreciation. They are less precariously placed in terms of cash flow as compared to the emerging growth companies. Their ability to borrow is not hampered by falling revenues or extreme competition in the market.

Mature industry companies, such as Infosys Technologies or Tata Consultancy Services Ltd, two of the leading software exporter and world leaders in their business space, are consistently increasing cash flows from operations. Occasional fall in revenues do not affect their operations. The cash flow from depreciation alone more than covers their capital requirements. They usually have a huge cash reserve for acquisition opportunities.

Declining industry companies struggle to earn sufficient cash due to meager revenue performance. Their products and services have outlived their usefulness or have been the victim of disruptive technology force. In an earlier section, we have discussed the cash flow pattern of a somewhat imaginary company called BTC Ltd. An incumbent landline operator with a large presence, its decline started when it had to compete with the mobile operators. The revenue from landline which formed 80% of its total income starts declining year after year. However, its legacy systems established for the landline network continue to act as a cost on its income statement. Cash flow from operations though substantial will not be sufficient to cover the losses and requirements of continuing operations. Polaroid Corporation, manufacturers of film cameras, faced a similar situation by 2000. Its profits had vanished three years earlier, and the cash squeeze became severe due to the deterioration in its core business. Digital photography was the new craze and customers abandoned film-cameras. As a cost saving measure, company slashed employee benefits like medical re-imbursements. In 2001 it filed for bankruptcy.

The Concept of Financial Flexibility[1]

Understanding a company's cash situation takes a lot more than a mere reading of its statement of cash flows, as the foregoing discussion reveals. However, the statement itself makes you ask the right questions. The first thing you would like to know is where the cash is coming from. Is it from operations of its core business? If so it is a good thing. Where is the cash going? Is the size of the investing activities a reasonably large negative number? (*Negative, because it is an outflow*). If so, it is a good thing. Well, wait a second. Where is the money for investing coming from? If it is from operations, your company is ok. If not, is it merely selling stock to finance all its investments? Is your company desperately selling stock to stay afloat? I am mortified at this point to state that the cash flow statement generates lots of questions. But they are the right ones to be asking. The answers to these and similar questions tell us the all-important concept of financial flexibility.

Put very simply, financial flexibility explains the ability of the management to continue to do the following operations: They are:

1. Pay dividends to its shareholders
2. Invest for future from funds that are internally available, even if external funding dries up or becomes extremely costly
3. Carry on its normal operations and meet regular obligations even if there is a downturn in the business

During difficult times the management must resort to cutting various expenditures to conserve cash. The key objective of the management must be to maintain the long-term health of the organization. If they fail to maintain the dividend, it acts as a signal to the market and subsequent efforts of the company to obtain capital from the market may prove difficult and costly. If the downturn in the market is temporary due to competitive pressures, long-term investments must not be allowed to suffer, while at the same time trying to keep up the level of operations. If expansions and modernization is cut back to conserve cash, future profitability and competitiveness could take a beating. In short, loss of financial flexibility leads to further loss of financial flexibility.

If the strain on cash becomes extreme, the board may decide to eliminate dividend. This may be a better option as compared to severe retrenchment of employees, after resorting to cutting their benefits or selling of core assets to generate cash and default of payments to third parties. Although dividend is a discretionary item for the management, it has wide ramifications in terms of the signalling power it commands in the market. It has the ultimate effect of increasing the cost of capital for the company. We therefore come to the conclusion that financial flexibility is the ability of the management to meet its present level of operations and investments from its own internal resources, while maintaining the current level of dividends.

The best way to gauge the degree of financial flexibility is to keenly observe the difference between the operational cash flow and the outflow on account of investing activities. The positive balance that remains after investing activities is called the free cash flow or the discretionary cash flow. This is cash in the hands of the management to use as it deems fit. The ideal situation exists where the free cash flow covers dividend.

A further factor in assessing financial flexibility relates to the changes in adjusted working capital. A growing company generally finds its stock of goods and the number of customers yet to make payments for services purchased increasing steadily. A moment's reflection will reveal to you that this in fact is a usage of cash from the company's point of view. These two items represent a cash outflow, as cash gets locked up either within the company (more inventories) or is lying with the customers (increase in receivables). If there is a more-than-proportionate increase in these items as compared to sales, external borrowing will become necessary. A very large company may be able to put off paying its suppliers for some time. But this cannot continue for a long time. Thus deterioration in operational cash flow will lead to borrowing, resulting in increased interest pay outs. In short, again, loss of financial flexibility leads to further loss of financial flexibility.

Managers everywhere therefore need to guard jealously the usage of cash. Failure to understand the importance of cash is a surefire method to messy managerial culture.

Is Hoarding Cash Good?

However, there are people who frown on the practice of managers who retain cash as a cushion. The basis of the argument here is that there is no need to preserve cash in excess of that which is required to fund all opportunities which have positive future cash flows. It is better to distribute the excess to shareholders in the form of dividend. We have seen the other side of the coin earlier when we discussed the idea of dividend signaling. We saw that some people perceived dividend as a last option where the management has run out of investment ideas. This appears to be logical. Managements prefer to continue investments even though it might not appear to be in the company's best interests. Mindless acquisitions to boost egos immediately spring to mind, which have destroyed long-run profitability of a few robust companies.

There is a word of caution due here. The argument appears valid only in hindsight. Managers appeared to have over invested when indeed the subsequent turn of events led to an economic downturn. Had they turned out to be otherwise and indeed the economic activity in general took-off, the same decisions would have turned out to be brilliant. If they had not invested in additional capacity, the subsequent shortfall in capacities would have left the firm non-competitive and vulnerable to their competitor's aggressive merger plans. This was certainly true of India's largest Telecommunications player, BSNL, the public sector giant during 2006-07. Though the company had large reserves of cash, it failed to invest in the new and emerging mobile sector. This was among the main reasons why it lost competitiveness in subsequent years. However, it would have been difficult to arrive at this very conclusion (*without the benefit of hindsight*) during the early years of mobile revolution in India. The hyper-growth of the mobile market in India during the decade from 2007 to 2010 confounded even the most seasoned pundits.

Perhaps, the subtler and more important aspect of cash as a cushion is that financial flexibility can and must translate into operational flexibility. We shall make this point very clear. It is not the amount of cash-hoard but the degree of manoeuvrability that really matters. Real cash deployed in 'marketable securities' will assist the company when credit conditions are really tight. The other obvious risk of not having this cushion is the permanent loss of skills and deterioration of plant and machinery if they are to be shut down due to lack of funds. Reviving these operations will later cost more dearly.

Getting to Cash from Other Statements

We have been emphasizing the 'real' part of company-reporting. We are agonized over the concept of value as presented in the balance sheet. Financial intelligence involves the ability to spot the real profit from the operations. As part of the exercise, we have now understood how assumptions and biases affect all reports and how we need to guard against arriving at conclusions too soon regarding the net worth and the real financial position of a business. In this section we are proposing to delve a little deeper into the concept of cash and how it can be found from the financial statements. In fact, arriving at *real cash transactions* simply involves reversal of some of the non-cash transactions that found their way into the income statement and the balance sheet. We can do this if we have an income statement and two balance sheets (current and previous). We will not here go into the actual mechanics of how it can be done. (*The interested reader will gain immensely if he now immediately turns to Appendix II where we have worked out a sample cash flow statement for an imaginary company from its two statements.*)

Real Cash Transactions

We stated that Cash is real. Well, almost.

Ramalinga Raju, chairman of Satyam Computers shocked the world, by revealing that he had overstated cash balances in the company accounts. He claimed that there was ₹53.61 billion in the bank when actually he had none. (*Although he was not the first businessman to do this!*)

He did this by issuing fictitious invoices, which were paid for in fictitious cash and then making fictitious documents to show that these were deposited into the bank.

The Language of Cash Flow

Any business undertakes three types of activities. It runs the day-to-day operations. It invests for the future. To do both of this it needs some form of financing activities. The main purpose of the cash flow statement then is to provide its users with information regarding the amounts used for these three activities in the form of cash inflows and outflows.

Those dealing with the business enterprise, the shareholders, lenders, suppliers, employees, regard the firm as a source of cash. They look forward to dividend, interest, payments, and salaries. They are directly interested in knowing whether the business will be able to do this now and continue do so in future. The cash flow statement enables them to assess the liquidity, profitability, financial flexibility and risk associated with the business.

Unlike the other two financial statements, the cash flow statement has a few peculiarities. Non-accountants generally find this confusing. There are basically two typical reasons. The first is that, the most common form of the statement of cash flows is like the crab. It seems to walk backwards, when it actually is walking forwards! The second reason is that it is not immediately clear why some items are shown as negative figure when it must indeed look like a positive figure. Let me attempt to clear up this backward-forward walking animal's behavior.

The Backward Looking Forward Walk

We have stated earlier that profit is not equal to cash as shown in the balance sheet. There are fundamentally several reasons for this. Firstly, customers don't pay cash immediately on sale and all expenses are not in cash. Further and most essentially, the company is like an organism in which the cash flows like its life blood through the arteries of its business operations, which are interconnected to several points outside itself. Therefore, 'inflows' and 'outflows' happen not only through sales to customers and expenses to employees, but also through purchases and owners putting cash into the system. If cash does not 'go-out' it 'stays' within the system.

Profit is arrived at after deducting all matching expenses for the period, some of which are not cash expenses at all. Therefore, to arrive at the cash profit, we need to add back all non-cash expenses and subtract all non-cash sales and calculate all inflows and outflows. This backward process of deducting non-cash sales and adding back non-cash expenses is known as the indirect method of arriving at the operating cash flow. This is backward-looking but is indeed a forward walk towards cash.

A further aspect of the cash flow statement is that it categorizes a company's cash outflow into 'operating', 'investing' and 'financing' activities. Non-finance executives might find this sometimes daunting. For example dividend distribution is categorized as financing activity, which if you really think about, is actually what it is. Again selling of assets is categorized as 'investing' activity even though it might seem like merely an operational hazard to many of us. What is sometimes really disconcerting is the usage of positive and negative numbers to denote cash inflow or outflow. For example under operational activities one might see that the figure for depreciation is a sizeable amount of cash inflow with a positive tag. The confusion arises because; we have all along been insisting that depreciation is an expense. Yes it is so. But it being a non-cash expense, no cash has gone out of the company when we depreciate an asset. Therefore we add back this figure to the profit-figure to get to the actual cash available in the company.

Does that make sense? Probably not! This is the reason why you would benefit immensely if you make an effort to go through the actual cash flow statement (*simplified for your benefit*) given in Appendix II of this book. But it is not yet time to panic. By the time you have finished reading this chapter you will feel more confident. We will introduce you to the basic concepts by starting with a few definitions.

1. Cash from Operating Activities

This category includes all cash used and received from a company's normal operations. It includes inflows from customers who pay their bills and the amount of money that is not yet paid to the vendors and other creditors. All outflows like salaries, rents, payments made to suppliers, postage and even the costs of telephone calls you made are listed here.

2. Cash Flow from Investing Activities

Please note at the outset that 'investing' here refers to the activities undertaken by the company and not the activities undertaken by the owners of the company. This will tell you that cash goes out of the company when it buys machinery and equipment to cater to a bigger market or for replacement of existing plant. Whereas, when the owners make investments then it will bring cash into the company in the form of share-capital. Thus purchase of assets is the main line-item in this section, showing a large negative figure. If the company sells off its assets, it will bring in cash. In general large outflows of cash for investing augur well for the future of the company. You must look for a figure that is considerably larger than the depreciation figure we mentioned earlier. This is because a company must invest in new technology and equipment to stay competitive in the long-run.

3. Cash Flow from Financing Activities

Financing activities refer to the transaction between the company and its owners on the one hand and its lenders on the other. If your company borrows money or pays back a bank loan taken earlier, these transactions appear here. If a shareholder invests money in the company it will show up as a receipt of cash in this section. If again your company buys back its own shares from open market, or pays a dividend to the shareholders, these are cash outflows which will appear in this section.

> **Financing a Company**
>
> A company gets money for its various activities only from two sources.
>
> First, from its owners. This is variously called as 'owner's capital', 'share-capital' or 'equity'. Second, from lenders. This is 'borrowings' by the company or is a 'debt' in the books. All other forms of financing the company are categorized under either 'Equity' or 'Debt'.

Looking for Cash in Your Own Company

It will be apparent to you that the cash flow statement reveals a lot about the company. An intelligent executive can translate much of this information into concrete action in the workplace. You would have by now figured out that among these, the critical thing to watch for is the operating cash flow. It represents the cash flowing into the company from its day-to-day business operations. This would mean that the company should aim at financing its operations and expansions with cheaper internal resources. We have explained this in detail in our discussion on financial flexibility.

If operating cash is not a healthy figure or it is decreasing from quarter to quarter, you must indeed raise a red flag. You must pin-point the reasons. The first place to look is in your company's sales figure or the top-line. May be all sales reported are not actual contracts with customers. May be your customers are defaulting on payments. Or somewhere the cash is leaking through the system. These are not all imaginary propositions. Reebok India Ltd executives, in order to achieve quarterly sales targets, shipped cartons of shoes to dealers, and reported sales to their parent company. But these were not contractual agreements with them resulting in payments. No cash was received and on closing of accounts the parent company had to write down nearly ₹800 million in its income statements. Even as we write this a detailed investigation is in progress. However, a closer scrutiny of the cash flow figures by the parent company would have revealed the fraud much earlier.

The second place to look for is in the inventory levels. Whether you are a manufacturing company or a trading and service company, you will have a stock of goods. A manufacturer will have idle stock both during the production process itself and stock of finished goods yet to be shipped to dealers. You will see clearly that such stock is nothing but cash in another form. Your company does not get any margin on those stocks unless raw materials are converted to finished goods and then shipped to customers. So long as they lie in your factory premises it is pure cash locked up and unusable till sold. Look for the inventory figure in the balance sheet. If it is proportionately large as compared to your sales figure, there is trouble. You will learn to analyze these numbers when we teach you about the practical ways of using financial skills, in working out ratios.

The category called investing activities shows whether the company management is milking the company for cash or is worried about its sustainability and future competitiveness. Merely generating cash and using it to pay dividends to please the stock market cannot go on forever. Sooner than later the operation is bound to fall through. Hoarding Cash as a strategy is feasible only in the short term. We need to see the big picture about the company and its environment before judging its usage of cash. However, the critical importance of reading and understanding cash cannot be brushed aside. A financially intelligent executive can employ these skills more than others to navigate the turbulent seas of business.

The third category of cash flows will show you whether the company is able to manage with its own cash flows or needs to depend on external sources. You can see over several periods whether the company is a net borrower (borrowing more than it is paying off). You can see whether it is selling shares frequently to raise cash. Any company perennially in need of cash is facing serious problems with its operations. Shareholders do not appreciate expansion of the equity base as it dilutes their dividend share. Lenders hesitate to offer money to a company that is frequently issuing bonds as they fear that interest burden will reduce the ability to pay back the principal and interest. It points to the management's inability to use precious cash resources judiciously.

Finally, the purpose of analyzing the cash flow statement is to understand the level of financial flexibility that a business actually enjoys. We can arrive at the cash flow through the company by analyzing and listing the major sources and usage of cash. But such a statement will be of little use to the categories of people, dealing with the company. Further, it will throw no light on whether a company can meet future obligations like dividend payments. It can reveal very little about the sort of external financing that the business may require. Perhaps a better approach will be to see whether the cash that the business uses comes from its operations or its investing and financing activities. Then we could observe the trends in cash flows and make comparisons with similar businesses.

The Concept 'Free Cash Flow'[2]

Prior to the advent of the cash flow statement and its being made mandatory under the Indian GAAP, Accounting Std No. 3, analysts and stock market watchers struggled with the income statement and the balance sheet to arrive at recommendatory findings about the company. This statement has made life easier for a large number of users. It became ever more relevant since the concept of 'profit' became more and more muddled not less so at the hands of inventive accountants finding legal ways around the GAAP. Since in many instances 'profit' figure as a single index became unreliable, other useful pointers had to be discovered. One such concept was called the EBDITA (earnings before depreciation interest taxation and amortization). It is easy to arrive at, as it is the figure in the income statement before deducting all these items. However, it must be emphasized here, as we have done already several times before, that depreciation is subject to the assumptions underlying the use of assets and therefore malleable at the hands of the accountant. Again Depreciation is not cash available to cover the cost of borrowing or any other investment program. It merely is a matching non-cash expense that does not represent a cash outflow. That's all!

Even though no single index can point to a company's financial position, managers everywhere continue to search for the gold and mount expeditions to El Dorado. One such attempt is the concept of 'free cash flow' popularized by the maverick Warren Buffett. He calls it 'owner earnings'. He defined it as the cash that remains out of the cash flow from operating activities after deducting the cash outflow from investing activities. Free cash flow according to Buffet is the cash generated by the business less the amount needed to keep it running.

This is intuitive and simple. If your business does not generate enough cash to maintain itself presently, how could it sustain operations in the future? Dotcom companies during the internet booming years had only this one peculiarity. It generated no cash but promised a pot of gold later. Investors who believed that the whole mantra of business had changed overnight, because a new world had emerged out of the 'cloud' were willing to pour money into such companies. Warren Buffet was among the very few who refused to do so. The mantra in truth never changes. Your operations must generate enough cash to keep you running. And that's just not enough; you must be able to spare enough cash to keep on running in future also.

....they say love is more important than money...but no matter how hard you hug your money, it never hugs back....

Summary of Chapter Four

In this chapter we tried to demonstrate how cash connects everything in business. We now know that profit as it appears in the income statement is not equivalent to cash. But without profits no company can generate cash. The statement of cash flows is a very interesting addition to financial reporting. It needs careful analysis to understand how the figures are arrived at. These are just additions and subtractions logically made from figures appearing in the balance sheet and P&L statements. This statement then becomes invaluable in situations where the balance sheet and the P&L statements provide only limited insight. The cash flow statement must however, be understood in the context in which the particular company is operating. The conclusions arrived at will vary depending on whether the company is in its start-up phase or in its maturity phase. It has ability to reveal the risks and opportunities that the company is going through, and the attitude of the management in guiding the organization through its future.

The key take-away from this chapter is most emphatically the concept of financial flexibility. Whatever the challenges a company is facing in its various stages in the life-cycle, financial flexibility is essential to meeting them. Financial flexibility is not merely a cushion or a security envelope to protect the investors. It has the essence of potentiality as in a tiny seed that grows into a mighty tree, in the hands of an aggressive but prudent management to nurture the company for the future, spending when competitors are forced to cut back, growing when others wither.

Find the Needle in the Haystack

Issues Based on Concepts in Part One

1. Looking at the Income Statement

When you come across a statement of profit and loss account, either in newspapers or in a business publication you can start with the following steps:

Look first at the balance sheet figures to see where the company stands at present. Then look carefully for the following:

(i) Do you see any trends in any of the line items, sales, employee costs, net profit? Do you think the raw numbers are telling you something?

(ii) You may find it easier to calculate some percentages for these items. (Percent change over previous years, or percent of some item over the sales figure)

(iii) Can you compare some major line items with any similar company?

(iv) Look at the reporting period. Are they same for the two companies which you are trying to compare? Are the denominations used by the companies the same?

(v) Are the nomenclature used for the line items the same? If they are different does it mean the same thing in each case?

If you have questions at any stage, read through the management analysis first, then look for notes to accounts, schedules for possible answers. If you notice any red flags at this stage you must pursue it to the very end till a possible satisfactory explanation emerges.

2. Reading and Understanding the Balance Sheet

(i) Balance sheet is the most important document that accountants produce.

(ii) When you look at balance sheets do you notice a pattern or order in which the items are listed? Is it the same for all companies?

(iii) Can you find the net worth of the company from the balance sheet? Where can you cross check this figure? Does the share-price of the company in the market equal this figure? Is the market price more than or less than the figure? What does it mean to you?

(iv) How much debt does the balance sheet show? Is the company able to pay back its debt?

(v) Is it generating enough profits through operations to finance its debt?

(vi) What do you think of a company that has little or no debt?

(vii) What are the company's assets? Is it worth what the balance sheet says it is? Would you pay more for it than the figure shown for the items like receivables and inventory?

(viii) Is the company adding to the assets?

(ix) How much does the company owe to outsiders?

(x) What do you think about its ability to meet day to day obligations like salaries, paying to suppliers?

(xi) Would you do any work for this company if you got an order?

Please remember that understanding the financial situation of a company is much more involved process than asking the sample questions listed above. You will need to carefully use the tools described in chapter seven of the book, even after which you would have merely arrived at a preliminary opinion. Further information about the company both inside and outside will need to be gathered.

3. Looking at the Cash Flow Statement

(i) Where does the bulk of the cash come from? Is it from operating activities or financing activities?

(ii) Is the company an established player or a new entrant? What is its main line of business? Is it having a stable model which will bring in cash regularly?

(iii) Is there a large difference between the sales figure and net cash from operations? Similarly between net profit and net cash from operations?

(iv) Is the company financing its purchases of assets with cash available from operations or by cash obtained from outside sources?

(v) What about depreciation figure as compared to purchases of assets? Is it more or less in comparison? What do you think it should be?

(vi) Does the company have financial flexibility as defined by Warren Buffet?

PART TWO

TOOLS IN YOUR SKILL-KIT

5
The Power of Interrelationships among Numbers

THIS CHAPTER DEALS WITH NUMBERS IN THEIR RAW FORM. However, before we actually go into the nitty-gritties of calculations, we must gently introduce the subject. But the purpose is to tell you that numbers can reveal a lot provided you have clarity of purpose and ability to look beyond the numbers themselves. We deal only with the numbers that are produced by the accountants in their three statements; namely, the balance sheet, the income statement and the statement of cash flows. The method we use below is called ratio-analysis by management experts; because they are in fact analysis of percentages and ratios, which uncover interrelationships among the various numbers that appear in these statements.[1]

The Number-Talk

Profile

Sachin Tendulkar has been the most complete batsman of his time, the most prolific run maker of all, and arguably the biggest cricket icon the game has ever known. His batting is based on the purest principles: perfect balance, economy of movement, precision in stroke-making, and that intangible quality given only to geniuses: anticipation. If he doesn't have a signature stroke – the upright, back-foot punch comes close – it is because he is equally proficient at each of the full range of orthodox shots (and plenty of improvised ones as well) and can pull them out at will.

An Economist's View

In 2011, a list of the top Test batsmen who ever lived was compiled by Griffith University's Dr Nicholas Rohde. Using data up until December 2011, the top of the list was Sachin Tendulkar, only just above Donald Bradman.

Wisden's Greatest Ever Player

In the early 2000's, Wisden released a list of the all-time top 100 greatest Test players using a unique rating system. The highest ranked batsman was Donald Bradman, a clear leader above Sachin Tendulkar.

Highest Test Run Scorers

The aim of a cricket batsman is to make as many runs as possible. Ranking the best batsman is by listing the total runs scored. The highest test run scorer is the Indian player Sachin Tendulkar, though the other commonly nominated greatest batsman, Bradman, is not

	Player	Played	Matches	Inns	Runs	Highest	Ave	100	50	duck
1	SR Tendulkar (India)	1989 +	177	290	14692	248*	56.94	51	59	14
2	RT Ponting (Aus)	1995-2010	152	259	12363	257	53.51	39	56	14
3	R Dravid (ICC/ India)	1996 +	153	265	12314	270	52.4	32	60	8
4	BC Lara (ICC/ WI)	1990-2006	131	232	11953	400*	52.88	34	48	17
5	JH Kallis (ICC/ SA)	1995 +	145	246	11947	201*	57.43	40	54	10
6	AR Border (Aus)	1978-1994	156	265	11174	205	50.56	27	63	11
7	SR Waugh (Aus)	1985-2004	168	260	10927	200	51.06	32	50	22
8	SM Gavaskar (India)	1971-1987	125	214	10122	236*	51.12	34	45	12
9	DPMD Jayawardene (SL)	1997 +	119	196	9630	374	52.62	28	38	11
10	S Chanderpaul (WI)	1994 +	133	227	9367	203*	49.04	23	55	13

even in the top 10! The Don was ranked 39th as he did not play anywhere near as many Test matches as these players. The table below was created in July 2011.

Greatest Test Averages

As the list above of top Test run scorers did not include what many consider to be the greatest batsman ever, here is a list that does have him on top. Below are the top test batting averages for players who have batted for 10 or more innings in Test matches. Now the highest run scorer does not make the list, though he would not be far off the top 10 with a current average of 56.94 (July 2011).

Player	Played	Matches	Inns	No.	Runs	HS	Ave	100	50	ducks
DG Bradman (Aus)	1928-1948	52	80	10	6996	334	99.94	29	13	7
CS Dempster (NZ)	1930-1933	10	15	4	723	136	65.72	2	5	0
SG Barnes (Aus)	1938-1948	13	19	2	1072	234	63.05	3	5	1
Taslim Arif (Pak)	1980-1980	6	10	2	501	210*	62.62	1	2	1
IJL Trott (Eng)	2009 +	21	34	4	1867	226	62.23	6	6	1
RG Pollock (SA)	1963-1970	23	41	4	2256	274	60.97	7	11	1
GA Headley (WI)	1930-1954	22	40	4	2190	270*	60.83	10	5	2
H Sutcliffe (Eng)	1924-1935	54	84	9	4555	194	60.73	16	23	2
E Paynter (Eng)	1931-1939	20	31	5	1540	243	59.23	4	7	3
KF Barrington (Eng)	1955-1968	82	131	15	6806	256	58.67	20	35	5

Below are some of the greatest cricketers ever, compiled using other published lists. The players are listed in no particular order. This list is not complete.

Name	Notes
Adam Gilchrist	Australian wicket keeper
Alan Border	Ex Australian captain was fifth on the Wisden all-time batsman list
Brian Lara	West Indian batsman
Clarrie Grimmett	Australian, cricketer fifth on the Wisden all-time bowler list

Name	Notes
Dennis Lillee	Australian fast bowler
Don Bradman	Australian legend batsman. Highest test average of 99.94. First on the Wisden all-time batsman list
Glenn McGrath	Australian fast bowler
Joel Garner	West Indian fast bowler
Mutthiah Muralitharan	First on the Wisden all-time bowler list
Rahul Dravid	Indian cricketer fourth on the Wisden all-time batsman list
Ricky Ponting	batsman
Richard Hadlee	second on the Wisden all-time bowler list
Sachin Tendulkar	second on the Wisden all-time batsman list
Shane Warne	Australian leg spin bowler. fourth on the Wisden all-time bowler list

Comment 1

Yes Bradman is great but Sachin is God.

1. Pressure

Tendulkar plays under huge pressure. Bradman never had such pressure in his whole career apart from bodyline series and in his last innings against England.

2. Fitness

Bradman played 52 tests in 20 years but Sachin played 162 Tests in the same number of years. During the Bradman-era, players easily got 7-8 days of gap in between 2 tests of a series. During the Sachin-era, 5 ODI get completed in 12-13 days and the Test series starts after a gap of just 3 days.

3. Opposition

Bradman played mostly against England and he got used to their bowling. One series against each minnows [India, South Africa and West Indies who were new to cricket that time] and scored heavily. Other than Larwood, Bradman never played any quality bowlers (*the others were CV Grimmett and RR Lindwall, who were friendly fellow countrymen!*). Sachin faced the likes of Ambrose-Walsh-Bishop, Wasim-Waqar-Akhtar, McGrath-Lee-Gilespie, Donald-Pollock, Warne-Murli and many more. The swing and reverse swing were unknown during the Don's time.

4. Technology

The average of 99.94 is phenomenal and is definitely considered a great feat, statistically. However, Cricket is not just a game of statistics, and averages. There are many other aspects which should be considered. For example, the level of playing cricket, the level of technology used to analyse each player's weaknesses, and the standards of fielding. The Media hype and expectations from fans is very high.

Sachin played lot of cricket, scored in every part of the world, consistently. Public and Media call him 'little master.'

If it is unfair to compare two batsmen of different era, then it would also be unfair to call Sir Don as the 'greatest batsman of all times.'

Comment 2

What I find staggering is that Indians tend to swamp websites with posts that almost deify Tendulkar.

Tendulkar worshippers will have to stomach historical facts.

Batting technology. Don didn't have the luxury of choosing the bats. Tendulkar had a bat that was much more powerful with less chance of mis-hitting the ball, and a 'sweet spot' that covers at least half the bat.

Pitches. When Don played pitches weren't covered when it rained. The weather could turn the pitch from a batting paradise to a bowler's dream in the course of a session. Tendulkar played most of his career on the batting paradise pitches that India has.

Bowling standards. According to Tendulkar fans, bowlers were slower and didn't really spin the ball. This is far from reality. During the Don's time, bowlers were brutally quick, dangerous, beguiling. The Don was often facing a bowler he had never seen in his life.

Bradman's genius. The Don averaged 99.94 in a sport where averaging above 45 is phenomenal. Now, he batted 80 times in Test cricket. Since 1877, when the First Test was ever played, the Don's performance as a batsman is 64% better than the second best average.

World War Two. When the Don was at his peak, WWII halted Test cricket for 8 years. If WWII hadn't occurred his statistics would be so far beyond compare that this discussion wouldn't have occurred.

Making Financial Numbers Talk

I have gone to some length in citing the numbers from cricket statistics. The purpose is to demonstrate what the numbers can do. The question as to who is the greatest cricketer still remains unanswered, despite all the numbers which are there for all to see. The intelligent reader would have somewhat guessed the reason why this is so. We shall presently elaborate.

1. The Purpose for Which the Numbers Are Used

The numbers speak only when the specific objective of using them has been clearly defined. If the aim of the analysis is to discover the greatest batsman in the history of cricketing, 'greatness' needs to be defined in clear and objective terms. Batting is all about scoring runs. The game itself, its rules and techniques of playing undergo changes from time to time. Defined in this way the only number that would matter to the analysis is of course, the number of runs scored by the batsman. Talent, genius and elegance are all attributes of greatness, but in a context.

Financial analysts often fall prey to this aspect of using the numbers. Clearly defined objective of rating a company for its creditworthiness would involve looking at the numbers that would enable the lender to ascertain whether the company has sufficient ability to meet its interest obligations. An important observation here is that beyond a certain point, calculating and comparing companies based on additional financial numbers would add little information to the objective establishing its creditworthiness. These numbers though indirectly related to the profitability aspects of management, does not carry any relevance to the lender.

2. The Line of Business

The greatest cricketer need not be a batsman. Therefore analysis of batting scores or long-run averages of batting figures would not yield the satisfactory answer. Comparing of two firms which operate in different nature of industries not only produces meaningless results, but ignores the all important fact that different industries have different financial characteristics. A machinery manufacturer's results will fluctuate significantly over the capital goods cycle. But a packaged foods industries player gets its revenues from goods that are in demand throughout the year. His cash flows and earnings are more predictable and therefore may be able to take on more debt. Comparing the two firms on debt burden or earnings or risk of default may therefore look rather off-color. The important principle here is to ensure that numbers can make sense and answer important questions only when they are kept within the boundaries of comparability. Industry numbers across economy borders like financial, utility, transportation, construction and food may look the same with similar nomenclature, but have widely varying underlying meanings.

The solution to this problem may partially be found in grouping industries under similar peer groups, virtually engaged in producing somewhat identical products. Even here, a producer of coated white paper is not strictly comparable to a producer of soft tissue paper or even a manufacturer of fine writing paper.

A word of caution is due here. It would be too zealous to compare only left-handed batsman who played between 2002 and 2010 in order to rank the best batsman in that category, even though it would satisfy stated goals of comparison.

3. The Interrelatedness of Data

A magical aspect of numbers in general is their interrelatedness. It is no surprise that the highest run-getters in cricket also have higher number of 'ducks' (*getting out without scoring a single run*). Again the highest run-getters also have larger number of 'centuries' to their credit. The 'averages' are better for those players who have played far fewer matches.

This is not a chance result. It is not easy for a company to have a comparatively high amount of debt and at the same time to have a large amount of income to cover the interest payments. It would again be near impossible for a company to grow at a fixed high percentage year after year. Increase in sales figure must be accompanied by increase in cash flows. If not there is a chance that sales are not real or customers are dissatisfied with the product or both.

Behind the Numbers

As by now you have realized, ratio-analysis or the art of drawing conclusions from financial figures produced by companies is both interesting and hazardous. If used with the above guidelines it can be interesting and meaningful in arriving at desired conclusions. If not it is hazardous and misleading, easily falling into the whirlpool of endless argumentation. A careful understanding of the purpose of financial reporting and its risks founded on assumptions and estimates will open up a world of well meaning conclusions which are useful. It may even help you to uncover frauds in the making, as leading practitioners of this art have done.

The following chapter then invites you to understand the basic tools of ratio-analysis. But we invite you to complement your conclusions with your own judgment on matters which are beyond the ken of the numbers themselves. Merely relying on numbers to arrive at a conclusion is as foolhardy as rejecting all the information the numbers are telling you and relying solely on your gut-feeling or instinct. This is true for all quantitative techniques. In short, equip yourself with these tools but do not be complacent about them.

Inconsistencies Stick Out

Andrew Shore (a financial analyst at Paine Webber and Company, now part of UBS group), not to be confused with the famous English baritone, used the numbers from the three statements to expose the accounting tricks of the notorious CEO 'Chainsaw Al' Dunlap of Sunbeam. Here is the story as it has relevance to our topic here.[2]

> In little more than four years, Albert Dunlap made more than $100 million, ran two well-known public corporations, wrote a best-selling vainglorious autobiography, and axed some 18,000 employees. His modus operandi was simple. He parachuted into poorly performing companies and made tough decisions that quickly brought shareholders sizable profits. 'We're all seduced by the possibility of big wins,' says PaineWebber Inc. analyst Andrew Shore.
>
> Wall Street lustily cheered his arrival at the $1.2 billion maker of electric blankets and outdoor grills. Sunbeam's stock surged nearly 50%, to 18 5/8, the day after his July 18 appointment. Less than four months later, Dunlap lived up to his reputation as a corporate demolition expert. He announced the shutdown or sale of two-thirds of Sunbeam's 18 plants and the elimination of half its 12,000 employees.
>
> When the stock spiked after Dunlap was appointed, Shore thought the reaction irrational and said so. His candor hardly pleased Dunlap, who would claim that Shore was biased against him because PaineWebber didn't get Sunbeam's investment banking business. (Shore denies that charge.) With each new earnings report, however, he carefully dissected Sunbeam's ever-improving results.
>
> The numbers showed that Dunlap was building what Shore considered abnormally high inventory levels and accounts receivable. His trade contacts confirmed his suspicions that Sunbeam was giving lucrative terms to dealers to ship products aggressively. As the company later acknowledged, he began to engage in so-called 'bill and hold' deals with retailers in which Sunbeam products were purchased at large discounts and then held at third-party warehouses for delivery later. **By booking**

these sales before the goods were delivered, Dunlap helped boost Sunbeam's revenues by 18% in 1997 alone. In effect, he was shifting sales from future quarters to current ones. The approach was not illegal, but the extraordinary volume made it unusual. Dunlap defended the practice, saying that it was an effort to extend the selling season and better meet surges in demand. Sunbeam's auditors, **Arthur Andersen & Co., later insisted it met accounting standards.**

Two weeks later, on Apr. 2, Shore heard more disturbing news: Donald R. Uzzi, Sunbeam's well-regarded executive vice-president for worldwide consumer products, had been fired by Dunlap. Not able to reach Uzzi or Dunlap for confirmation, Shore sought out investor-relations chief Richard Goudis, only to discover that he had quit.

Finally, the analyst thought, it was time to advise his clients to get out of the stock. He frantically downgraded the stock on Apr. 3 at 9:00 a.m., and it quickly fell by 4 points. Some two hours later, Sunbeam disclosed that it would post a first-quarter loss. **By day's end, the stock fell 25%, to 34 3/8, and shareholders soon filed lawsuits charging deception.**

Andrew Shore was not a prophet. He merely followed the simplest rules of financial ratio-analysis. He began noticing the gap between sales and cash by analyzing the abnormal increase in the number of customers who failed to pay up. Simultaneously he observed that sales of electric blankets and grills were completely out of tune with the seasonal behavior of these products. The sales which would normally have taken place during the first and second quarters were already recorded through the strategy of 'bill-and-hold' which was nothing but a euphemism for channel stuffing.

Channel Stuffing

A deceptive business practice used by a company to inflate its sales and earnings figures by deliberately sending to dealers more products than they are able to sell to the public.

By channel stuffing, distributors temporarily beef up their accounts receivables. However, unable to sell the excess products, retailers will send the excess items instead of cash back to the distributor, who must readjust its accounts receivable and ultimately its bottom line. In other words, stuffing always catches up with the company, because it cannot maintain sales at the rate it is stuffing.

This is usually done fraudulently to raise the value of the stock.

Ratio-analysis provides you with sufficient pointers to draw meaningful conclusions if you can detect them. The inconsistencies in the numbers usually stick out for the astute analyst to sense that something may be wrong somewhere. It does not tell you what.

Analytical Applications for the Interrelationships

Users of financial statements have various objectives for looking at the numbers. Bankers and lenders may like to get an idea of the overall debt repayment capacity of the company before making further loans. Suppliers and vendors would necessarily assess the liquidity position of the company before signing agreements to make large supplies. Senior management, on the other hand, makes careful note of the gross profit margins, the operational efficiency and return on investment ratios. Employees are indirectly concerned with the profitability of operations and their own job security. They would like to continue getting the salaries on time and bonuses and incentives. Shareholders have altogether different viewpoints. They are primarily concerned with stock appreciation in the market and the rising net worth of the company over a period of time. Financial analysts and investment firms closely monitor company rating as compared to its peers in the industry. They have clients to advice and they wish to be right in their recommendations. They therefore follow up their analysis of the numbers with as much information about the company as possible. They speak to the management at all levels as soon as they see any inconsistencies in the financial numbers for a plausible explanation. They also possess a sound knowledge of what is legal and permissible under the accounting standards, to see how far the companies are involved in creative accounting practices that stretch the standards into the grey area between legality and fraud.

Financial ratios offer more than the numbers themselves in their raw-form. The power of percentages is far beyond the absolute numbers. For example, profit as a percentage of sales, total assets or the total shareholder's equity will tell a different story each time. Each of these percentages has a different meaning for the stakeholder involved. Merely stating that your company made ₹10 million in profits means nothing to the intelligent observer, in judging whether it is a good or bad story. It is just like the woman when asked how her husband was, she replied, 'Compared to what?'

These ratios, on the other hand, can tell the management whether pricing is right or too many discounts are being offered in order to achieve sales. It points to the efficiency of assets utilization on the one hand and the return to the shareholders after all other obligations has been met. The ratios can be compared to themselves over a period of time to form trend lines which are powerful tools with some predictive properties. Ratios can be used as control levers to manage outcomes with regard to inventory, debtors and costs. Ratios are used to compare companies within the Industry. Peer group analysis as we have discussed earlier throws considerable light on managerial skills of particular firms. A good example of this is from India's Telecommunications sector. Airtel, under the control of Sunil Bharti Mittal, was able to cut costs of operations per employee by extreme innovation. He outsourced the management of switching capacities to third parties. The peer companies found themselves outfoxed by this innovation and lost competitiveness in a low-priced telecom market.

The use of ratios gives power to all stakeholders. Financial statements are somewhat opaque to even experts in finance. Ratios throw light into the dark corners. It is like looking into a locked up house through the windows which are open.

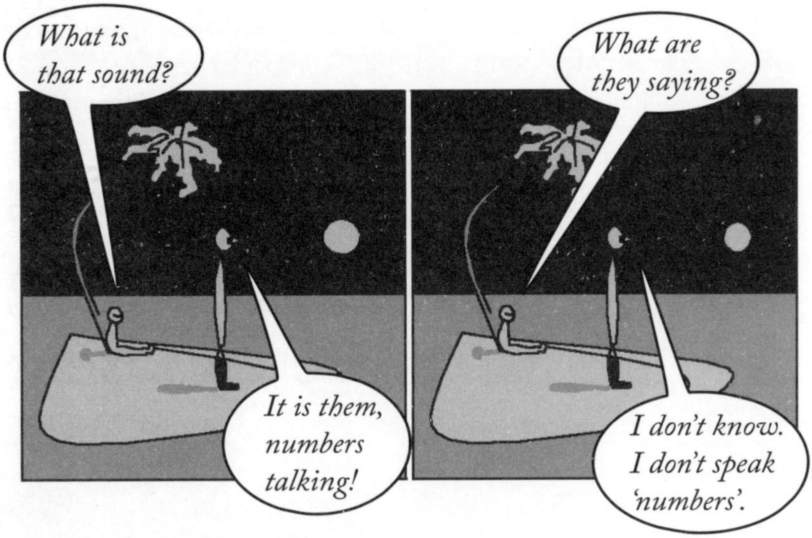

Summary of Chapter Five

The use of ratios in financial statement analysis is based on percentages and interrelationships. In this chapter we have not gone into the ratios themselves. But we attempted to give a foretaste of what they can do and how they ought to be used. The art of making the numbers speak is through the technique of squeaking them. Clarity of purpose to get at the specific facts is important. Looking for attributes in statements which cannot be revealed by numbers will not take the analyst any distance. Ratios if used with skill and clarity can reveal a lot more than the raw statements themselves. The aspects of a company with regard to profitability, creditworthiness, liquidity and efficiency are all hidden in the numbers which can be brought to light by ratios.

We have cautioned the reader that ratios by themselves do not constitute the end of analysis. Information about the company, its managerial culture and environment and other information related to the nature of business and its cyclicality are vital. It is also important to remember that accounting numbers carry biases inbuilt in their very nature. But abandoning the powerful tools of ratio-analysis because of this would not be wise, just as complete reliance on it alone would be rather odd.

6

Can Accounting Tricks Be Exposed?

FINANCIAL STATEMENT ANALYSIS IS AN ESSENTIAL PART OF financial intelligence. Business acumen and the ability to diagnose what your business needs at particular inflection points cannot be separated from each other. These skills are essential in a variety of professions, investment, management, corporate finance and commercial lending are some examples. But the ordinary executive in a business needs these skills to be effective and advance his career. For individuals, who engage in such activities, and analyze financial data for personal investment decisions, the distinct priority is to avoid being caught on the wrong foot. It is hard to digest the ebbing away of personal net worth as a result of having relied on dubious financial information.

The reader may at this point imagine that this view of the financial information is overly pessimistic. He may indeed argue that the superstructure of accounting rules and regulations and the elaborate discipline of accounting that has evolved over the historical past guiding corporate reporting practices are safeguards for the individual user. Further an elaborate legal system surrounding the corporate behavior prevents or at least effectively exposes the misdeeds of the few who attempt them. These then should in no way form the basis of the premise that all reporting is suspect and tinted with fraudulent intent. This is undeniably true.

The inconvenient fact that confounds all such views is that financial *statements do not invariably* reflect the true performance of the issuer faithfully. They reflect the financial position as intended to be reflected. Herein *lies the great truth* that the purpose of financial reporting is not *accurate* measurement of financial position, but projecting a *feasible* financial position. A large majority of managements use the financial statements as banners to propagate the message of well-being within the company, not infrequently using the numbers as advertisements in business publications. They employ investor relationship managers, frequently hold press meets and communicate with existing and potential customers and investors. If the sole purpose of these exercises were to report the accurate financial situation, the three statements contained in the annual reports and quarterly results might have served the purpose.

Is All Financial Reporting Tainted?

This book is not adversarial to the practice of financial reporting. This book is rather overly concerned with the concept of financial skills, which involves the accurate discernments of such reporting. This is essential intelligence for individuals and employees everywhere, because without it, the implications of understanding financial statements and getting behind the numbers to peal-away the covers to expose the accurate picture presented will not be possible. This book does not claim that all financial reporting is inaccurate or fraudulent. If it were so why write the book at all? Let us make our position explicit.

A corporate body exists chiefly to create wealth for its stakeholders. Its main objective is not to educate the general public and all who may care about its financial situation, but to increase the net worth of its shareholders. If accurate financial reporting helps in achieving this goal, the management certainly will report its financial position. But corporate bodies registered under the company's act are legally bound to report earnings periodically. In doing so, they have to follow the regulations advanced by the national governments and regulatory bodies under them. This is perhaps the only reason why corporate bodies report earnings and financial position; not to enlighten the general public, but because it is mandatory.

The astute reader will immediately raise two objections. First, they will challenge the position that mandatory requirements alone explain the reporting practices of companies. They remonstrate perhaps rightly so, that if authorities alone are to be satisfied, the efforts put in to present a picture that appears slightly awkward on careful scrutiny is neither in the company's interest nor sustainable in the long-run. Investors and lenders who rely on such statements eventually arrive at the conclusion that the picture presented does not conform to reality and will abandon the company. This is self-defeating. Therefore, by force of economic and business reality, companies must report their financial position honestly and as accurately as possible.

Second argument may appear even more persuasive. It runs thus. Fraudulent reporting to maximize shareholder's wealth is a crime. Crime does not pay.

The answer to these positions is merely to examine the past history of reporting of financial statements. Users of financial statements over the years have disconcertingly discovered time and again that financial data that produce numbers that conform to all GAAP and regulatory requirements can be yet misleading and convey distorted picture of the company's financial position. Worse still, frequent violations of financial rules are very frequent. The certification by independent auditors do not authenticate the fact these numbers are reliable.[1]

Notable Accounting Scandals

Company	Year	Audit Firm	Country	Notes
Phar-Mor	1992	Coopers & Lybrand	United States	mail fraud, wire fraud, bank fraud, and transportation of funds obtained by theft or fraud
Informix Corporation	1997	Ernst & Young	United States	Channel stuffing
Sybase	1997	Ernst & Young	United States	False sales figures
Waste Management, Inc.	1999	Arthur Andersen	United States	Financial misstatements
MicroStrategy	2000	Pricewaterhouse Coopers	United States	Falsification of sales
Computer Associates	2000	KPMG	United States	Misstatements
Lernout & Hauspie	2000	KPMG	Belgium	Fictitious transactions in Korea and improper accounting methodologies elsewhere
Xerox	2000	KPMG	United States	Falsifying financial results
Enron	2001	Arthur Andersen	United States	Transactions between a web of related companies
Adelphia	2002	Deloitte & Touche	United States	Misstatements
AOL	2002	Ernst & Young	United States	Inflated sales
Bristol-Myer Squibb	2002	Pricewaterhouse Coopers	United States	Inflated revenues
CMS Energy	2002	Arthur Andersen	United States	Round trip trades
Duke Energy	2002	Deloitte & Touche	United States	Round trip trades
Dynegy	2002	Arthur Andersen	United States	Round trip trades

Company	Year	Audit Firm	Country	Notes
El Paso Corporation	2002	Deloitte & Touche	United States	Round trip trades
Freddie Mac	2002	Pricewaterhouse Coopers	United States	Understated earnings
Global Crossing	2002	Arthur Andersen	Bermuda	Network capacity swaps to inflate revenues
Halliburton	2002	Arthur Andersen	United States	Improper booking of cost overruns
Homestore.com	2002	Pricewaterhouse Coopers	United States	Improper booking of sales
ImClone Systems	2002	KPMG	United States	Fraud accounting
Kmart	2002	Pricewaterhouse Coopers	United States	Misleading accounting practices
Merck & Co.	2002	Pricewaterhouse Coopers	United States	Recorded co-payments that were not collected
Merrill Lynch	2002	Deloitte & Touche	United States	Conflict of interest
Mirant	2002	KPMG	United States	Overstated assets and liabilities
Nicor	2002	Arthur Andersen	United States	Overstated assets, understated liabilities
Peregrine Systems	2002	KPMG	United States	Overstated sales
Qwest Communications	2002	1999, 2000, 2001 Arthur Andersen 2002 October KPMG	United States	Inflated revenues
Reliant Energy	2002	Deloitte & Touche	United States	Round trip trades
Sunbeam	2002	Arthur Andersen	United States	See main text
Tyco International	2002	Pricewaterhouse Coopers	Bermuda	Improper accounting
WorldCom	2002	Arthur Andersen	United States	Overstated cash flows
Royal Ahold	2003	Deloitte & Touche	Nether-lands	Inflating promotional allowances

Company	Year	Audit Firm	Country	Notes
Parmalat	2003	Grant Thornton	Italy	Falsified accounting documents
Nortel	2003	Deloitte & Touche	Canada	Distributed ill advised corporate bonuses to top 43 managers
Chiquita Brands International	2004	Ernst & Young	United States	Illegal payments
AIG	2004	Pricewaterhouse Coopers	United States	Accounting of structured financial deals
Bernard L. Madoff Investment Securities LLC	2008	Friehling & Horowitz	United States	Massive Ponzi scheme
Anglo Irish Bank	2008	Ernst & Young	Ireland	Anglo Irish Bank hidden loans controversy
Satyam Computer Services	2009	Pricewaterhouse Coopers	India	Falsified accounts
Lehman Brothers	2010	Ernst & Young	United States	Failure to disclose transactions to investors
Sino-Forest Corporation	2011	Ernst & Young	Canada-China	Falsified statements
Olympus Corporation	2011	Ernst & Young	Japan	*fraud*

A few examples of accounting tricks can throw light on how users could be misled. Let us begin with the choice of the fiscal year itself. One reason companies choose different fiscal year-ends is that their industries fluctuate at various times. Thus, by being able to adjust the timing of their earnings reports, companies can minimize the negative seasonal effects that occur within their specific industries. For example, a company that has to buy inventory during the summer months probably won't want to report its earnings during this time because the inventory purchases will decrease its earnings. Not all of these practices are either illegal or wholly tinged with fraudulent intent. But there are several other ways that may fool the casual reader of statements, unless he uses the methods of financial intelligences discussed here.

There's more than one way to make financial statements look pristine. We take a look at two ways in which companies can fool investors, so that you can learn to spot accounting manipulation: 'one-time charges' and 'investment gains.' This isn't to say it is a bad thing every time a company writes down charges. The problem lies with those companies that continually resort to this practice. Firms sometimes use one-time charges to blame previous management for leaving problems. We have referred earlier to the incoming chairman of the State Bank of India, the leading nationalized bank in India, who decided to write back some of the revenues as soon as he took over as the new chairman. In truth, these charges may be an indication that something is wrong with the company.

Also, we need to keep a close watch, when companies use restructuring charges to improve future earnings and profitability. By taking huge restructuring charges when times are bad, the company reduces depreciation in future periods and ultimately increases income.

At the peak of the dotcom boom, a lot of investment gains were showing up on financial statements. This happens whenever things are going well in the markets. An investment gain is definitely better than a loss, but these gains are typically unsteady.

Investment Gain or Capital Gain

A profit results when the price of a marketable security held by a company rises above its purchase price. If the security is sold it is realized gain, In not it is unrealized gain. In both cases the accountant can show the profits in the income statement. A capital loss would occur when the opposite takes place. Many companies hold excess cash in the form of capital assets that can easily be converted into cash when needed.

Take for example, Intel's experience. Its investment and interest gains during the second quarter of 2000 were just over $2.3 billion. One year later, in the second quarter of 2001, they sank to a paltry $115 million. A company that aims for investment gains can pose another problem: a company having trouble meeting earnings expectations may try to boost investment income to meet shareholder and market expectations. This can mean that the core operations of the company are left behind. The moral of the story is, not to put too much faith into investment gains. These gains flourish when the market sentiments brighten, but shrink when the financial markets head south. While you analyze the financial statements of a company, take a close look at the one-time charges and investment gains. Spotting these two accounting tricks can help to tell the story behind a company's numbers.

Management and communications teams are known to use some of the following in their companies' releases.

1. They Don't Hide Information. They Bury It

Communication teams looking to 'bury' a bad earnings report (*or bad news in general*) will sometimes seek to disseminate the release at a time when it suspects the lowest number of people are watching, perhaps on a Friday afternoon after the close of the markets. An innocuous looking statement somewhere in a voluminous report regarding expenses or revenue is another common trick. Language that includes 'challenging', 'pressured,' 'slipping' and 'stressed' should not be taken lightly and could even be red flags. For example, rather than say in a release that the company's gross margins have been declining and that as a result the company's earnings may get pinched in the future, management may simply say that it 'sees a great deal of pricing pressure.' The intelligent reader may calculate gross margin percentages from the income statement provided – something that few retail investors generally ever do.

2. Enhancing Preferred Information

Some companies' investor relations teams will **bold** or *italicize* headlines and information in an earnings release that they want the investment community to focus on. This isn't a trick designed to fool you, but it can take advantage of reader laziness (for example '*Q3 EPS Increases 30%*') to read between the lines.

3. Increasing Stock Buybacks

While stock buybacks are often a good thing, some boards will authorize a buyback as part of an effort to make their stock appear more attractive to the investment community. These boards/companies may have every intention of completing such a repurchase, but you may notice that companies tend to announce such repurchases in conjunction with or just after bad news is released. It just smacks suspicious timing and appears disingenuous.

4. Announcing Good News to Offset Bad News

Some companies will announce a major new customer, large order, store opening, product launch, or new hire around the same time that bad news is released. Again, the idea is to convey the image that things aren't that bad. There are a number of tricks or actions that companies take to make themselves appear solid and to reduce the impact that bad earnings can have on their share price. Thorough investors who study all the facts and read all earnings releases in their entirety need not be fooled.

Readers, who have been waiting for a complete answer to our core issue raised in the sub-title of the section, are getting impatient. We no longer wish to delay the answer. There are two possible answers to the question whether all accounting statements are tainted. Yes, or No. But a moments' reflection brings us to the point when neither answer seems satisfactory. An affirmative answer assumes the existence of untainted financial reporting in its purest form. This is neither possible nor practical because of the very nature of financial reporting, even as it has to make a whole host of assumptions and estimates which rely solely on the judgmental leanings of the accountant. An affirmative answer brushes the entire financial reporting fraternity, with its highly erudite practitioners, black. This is neither true nor fair. The confusion even if unwittingly, arises because of our inadequate definition of a tainted reporting.

We must at the outset distinguish between outright fraud and embellishments in financial statements. Fraud happens before fraudulent reporting takes place. Fraud is a fact and reporting is a cover-up. But Embellishments and distortions may ultimately result in defrauding the users that rely on them.

This book has scatterings of examples that constitute both types of reporting. As the preceding deviations demonstrate, neither the fear of fraud investigation or violations of GAAP based regulations prevent frauds. Self interest as defined earlier for the long run benefit of the companies themselves does not seem to be sufficient motivation for the managements to report accurately and painstakingly the actual financial situation. Corporations of all hues do not hesitate to smooth earnings, to create the impression of a steady growth in revenues, rather than the haphazardly behavior of the numbers in the real world. Auditors often co-operate with this as it does not specifically infringe on the GAAP rules, but keeps the stock market pundits free of surprises in results. These are not simple tricks used by fly-by-night operators alone. General Electric officials have admitted to hunting for lucrative acquisitions when a division is in danger of facing revenue target shortfall.

A further but well recognized aspect of management of public corporations is that managers that actually run the company on a daily basis may have objectives of their own, which may not be in line with those of the owners. Their compensation levels and the bonuses they receive very often depend on the financial results presented by them. This divergence of objectives sometimes drive them to artificially inflate earnings figures, by manipulating depreciation rates for example, which in fact has neither an impact on the stock market, nor on the cash flows within the company, but has the ability to show net profits and earnings per share in a better light. The surprising outcome of this behavior is that it is not only among the listed private companies that this attitude is visible, but also among CEOs of public sector companies owned by the government. Here the objective may not be to maximize personal wealth, but to achieve personal gain through advancement of career prospects taking advantage of such compensation systems through financial reporting gimmicks.

Auditors Don't Expose Frauds

Why do auditors don't forbid such accounting gimmicks? After all, embellishments in financial reporting is distortion of the actual position within a business and not the accurate projection of it. There are some foundational reasons why such a state affairs persist in the accounting world.[2] We wish to present some of them.

In the real world of business politics, financial reporting standards are framed by a representative body of accounting professionals, issuers of financial statements themselves, theorists and users among others. In India, **National Advisory Commission on Accounting Standards (NACAS)** is the Government body that approves the standards. The theoretical foundations of the standards are laid by the Institute of Chartered Accountants of India (ICAI), who defines them well in advance.

The actual process of standard formulation and approval may take a few years. During this period of meetings and discussions, the business community pursues the matter on a more practical level. They continuously confront the government bodies by raising issues and concerns. The journalist's community and the media contribute in no small measure. Parliamentarians and businesses who have a nexus based relationship, are capable of mounting veiled threats on the law making body. This might result in curtailment of the authority of NACAS. These activities may even result in change of the membership and leadership of the law-making body. The inevitable outcome of these forces is the compromises that emerge. They fail to satisfy the theoretical formulations, as originally conceived by the ICAI. At the time of writing, the IFRS convergence law in India is pending for final approval about three years, for assorted reasons as above.

Modern day corporations are highly competitive in its working environment. This creates a spirit of extreme pressure both within and outside the corporation. Individuals involved in such pressure cooker atmosphere believe that their careers and success depends on winning at the workplace. To the emerging manager it becomes eventually clear that superior knowledge and management skills do not produce better business results. They know that what matters is not only the ability to garner monetary rewards, but also the prospect of making a reputation in the business world. The benchmark for creating such successful careers is based on financial performance of the businesses they manage. Reputations and inter-peer comparisons get brandied about in business journals and glossies. The challenges are not different from the targets set for athletes. Profits and growth are then the constantly moving goal-posts for these men. The balance sheet is the overall record of wins and losses.

The analogy can be extended further to encompass the entire system. A cricket administration run with large amounts of funds and political clout can browbeat the visiting country's team into accepting terms which are not very favorable. For example, home teams can prepare flat pitches to suit spin bowling if their best chance depends on spin. They can shorten the length to the boundary of the home stadium if they have pinch-hitters to carry on the slog-over. They intimidate umpires by mounting a heated campaign against his decisions in the popular media and complaining to the international cricket control board. Collectively a group of cricket playing nations can arm twist the ICC to frame new rules.

Such methods are equally applicable to the practical use of financial rules of accounting. Managers whose bonuses and promotions depend on earnings levels use every trick in and outside the book to produce higher earnings even if some of it is through the accounting sleight of hand. Financially savvy readers who recognize such intentions and understand the process should be vary of the reported numbers for their own sakes.

The case of the Auditor is not entirely different. Auditors are given the task certification of the annual accounts of a company by the Board of Directors. They then undertake the onerous task based on compliance to the accounting standards and materiality of facts. But they are fully aware that it is eventually the management which will authorize their fees. They work in close proximity to the accountants and staff within the company who report their every action to the Board. In such a situation it will be precarious for the auditor to earnestly dig in deep into the numbers to uncover the real financial position within.

They are hard-nosed practical men with an eye on further employment as well fidelity to the profession. This involves a tight rope walk, not to displease the management but at the same time stand up to peer-review of their work, if any. They wish to appear as true professionals. They question the management as to why some numbers and assumptions appear to stretch the accounting rules. The resulting arguments and hard-nosed negotiations with the auditors, generally end with the management side winning, by a handsome margin.

Junior Auditors, who joined the firm with idealistic and romantic view of the world they acquired during their school days, have initial difficulty in adjusting to this reality. They are unable to grasp the fuzzy-logic of the managements who wish to 'get on with the washing'. Their initial stand gets overruled by the senior partners in the audit firm. They quietly nurse their fresh wounds and eventually get over them by using the excuse that after all, their job ends in ensuring that the numbers confirm to the accounting standards and not beyond. The attitude suits the managements extremely well. The senior auditor smiles knowingly and earns another term as extension.

Highly professional Auditors sometimes refuse to tow the management line and don't buy the argument that everything in life is open to negotiation. The outcome is again a lesser than fair view of the financial position within. Auditors use a method known as random sampling to check the figures. This is because a 100% check of every voucher or item of inventory is neither possible nor cost-effective. Samples sometimes miss the important items that contain less than true version or fraudulent figures and vouchers. Devious managements can sometimes put in place schemes that are capable of spoiling the scientific random sampling methods to defeat auditors, even if they are sincerely hoping to complete the job in a professional way.

Fraud is a crime and extreme violation of accounting rules. But auditors do not catch it.

On 14 January 2009, Price Waterhouse, the Indian division of PricewaterhouseCoopers, announced that its reliance on potentially false information provided by the management of Satyam Computers may have rendered its audit reports 'inaccurate and unreliable'. Such reply was disappointment for the general public at large as The Chartered Accountants Act, 1949 clearly states that an auditor is responsible towards the information provided to him by the management.

Is Fraud Detectable?[3]

It is essential at this point to recall the earlier position we expressed. While there are many ways the managements use to embellish earnings figures and downplay expenses, they do not at the same time find themselves in jail except in extreme cases. This is because, there are several ways of doing this by stretching the concepts and convincing the auditors about their legality. Here the fear of retribution or exposure is not illegal. However there are several occasions where the corporate executives step beyond the line into illegality.

Misrepresentation of facts is illegal, if it results in loss to the persons who rely on them. Since financial numbers are widely used by the investor community and individuals, this clearly is an offence. The Roman Catholic Church declared in 1992, that fudging of financial accounting numbers is a 'sin' in its new catechism. Auditors, who conduct their study in good faith, relying on the management side of the story, sometimes fail miserably in exposing deliberate misrepresentation.

There is no fool-proof method for uncovering frauds. The reason is that fraud is a deliberate act and fraudulent reporting is an act of cover-up. This does not imply that the users of financial statements are obliged to accept all that is written in the annual reports. By using the tools that are available to all and employing the techniques which are about to be described in subsequent chapters, one can arrive at an independent opinion about what the numbers are trying to say. At the very least, the exercise will reveal valuable clues regarding the integrity and consistency of the statements.

We present a small list of tell-tale signs that may point to either outright fraud or embellishments in earnings. These are not irrefutable attributes of fraud. They are like sign posts pointing to the road ahead. The financially intelligent reader must travel down the road and look beyond into the thickets to identify the animal. Here is the list.[3]

1. Increasing gap between sales and cash received
2. Growing sales
3. Decreasing rates of depreciation
4. Increase in the proportion of non-current assets in total assets
5. Decreasing gross margins
6. Presence of a web of interconnected companies

It would be unfortunate to view these factors independently and without supporting evidence of manipulation. All companies that grow are not increasing the sales by embellishments. But a company that shows increases from quarter to quarter relentlessly needs to be established as such by other data. A host of companies interconnected by ownership in each other, in the Indian context, are known to have carried out transactions that need a lot of tracing. Ramalinga Raju's companies and Enron Corporation are known to have engaged in this type of manipulations. They also fulfill the criteria listed at number one.

Shortcuts to Safety of Your Assets

At several points in this chapter we laid adequate emphasis on the fact that readers must not rely solely on what appears in the disclosed numbers. They must keenly observe the interrelationships among data by analyzing the numbers through percentages and ratios.

1. Obtain information about the company and its economic environment
2. Understand the management's attitude to financing and internal performance
3. Discover little tricks companies use to hide or bury information
4. Look for visible signs of manipulation in earnings or expenses
5. Check out extraordinary items and restructuring costs
6. Work out trend line and watch for sudden shifts
7. Compare with peer groups but be careful with your selection of peers
8. Pursue any signal that raises a red flag to the very end

....actually I never committed any crime...
All I did was fail to comply with the law....

Summary of Chapter Six

Because corporations hide the motives for financial reporting it is quite possible that managements have interests of their own motivating them to present a performance picture that may not be entirely in tune with reality obtaining within the companies they manage. This tendency is much more widespread than imagined by most users of these statements. Some of these are mere embellishments to the earnings figures, just like putting on a Sunday-best appearance while posing for a wedding photograph. But at times such embellishments can cross the threshold of legality as defined by the GAAP and step into dangerously fraudulent reporting. Fraudulent reporting is a crime, because it causes the loss of money and other assets of those of who rely on them.

It is not often neither feasible nor wise to depend on auditor certification as ultimate proof of correct reporting. There are practical reasons why this is so. The onus then falls on the user to come to a conclusion regarding the numbers and what they are telling. Towards achieving this goal the user must develop a few tried and tested analytical tools, like ratio-analysis. It is not easy to detect frauds in the making. Because frauds often are accompanied by elaborate cover-up operations. But there could be tell-tale signs that point towards such activity within a company. If misstatements and falsified accounting practices were isolated rare events, users could safely depend on them, without anxiety. But due to the gap between theory and practice as in all things, users must provide themselves additional protection in the form of thorough scrutiny. But extreme caution is advised before drawing such conclusions purely based on financial statements alone, as they are not sufficient. The conclusions are not easy to arrive at, but with practice and acumen developed over experience, it is possible to see through the accounting tricks to draw reasonable assessments of the validity of the numbers and what they are telling.

7
Diagnostic Use of Ratios

USE OF CLUES, BY ARTHUR CONAN DOYLE (*A TRAINED MEDICAL DOCTOR himself*) who created the immortal detective Sherlock Holmes captivates readers and television audience even today. Part of the explanation perhaps can be found in the apparent superhuman ability to smell out the trail left by the hapless criminal by examining seemingly trivial tit-bits of information garnered through an uncanny ability for observation. While the bits of clues are by themselves insignificant, the conclusions arrived at are dramatic. However, to the trained mind it is 'elementary dear Dr. Watson!'

The use of financial ratios can achieve similar dramatic results because of the interrelationships that exist between the various parts of the three financial statements themselves and characteristics that must somehow accompany them. The absence or presence of certain characteristics can therefore become indicators of distortions, that must be examined and cross-verified with other data to arrive at definitive conclusions. In this chapter we propose to introduce the reader to those clues and how to link them together to arrive at a conclusion as to the reliability of financial statements as representing the true financial position of a company.

Financial Ratios and What They Can Do

Our aim is to examine whether the financial numbers put out by the companies are saying what they actually mean. In other words, whether they reflect the true financial picture of the company and as such are reliable. This skepticism of the numbers is based on the experience observed in the past where companies have presented distorted picture of their position. The other use of ratios and perhaps the more elusive one is to use ratios to predict future prospects of the company. Looking forward into the future is the riskiest form of analysis, since there is no correct answer till the future emerges. The prominence of chance events of extreme nature (*what is now known a 'Black-Swan-Events' after Nassim Nicholas Taleb*[1]) can completely invalidate the projections. These and other related aspects therefore do not form part of this book, and the reader is advised to the fact no matter how refined the methods of prediction the future will always remain unpredictable. Before committing large sums of money in the face of greatest uncertainty, investors do well to understand the odds.

In this chapter we deal with ratio-analysis mostly for their power to point to possible distortions and incongruities in financial statements, so that further investigation can be done to get to the bottom-most reality. Unlike a medical practitioner, dealing with real live data, the financial-analyst deals with data that is often riddled with assumptions and biases of the accountants and managements. It is not possible for ratio-analysis alone to uncover incongruities without other supporting data. Ratios can at best raise the antennae and send a curious feeling down the spine, or perhaps point the direction to the problem area. The reader must use his skills to collect other data regarding the company from inside and outside sources to arrive at a definitive conclusion.

The Basic Analytical Approaches

To arrive at the true picture, analysts must rely on all the information they can get. But unfortunately they do not have all the information they need. They must therefore make the fullest use of whatever details the company has disclosed in their annual reports and public statements. There are in effect two basic approaches to financial statement analysis, whatever the methods that may be employed. First is to look at the company affairs from an internal viewpoint, a sort of mirror reflection of what appears from within itself. The second approach is to view the company from an external angle, as investors and stakeholders would want to see it despite what the management has presented, in their public disclosure. For readability's sake we have presented the material in this chapter in two parts: Internal Viewpoint and External Viewpoint. We shall presently deal with both these viewpoints in some detail.

Part One

Internal Viewpoint

The dotcom era has demonstrated that deterioration in a company's financial position occurs gradually over a period of time, but disclosures related to it come as a total surprise. At other times risk factors creep up on the company gradually, but analysis of these factors becomes clear only after the risk has become quite real. One method of spotting such situations well within reasonable time-periods is to prepare common-size statements, such as the one presented below.[2]

Idea Cellular

Balance Sheet as at March 31, 2011 (₹ in Millions)*

	March 31, 2011	%	March 31, 2010	%
Sources of Funds				
Shareholders' Funds				
Share Capital	33,032.72	14.25	32,998.38	17.55
Outstanding Employee Stock Options	478.09	0.20	444.45	0.23
Reserves and Surplus	89,796.21	38.73	85,093.26	45.69
	123,307.02	53.24	118,536.09	63.44
Loan Funds				
Secured	77,600.39	33.49	59,886.08	32.15
Unsecured	27,974.21	12.04	5,378.05	2.87
	105,574.60	45.59	65,264.13	33.44
Deferred Tax Liability	2,870.15	1.20	2,256.36	1.20
Total	231,751.77	100 .00	186,056.58	100.00
Application of Funds				
Fixed Asset				
Plant and Property after Depreciation*	191,316.24	82.68	149,270.59	80.10
Capital Work-in-Progress	35,940.51	15.15	4,625.81	2.47
Investments	25,728.07	11.03	27,551.26	14.51
Current Asset				
Inventories	522.16	0.22	466.99	0.24
Sundry Debtors	4,614.46	1.99	4,301.17	2.31
Cash and Bank	4,515	1.94	2,804	1.50
Loans and Advances	22,902.76	9.78	30,002.81	16.16
Less: Current Liabilities and Provisions				
Current Liabilities	53,237.16	22.94	36,796.23	19.56

Provisions	**1,291.73**	**0.86**	1,377.62	0.69
Net Current Assets / (Liabilities)	**(21,233.05)**		645.18	
Profit and Loss Account			3,963.74	
Total	**231,751.77**	**100.00**	186,056.58	100.00

Source: Published annual Report of Idea Cellular, Suman Towers, Bombay: 2011
**** Data has been modified under fixed assets to show net assets after depreciation.***

This is also called the common form balance-sheet. In this form of balance sheet, each asset (*every component of asset*) and liability (*every component of liability*) is converted into a percentage of the total asset and total liability. We have presented the common form balance sheet for Idea Cellular as at 31-03-2011, above.[2]

The Percentage Balance Sheet and Income Statement

The immediate aspect of the balance sheet that strikes the reader is the increased borrowing levels. This has been necessitated by the increase acquisition of assets most of which are in the work-in-progress stage. Such addition to capital equipments may have been required because of the need to bid for 3G spectrum and also the hyper growth in the market for 2G services. The company is low on cash balances and had to write down general reserves to finance expansion of services. If the revenues do not pick up during subsequent years, the interest burden is sure to show up on the income statement and reduce profit-levels even further. But if such investments in new network elements result in fresh customer additions and revenue streams the strategy will pay off.

Financially skilled reader will learn if he looks for the subtle changes in percentages over several quarters and years to examine whether inventory is increasing as percentage of total assets. Such increases may be due to slowdown in sales or an economic downturn. In this particular case inventory has increased significantly over the previous year. The reader must then probe into the report to examine what these items of inventory are and the company's policy with regard to inventory management. Huge increases in fixed assets is a sign that the company operates in a highly capital intensive sector. Such a proportion of fixed costs to variable costs can make the earnings extremely volatile during unfavorable market conditions.

Fixed Costs and Variable Costs

Fixed costs are costs that will continue whether or not any units are produced. These costs are 'fixed' over a specified period of time or range of production. Variable costs are costs that vary directly with the number of products produced.

It is clear then that the higher the proportion of fixed costs the more number of units must be produced and sold to reduce the average costs of each unit.

Telecommunications networks are expensive to build and maintain. Telecom operators have to enroll a very large number of customers to overcome the problem of heavy network costs. But because of the competitive nature of the market, the margin of profit from each customer becomes very thin. There is one additional reason why telecom operators have to invest heavily into equipments. The reasons are technology changes, fast obsolescence of existing services and rapid shifts in customer preferences.

Yet another technique of using percentage form of P&L statement is to compare two companies based on the percentages. We present below a real life example of two telecom operators in India.

Idea Cellular & Reliance Communications[3]
(Period Ending March 31st 2011, ₹ in Crores)
Comparative Percentage Profit and Loss Statement*

	Idea Cellular		Reliance Communications	
	2011	%	2011	%
Income				
Service Revenue	15,332	100.00	12,130	100.00
Other Income	1,356	8.84	1,152	9.49
Total	15,388		13.286	
Operating Expenditure				
Personnel Expenditure	728	4.74	601	4.95
Network Operating Expenditure	4,679	30.51	9036	74.49
License and WPC Charges	1,772	11.55	(188)	
Roaming & Access Charges	2,475	16.14	-	
Subscriber Acquisition & Servicing Expenditure	1,642	10.70	-	
Selling, General and Administration Expenses	960	6.26	1,794	14.78
Finance and Treasury Charges (Net)	248	1.61	846	6.97
Depreciation adjusted against General Reserve III	-	-	(1,175)	
Amortization & Depreciation	1,972	11.69	2856	23.54
Profit Before Finance Charges, Depreciation, Amortization & Taxes	3,128	20.40	(860)	(7.08)
Profit /Loss Before Tax From Operating Activities	906	5.90	(860)	(6.54)
Tax and other adjustments	62	102		
Profit /Loss After Tax	844	5.50	(758)	(6.25)
Earnings Per Share				
Basic	2.56		(3.67)	
Diluted	2.55		(3.67)	

**Source: Published annual reports of Idea Cellular (2011), Reliance Communications (2011) (Table has been modified to make it comparable. Formats of presentation used by the companies and nomenclature of line-items used by the companies are different - author)*

Looking at the above two companies, what strikes the reader immediately is that the two companies are nearly of the same size in terms of sales revenues, and personnel costs. Idea Cellular has made efforts to disclose various charges in detail as compared to Reliance Communications. However, the network operating costs are substantially different for the two companies. While Reliance has splurged a higher amount on selling and administration expenses, it does not have seemed to have resulted in desirable outcomes. Finance charges have acted as a heavy drag on profitability in the case of Reliance Communications, which may be due to the higher debt levels and higher costs of borrowing. What is more interesting is the great gap between the two companies in the treatment of depreciation figure. A detailed examination by the interested reader will reveal that both *tangible* (plant and machinery) and *intangible assets* (Telecom licenses) have been written down by large amounts by Reliance.

The intelligent executive has his tasks cut out here. He must probe into this aspect of the Reliance's operations in the Telecom market, understanding the difference between CDMA technology (*that Reliance use*) and the GSM Technology (*that Idea use*) and the implications of this choice in terms of Licensing conditions and financial impact on its operating incomes. Reliance Communications is the only operator in India that operates services in both the technologies. The entry into GSM market was a subsequent decision which necessitated high cost of entry-licenses, and hence a larger amortization figure became inevitable in the income statement.

Overall the two companies are on different platforms in terms of operational efficiency and overall strategy. Reliance Communications' high network expenditure combined with a high-cost marketing effort to shore up a slightly less conventional CDMA technology has cost the company in terms of lower profitability and necessity to go in for high-cost debt to finance its operations. This type of analysis drawn from simple percentages to compare peer-group companies can yield satisfactory insights into the numbers. Here again, as elsewhere, the reader must be cautioned before jumping into conclusions without an in-depth reading of the entire report itself.

The Contrasting cost-structures of Idea Cellular and Reliance Communications, as evidenced by the percentage Income statement, highlights a key issue in such comparisons. A line-by-line comparison of the two companies does not in effect yield a satisfactory answer to the question of which one is more efficient. Idea Cellular is perhaps able to reduce its costs of operations, because it is a much smaller company with lower footprint in the telecom space as compared to Reliance, which has multiple products and an integrated infrastructure business. Its balance sheet is nearly three times that of Idea Cellular. Reliance has acquired futuristic business licenses like 4G capabilities and has near-ready infrastructure for deployment of BWA services. The financially savvy reader must take care not to confuse the differences with managerial efficiency which might in fact be differences in business strategy. We therefore invite the reader to explore other measures of managerial efficiency, which is the subject matter of our next section.

Managerial Efficiency Measures

The goal of the *managerial efficiency* is to provide a usable and accurate tool for maximizing productivity, profit, and shareholder value, among other multidimensional goals of the modern corporation.[4] At the outset it must be made clear that no textbook on management has as yet defined satisfactorily, as to what constitutes managerial efficiency, in practice. It is generally believed to be the result of the combined effect of management, teaming, and leadership skills on corporate productivity. Delving into the theoretical aspects of managerial efficiency and effectiveness can be an interesting pursuit in itself. But as our aim and purpose is to arrive at the real story behind the numbers presented by these managers themselves, we will deliberately refuse to walk down that lane. Instead we will focus on what a corporate body expects from the overall managerial inputs, in terms of results that are visible above the ground. Towards this objective we propose to present some ratios that may effectively point to the contribution of managerial inputs. These measures are by no means that final word on comparing corporate efficiency. As already stated, strategy and long-term game plans do constitute a key aspect of managerial contribution to overall corporate goals.

Productivity Measures

At the very beginning of this book we expended considerable quantity of word-space to grapple with what we considered the foundational aspect of a business. The concept was net worth. We understood it to mean the fair value of the business, which an investor would be willing to pay. It would automatically follow from the above, with a moments' reflection, that additions to the net worth of the company is the productivity enshrined in the operations of the company and perhaps its sole aim for the operating activities.

But the problem begins here. No matter how elegant the concept appears to be, measuring net worth in practice has proved very elusive. All that the user is left with is to fall back to reality as presented by the corporate bodies in their periodic reporting. He must then sift through the chaff and collect data which are a reasonably accurate reflection of the true financial situation within the company. The user can begin to work out ratios to measure and compare productive additions to the net worth of the company. This is what we propose to do here in the following sections.

Return on Assets

The reader must be warned that he is entering a very shifty ground here. He must be cautioned that it will be very nearly like walking on quick-sand – there is no guarantee of immediate rescue at hand. But skillful negotiation of this section and chapter is essential for achieving our original goal of attaining the *nirvana* of basic financial skills of analysis.

We have chosen Return on Assets (ROA) measure as an overall measure of total productivity of the company. The formula is straightforward:

$$\text{Return on Assets (ROA)} = \frac{\text{Net Profit}}{\text{Total Assets}}$$

Based on the numbers the formula represents what percentage of every rupee invested in the business is being returned as a surplus. The concept seems clear enough. Every business activity makes use of machinery, cash, facilities, vehicles, inventory, and software and so on to make a profit at the end of the period and to add to such existing useful resources over several periods. The type of resources used varies with the nature of the business. The ROA measure shows how productive these assets have been at the hands of the management.

Like all measurements, the ROA throws up some immediate issues. Having gone through the skepticism the author has managed to generate in the numbers themselves, the measurements based on such numbers itself generates further skepticism. Apart from this general problem, which applies to all the ratios being discussed here, two issues can come up. Firstly, should we use the profit figure or the cash earnings, which is a better representation of reality? Given the adversarial nature of managerial reporting of accounting profits, this argument may appear somewhat justified. Secondly, the balance sheet that lists the assets misses out the most important asset that makes all productivity possible, the manpower and their embedded skills.

Notwithstanding the above arguments, the reader will recognize that introducing qualitative factors into the analysis of numbers which are mostly objectively formed (*even though good many of those numbers have assumptions and estimates supporting them*) and based on regulatory guidelines, substantially devalues the methodology of such analysis. The analyst has the option to modify the ratio based on his findings. Substituting cash earnings in place of accounting profits certainly enhances the understanding of the return concept. This modified ratio is something the analyst may rely on. But as a standard usage, ROA, as defined above, serves the purpose and is a very good starting point for understanding a company's overall productivity. Elsewhere in the book we have defined bona fide profits as that which makes the owners wealthier than before. If the analyst can come up with a number that accurately represents the bona fide profits of the company, and another number that states the actual value of assets owned, he will then be able to discover the true return on assets as intended. However, the task is fraught with immense difficulties. Even if the intelligent reader can somehow arrive at a satisfactory figure for bona fide profits, he would not be able to reach a conclusive value for the total assets as that will come to light only in a transaction, involving the sale of such assets. For a company that is never involved in such a transaction, the true value of assets remains hidden. ROA as defined in its simplest form then must satisfy the immediate requirement as an overall indicator of a corporate entity's productivity.

The DuPont Formula[5]

With the aid of the *DuPont Formula*, the reader may be able to advance a bit further in understanding the sources of a company's productivity and consequently the concept of return on assets. The idea is generally attributed to Donaldson Brown, who developed the concept while working at E.I. du Pont de Nemours, (*world's third largest chemical company based on market capitalization in 2009*) and later successfully applied it as Vice-president Finance in General Motors. He defined return on assets:

Asset turnover	×	Return on Sales	=	Return on Assets

$$= \frac{\text{Sales}}{\text{Assets}} \times \frac{\text{Net Profit}}{\text{Sales}} = \frac{\text{Net Profit}}{\text{Assets}}$$

In its simplest interpretation, the DuPont formula explains the two main aspects of efficiency. DuPont model tells that ROA is affected by:

- Asset use efficiency, which is measured by total asset turnover; (*sales/assets*)
- Operating efficiency, which is measured by net profit margin; (*net profit/sales*)

DuPont analysis helps to locate the part of the business that is underperforming. This analysis certainly answers some questions, but raises a few others. A company can improve its performance efficiency, reducing working capital requirements so that asset-turnover ratio improves. But such an action by the company may reduce its competitiveness in the market.

Working Capital and Efficiency

Working capital gives an idea of the company's underlying operational efficiency. Money that is tied up in inventory or money that customers still owe to the company cannot be used to pay off any of the company's obligations. So, if a company is not operating in the most efficient manner (*slow collection*), it will show up as an increase in the working capital. This can be seen by comparing the working capital from one period to another; slow collection may signal an underlying problem in the company's operations. If a company's current assets do not exceed its current liabilities, then it may run into trouble paying back creditors in the short term. The worst-case scenario is bankruptcy. A declining working capital ratio over a longer time period could also be a red flag that warrants further analysis. For example, it could be that the company's sales volumes are decreasing and, as a result, money due from customers (*accounts receivables number*) continues to get smaller and smaller.

On the other hand, cutting back on necessary capital expenditures will also improve the assets-turnover ratio (*in the short-run*) in two ways. It reduces the denominator (*assets*) in the equation by reducing total costs by refusing to build new assets. A further advantage is the ability to improve the return on sales due to lower costs as a result of lower depreciation. This happens because, consequent on the creation of lower amount of new capital assets, the business encounters lower depreciation costs in future. Such an improvement in ROA however, is obviously not desirable, because future market share is likely to decline for the company that spends lower than optimum levels on capital expenditure.

The intelligent reader therefore needs to be careful in looking at these ratios, to understand how they were achieved, rather than at the numbers themselves in isolation. Generally speaking, a higher return on assets, achieved through increases in efficiency based on better utilization of shareholder's equity investment than by increasing debt component of the assets base, is better appreciated by the market. This implies that a lower leverage and higher ROA is true managerial efficiency.

Adding more debt needs no skill and does not in any way improve operational efficiency, but introduces more volatility in the earnings number. The financially intelligent reader then recognizes that while the level of ROA achieved is of considerable significance, assiduously makes efforts to gauge the quality of ROA as reflected by the numbers. This aspect of the numbers is highlighted by a DuPont analysis of the four major telecom operators in India. The numbers are displayed below:

DuPont Analysis of Major Telecom Operators in India

Name of Company	Assets Turnover	Return on Sales	Return on Assets
Bharti Airtel	53.56%	20.12%	10.77%
BSNL	31.52%	–23.62%	–7.44%
Idea Cellular	50.02%	5.79%	2.81%
Reliance Communications	14.09%	–6.24%	–0.88%

Source: Compiled from the published annual reports of telecom operators 2010–11

Above Table shows two companies at the extreme ends of the DuPont spectrum, namely Bharti Airtel and BSNL. Even though the two are not strictly comparable because of the nature of their organizational structures and products, the contrast between the operational efficiencies of the two are marked. The reason for this visible divergence in returns performance both on Assets turnover efficiency and Margin of sales efficiency are not immediately clear to the general reader. BSNL is a predominantly wireline operator having large amounts of capital already sunk into its traditional telecom services, and having entered into the mobility segment. The new services in the telecom sector require heavy but far lower investments per line as infrastructural costs. Further, BSNL has far more establishment of previously employed staff who constitute a fixed cost of operations. This heavy baggage of existing commitments drags down its margin at the operational level, the resultant DuPont index overall a negative figure.

On a separate plane the two other companies, Idea Cellular and Reliance Communications present a somewhat different picture. Idea Cellular is able to maintain a positive DuPont Index even though slim, contrasts with Reliance which has a negative operational efficiency index. Further the return on capital employed is far lower than that of either the industry leader or of Idea Cellular. Reliance fell into this trap because of the adoption of CDMA platform for its services which did not prove to be successful and popular as GSM technology. Even though its capital assets are on par with

BSNL and Bharti, the efficiencies are dismal on comparison with either of them, because of far lower sales revenues. In contrast Idea Cellular has achieved much higher revenues with less than half the levels of assets invested into those sales.

Return on Equity

Shareholders of a corporate entity have one major goal. To make a reasonable return on the money they have invested, and prospective investors look out for the level of return they can expect from a company. Equity is what is left over to the disposal of the owners of a company. Return on equity then would be defined as:

$$\text{Return on Equity (ROE)} = \frac{\text{Net Profit}}{\text{Shareholder's equity}}$$

Shareholders in a company receive what is left over after all other claimants to the company's expenses have been settled off. They are usually the employees, vendors, lenders, government and shareholders, in that order. What is left over is in effect what the company actually owns or the more complete definition we had earlier given – the net worth. However, the usual definition that appears in standard text-books of finance and accountancy is narrower. It is usually the share capital contributed by the investors in the company. A little reflection would reveal that the original share capital grows little by little, each time the company makes a surplus in the form of net profit. These accumulations whether actually distributed or not in the form of dividends, represents growth of the original share capital.

Taking an external view of the company's operations, the investor may care little for the accruals in real assets unless he intends to remain invested in the company for subsequent periods. To such an investor, ROE then represents the dividend payments.

However, looking at the company from the internal viewpoint, all surpluses and reserves in the balance sheet constitutes shareholder's accumulated capital over several periods of successful operations. Both the return measures we have discussed above, ROA and ROE are known as combination ratios as the figures are derived from the income statement and the balance sheet. These ratio-combinations link the reader to the economic concepts of productivity of capital.

Here again we need to qualify the purity of these measures, since there could be several variants of the same measures depending on the analytical purposes for which they are employed. For example, ROE sometimes defined as:

$$\text{Return on Equity} = \frac{\text{Net Profit}}{\text{Common equity + Preferred equity}}$$

To arrive at the ROE generally the equity figures as on the last day of the financial year to which the net profit relates is considered. However, imagine a situation where the company has raised capital during the last month of the financial year. This results in a distortion of the ROE figure because, the net profit does not represent the result of new capital which has been employed only for a few days. This figure will then compare unfavorably with its peer company which did not raise any capital. To overcome this problem, we can use the average capital employed by the company as denominator {*(equity at beginning of year + equity at end of year)/2*}. A similar problem may arise with regard to the net income as nominator, if we are comparing a full year return measure with the first quarter of the next year. The user then needs to annualize the earnings figure.

How to Annualize

It is the process of converting a rate of any length into a rate that reflects the rate on an annual (yearly) basis. This is most often done on rates of less than one year, and usually does not take into account the effects of compounding. The annualized rate is not a guarantee but only an estimate, and its accuracy depends on the variance of the rate. This rate is also known as 'annualized return' and is similar to 'run rate' calculated by statisticians during a cricket match.

For example, an investment that returns 1% a month returns 12% on an annualized basis. If, however, the 12% value was computed after only one month of returns, it is not certain that the 12% will be achieved for the year.

The more immediately relevant issue here is that in order to arrive at meaningful measures such as the returns figures, the reader must develop a sense of what is intended, before attempting to arrive at a definitive conclusion. These words of caution have already been alluded to in the beginning of the section on the analytical power of ratios.

Profitability Measures

We have emphasized the importance of approaching the numbers from the balance sheet angle due to the fact that the balance sheet is the long term average and therefore the more reliable indicator of the company's financial health. However, the income statement is the driver of the balance sheet numbers. Without profitability, cash flows dry up; operations to produce, maintain and sell get scaled down. The balance sheet will then begin to shrink as the company is no longer able to purchase new assets or replace worn-out equipment. To use our earlier analogy from the cricket field, if the runs do not come at a reasonably good rate from every over that is bowled, it will be foolhardy to expect that the last-man standing at the wicket will hit all the required runs in the final over. If a business does not produce sufficient profits at a reasonably acceptable margin during every period, any sudden shifts in the market place or cost increases due to external factors will in turn begin to erode the balance sheet figures of total borrowing and shareholder's equity. One or two 'over with no runs' will increase the pressure during subsequent 'batting-overs' perhaps leading to a total collapse. One or two years with 'big-bath-losses' for a large company may not look alarming. But if these losses are due to superior competition or inability to strategize during a paradigm shift in the market conditions, recovery in subsequent periods may not be assured. A case in point is that of the biggest telecom operator in the Indian market, Bharat Sanchar Nigam Ltd (BSNL) an incumbent player whose inability to strategically place itself in the emerging market for mobile communications in India during 2007-10, led its downturn in revenues and profit margins. At the time of writing, its balance sheet is beginning to shrink albeit imperceptibly.

A key income statement focus for analysts is the profit margin measures (*profit as a percentage of sales*). The narrower the margin, the greater is the danger that slight volatility in earnings plunges the company into uncertain future. As already shown in our percentage income statement, the margin can be measured at several levels, either before or after deducting the various charges that gets us to the bottom line or the net profit. The most useful among these are listed below:

$$\text{Gross Margin} = \frac{\text{Sales} - \text{Cost of Goods sold}}{\text{Sales}}$$

$$\text{Operating Margin} = \frac{\text{Operating Income}}{\text{Sales}}$$

$$\text{Pre-tax Margin} = \frac{\text{Net Profit + Income Tax}}{\text{Sales}}$$

$$\text{Net Margin} = \frac{\text{Net Profit}}{\text{Sales}}$$

The different margin measures reflect managerial effectiveness on the level of profitability. Gross margin is of particular interest to traders and retailers who attempt to buy and sell at advantageous prices. Operating margins tell the story of how well the management has run the business, trying to obtain the best cost advantages in not only buying and selling, but also in controlling selling, general and administrative expenses, which are under their control and costs like interest expenses and taxation which are sometimes beyond their control spheres. The last two ratios progressively present the profitability picture, whether they are directly or indirectly controlled by the management. The only aspect which the reader should keep in mind while analyzing the margin is to isolate the effect of extraordinary items, to correctly conclude regarding the sustainable profitability margins of a company.

Part Two

The Outsider's Viewpoint

Two categories of users are keen to watch the performance parameters of a business enterprise from an outsider's stand-point, and they have higher stakes in the company than the commonly considered insiders themselves. They are the owners of the business and the lenders to the business. In the language of the professionals they are the equity holders and the debt holders. Equity holders analysis of the company's numbers is aimed at discovering the true value of the company as reflected in its market capitalization. He, therefore, wishes to make an independent judgment regarding the price he will pay for a share of the company. We shall call this process 'Equity' analysis. When the lender of monies to a business looks at the financial statements of the company, he has altogether a different focus. He wishes to confirm that the company's income is capable of supporting periodic interest payments and repayment of principal amount. We shall call this 'credit' or 'creditworthiness' analysis. In this first section we will take up methods of creditworthiness analysis of a business in detail.

A. Credit Analysis

Debt is perhaps the most important engine of business in the modern world. The credit market can make or break a corporation or even a country as recent experiences of the economic crises in USA and the European countries (*PIGS group-Portugal, Italy, Greece and Spain*) have shown. Lenders who extend credit to corporations and countries with their eyes half-shut not only invite doomsday to their doorsteps, but pull the whole economy down, if the scale of such lending is large enough. On a smaller scale, merchants exchanging goods based on promises to pay must evaluate the likelihood of repayments based on those promises. Banks extending short-term credits to businesses to finance their inventory purchases must evaluate the business for the probability of repayment. Commercial banks too have this problem of creditworthiness because they borrow from other financial institutions, when they issue certificate of deposits and bonds. Financial statement analysis can significantly influence such lending decisions.

The lender and the student of finance can draw valuable conclusions from the three financial statements put out by the companies regarding its creditworthiness. We have attempted, therefore, to present the basic techniques and ratios that must form a valuable tool to the diagnostic attempt.

Diagnostic Ratios from the Balance Sheet

The borrower must have cash to pay off its debt or must be able to raise cash when such payments are due. This is what we call liquidity. It implies that the company must have sufficient cash in its bank or must have assets that can be disposed of quickly to raise cash or have the ability to borrow more cash from others to pay off its obligations. Illiquidity is the contrasting condition of excess payments due more than currently available assets will support. We can then arrive at a ratio which measures liquidity thus:

$$\text{Current Ratio} = \frac{\text{Current Assets}}{\text{Current Liabilities}}$$

Typically a company with a ratio of more than 1 will be able to meet its obligations. However, some of the components of current assets may not actually fetch the values as shown in the balance sheet (*you may recall our earlier discussion on book value and market value*) in which case the ratio tells a different story in reality. The analysis can gain more confidence in the liquidity position by applying a more stringent measure of liquidity as defined below:

$$\text{Quick Ratio} = \frac{\text{Quick Assets}}{\text{Current Liabilities}}$$

Quick assets are here cash and those assets that can be quickly converted into cash (*such as marketable securities and receivables*). This ratio is more popularly known as the acid-test ratio because it indicates in no uncertain terms the actual liquidity position of the company.

Sometimes it is useful to calculate the difference between current assets and current liabilities which is termed 'working capital':

$$\text{Working Capital} = \text{Current Assets} - \text{Current Liabilities}$$

Such a measure is a pointer to the ability of the company to meet its obligations within the year. The reader is again warned that both these figures are in fact estimates of assets (*inventories, receivables, outstanding loans to employees etc*) and liabilities (*payments due to suppliers, bank overdrafts etc*) which are likely to materialize during the year. Therefore, the difference is also an estimate of the future position of ability to meet the obligations. Nevertheless it is a warning on impending illiquidity if the difference is a negative figure.

Despite all the precautions the lender may employ before loaning monies to the businessman, they frequently discover that they are saddled with bad lending that end up in default. Companies sometimes end up in bankruptcy and creditors are left standing at their doors hoping to recover at least part of the money. In a situation of liquidation, the creditors wish to estimate how much they can actually salvage from the sinking concern. There are many ratios that provide reasonable confidence to the lender. We start with the broadest.

$$\frac{\text{Total Assets}}{\text{Total Liabilities}}$$

This is the broadest measure of asset protection. The bigger the number, the greater is the sense of relief for the lender. Total liabilities can be easily discovered by subtracting shareholder's equity from total assets. Put in another way, if the owners have pumped in more capital than debt, the lenders feel safer. This is due to the fact that shareholders have lower preference than debt holders to receive payment in the event of liquidation. This brings us to the most common measure of the Lender's view of a business: Debt-to-Equity ratio.

$$\text{Debt-to-equity Ratio} = \frac{\text{Total Debt}}{\text{Total Equity}}$$

Finance companies generally exhibit a ratio higher than 1 for the D/E ratio. But conventional companies have a ratio less than 1. For banks however, the ratio most commonly used is called the 'Capital Adequacy Ratio' which is a measure of the bank's ability to meet all its depositors in case of run on the bank. (*The reader may understand here that in most countries, the Central Bank acts as 'a lender of the last resort' and consequently bank failures are less frequent. The reader is advised to read up the events in the USA related to the bankruptcy of Lehman Brothers and Bank of America. 'The Ascent of Money' by Niall Ferguson is an excellent account*)[6]. The cardinal failure in all these cases was the failure to maintain standard levels of Capital Adequacy Ratio.

What Constitutes Debt?

Here the intelligent reader would have raised this valid query. What constitutes debt? In the balance sheet you will notice two types of debt: long term borrowing shown just below the share capital number and short term debt, which is shown under current liabilities. Strictly speaking short term overdrafts is used to finance seasonal working capital needs such as festival season inventory buying. However, some businesses have revolving credit arrangements with their creditors. This must indeed be considered as long term debt. There is a danger to the company of exposure to interest rate fluctuations in such arrangements. Long term debt with floating rate interest rates is also subject to volatility of interest burden in the income statement. Yet another aspect of debt calculation is the existence of preferred stock.

Preferred Stock

Preferred stock generally has a fixed rate of dividend that must be paid out before dividends to common stockholders, if dividends are declared. Each company may have different terms and conditions for issue of such share. The best way to think of preference shares is to see it as having characteristics of both debt (fixed dividends) and equity (potential appreciation).

There are pros and cons when looking at preferred shares. Preferred shareholders have priority over common stockholder in the event of liquidation and they have a fixed dividend (paid before common stockholders), but they have no voting rights and less potential for appreciation.

Legally speaking preferred stock is equity as it ranks junior to debt in liquidation, and failure to pay dividend is not default. However, treating it purely as equity is not correct for the analysis of financial flexibility, because of the various conditions attached to preferred stock. Usually they have cumulative preference for dividend, at other time they may have sinking fund provisions just like bonds. Risk to the lender substantially changes when preferred stock is present in the capital structure.

The other important aspect is to find out if the company has any lease agreement in its financing of capital equipments, or in its operating arrangements. Lease arrangements are in fact debt obligations shown as 'rental expense' in the income statements. They are also called off-balance sheet items, as they do not appear in the balance sheet. The 'rental expense' on account of lease charges is fixed payments that constitute a prior claim on earnings and lenders must be wary of these before considering extending further debt. The total amount of debt in most cases would be equivalent to

7 or 8 times the 'rental expense' figure. In most instances leasing has only a thin cosmetic effect of disguising debt.

There are other ingenious ways through which some management disguises debt obligations by taking them off the balance sheet. A common method is to form joint ventures or affiliate companies whose operations are critical to the parent. They may receive dividends from these companies yet show no liabilities as matching their revenues. These are in fact *several obligations* as against *joint* obligations in legal language. Some parent companies may take over 100% of the debt of the joint venture partner since its operations affect the parent's performance. The reader should also be aware of emerging financing methods like 'sale and buy-back arrangements' which are nothing but debt in another form.

Sale and Buyback

A method of financing in which an owner sells an asset or property to an investor or lender on cash-basis, and immediately buys it back on a long-term mortgage basis to retain possession, title, and use. This method avoids selling-off of an asset and enables its owner to continue to enjoy depreciation and tax benefits. The reader will notice that the asset then will no longer appear in the balance sheet.

Another angle to the obligations that the company may have to meet in future is the issue of employee benefits, such as pension and post-retirement medical benefits. These are usually funded (*meaning thereby that investments in assets have been fully made for these eventualities*): however, the reader should look out for those obligations which are not fully funded or not funded at all. In the event of liquidation, claims by such groups of employees will take precedence over other creditors.

Like all analytical approaches, ratio analysis must be forward-looking rather than backward-looking. The reason is that past is seldom a yardstick of future events. The intention of the management to obtain more capital at cheaper rates overrides many of their decision making processes. They may even liquidate existing debt to convince creditors that they mean well and that they no longer intend to pursue the reckless course of borrowing heavily that got them into the financial mess. However, many CEOs betray this intention when they are tempted by acquisition prospects which they imagine will increase their net worth or sphere of influence. It is important for the intelligent reader to keep a lookout for signs such as these, before arriving at a conclusion regarding the creditworthiness of the company's numbers they are reading. There are also other ratios which the reader should cross-check along with those from the balance sheet, which we have discussed. They are from the income statement and the cash flow statement, which we propose to examine now.

Diagnostic Ratios from the Income Statement

Up until now we have placed emphasis on liquidity and risk assessment to the company's assets. Howsoever important that may be, the key inference related in effect to the overall profitability of the company. Without profits, no company can attempt to maintain liquidity or asset values. High flow of cash through the system is because the assets are productive, the managerial input is effective and company has ability to face the current market environment. The implication here is that credit analysis cannot ignore the income statement and its underlying ratios. Merely relying on the current ratio or the acid test ratio may distort the view presented to the prospective creditor and threatens the safety of the existing lender. In the ensuing section we propose to examine the profitability aspect of a business for drawing conclusions about its overall financial position. We use the P&L statement of Bharti Airtel as a starting point.

Bharti Airtel
The Profit and Loss Account
Annual Report 2011-12
(Millions, Except Per Share Data and as Stated Otherwise)

Particulars	For the Year Ended March 31, 2012	For the Year Ended March 31, 2011
Revenue from operations	**416,038**	380,177
Other income	**6,247**	3,212
Total revenue	**422,285**	383,389
Expenses		
Access charges	**58,086**	49,872
License fee and spectrum charges (revenue share)	**46,942**	42,903
Cost of goods sold	**183**	161
Employee benefits expenses	**13,915**	14,512
Power and fuel	**29,727**	25,233
Rent	**47,714**	43,337
Other expenses	**82,702**	70,466
Total expenses	**279,269**	246,484
Profit before finance costs, depreciation, amortization Charity and donation and taxation	**143,016**	136,905
Finance costs	**13,962**	3,241
Depreciation and amortization expense	**59,160**	46,116
Charity and donation	**332**	290
Profit before tax	**69,562**	87,258
MAT credit	**(5,227)**	(12,469)
Tax expense		
Current tax	**14,398**	17,315
Deferred tax	**3,091**	5,243
Profit for the year	**57,300**	77,169
Earnings per share (equity shares of par value ₹5 each) Basic and diluted	**15.09**	20.3

Source: Published annual report of Bharti Airtel

Here are the profitability ratios for Bharti Airtel for the year ended March 31st 2012.

$$\text{Operating Margin} = \frac{\text{Operating Income}}{\text{Sales}} = \frac{143{,}016}{416{,}038} = 34.37\%$$

$$\text{Pre-tax Margin} = \frac{\text{Net Profit + Income Tax}}{\text{Sales}} = \frac{747{,}89}{416{,}038} = 17.97\%$$

$$\text{Net Margin} = \frac{\text{Net Profit}}{\text{Sales}} = \frac{57{,}300}{416{,}038} = 13.77\%$$

Bharti Airtel's operating margins are typically higher than other telecom operators in India. This is largely due to the company's ability to keep its total operating expenses lower than its peers. The company achieved this remarkable feat by innovative cost management techniques unknown to the industry, especially the ability to outsource most of its network operations to Telecom equipment suppliers like IBM and Eriksson.

To get a clearer picture of the company with regard to its credit-worthiness, the reader must refer to the balance sheet. We have reproduced the company's corresponding balance sheet for the year as in March 2012.

Bharti Airtel
Annual Report 2011-12
Consolidated Statement of Financial Position (₹ in Millions)*

Particulars	March 31, 2012	March 31, 2011
Assets		
Non-current assets		
Property, plant and equipment	674,932	651,426
Intangible assets	660,889	637,317
Investment in associates	24	-
Derivative financial assets	2,756	1,998
Other financial assets	17,086	7,930
Other non-financial assets	15,568	9,255
Deferred tax asset	51,277	45,061
	1,422,532	1,352,987
Current assets		
Inventories	1,308	2,139
Trade and other receivables	63,735	54,929
Derivative financial assets	2,137	2,682
Prepayments and other assets	32,621	30,504
Income tax recoverable	9,049	5,280
Short term investments	18,132	6,224
Other financial assets	802	744
Cash and cash equivalents	20,300	9,575
	148,084	112,077
Total assets	1,570,616	1,465,064
Equity and liabilities equity		
Issued capital	18,988	18,988
Treasury shares	(282)	(268)
Share premium	56,499	56,499
Retained earnings	395,682	357,446
Foreign currency translation reserve	(6,026)	14,018
Other components of equity	41,252	40,985

Equity attributable to equity holders of parent	**506,113**	487,668
Non-controlling interest	**27,695**	28,563
Total equity	**533,808**	516,231
Non-current liabilities		
Borrowings	**497,154**	532,338
Deferred revenue	**2,892**	8,700
Provisions	**7,240**	6,085
Derivative financial liabilities	**401**	151
Deferred tax liability	**11,621**	12,487
Other financial liabilities	**23,076**	13,856
Other non-financial liabilities	**5,551**	5,371
	547,935	578,988
Current liabilities		
Borrowings	**193,078**	84,370
Deferred revenue	**43,282**	30,599
Provisions	**1,290**	1,180
Other non-financial liabilities	**10,811**	10,053
Derivative financial liabilities	**166**	317
Income tax liabilities	**7,596**	3,642
Trade & other payables	**232,650**	239,684
	488,873	369,845
Total liabilities	**1,036,808**	948,833
Total equity and liabilities	**1,570,616**	1,465,064

******Adapted by the author from the published annual report of Bharti Airtel***

Liquidity Ratios for Bharti Airtel are worked out from its balance sheet as on 1st March 2012.

$$\text{Current Ratio} = \frac{\text{Current assets}}{\text{Current Liabilities}} = \frac{148{,}084}{488{,}873} = 0.30$$

$$\text{Quick Ratio} = \frac{\text{Quick assets}}{\text{Current Liabilities}} = \frac{39{,}234}{488{,}873} = 0.08$$

Working Capital = Current Assets – Current Liabilities
= 148,084 – 488,873 = –340,789

$$\frac{\text{Total Assets}}{\text{Total Liabilities}} = \frac{1{,}570{,}616}{1{,}036{,}808} = 1.51$$

$$\frac{\text{Total Debt}}{\text{Total Equity}} = \frac{690{,}232}{533{,}808} = 1.29$$

Looking at these ratios gives a different picture. The company is likely to face liquidity issues during the year as it has a rather high negative working capital figure. It will have difficulty in meeting obligations and may have to fall back to further short-term borrowings which are already high. This view is further confirmed by the two ratios for assessing liquidity. The current ratio is less than 1 and current assets are just about 1/3rd of its current obligations. The quick ratio is precariously low as the cash and near-cash securities reserves are in fact less than 1% of its payment obligations. The overall picture which is a rough guide to creditworthiness also does not look good as its total debt exceeds total equity by nearly 30%. A further reading of the report shows that the weighted average cost of borrowing from the previous year has nearly doubled during the current year along with the more than doubling of the total outstanding borrowing figure. This position in the consolidated accounts is the result largely due to the company's overseas new acquisitions in Africa and Bangladesh Infratel Networks Ltd. which have been largely financed by borrowings.

At this point the reader begins to wonder whether the company will be able to meet its fixed payment obligations to its lenders. The margin measures we have discussed above reflect the management's efficiency in utilizing its resources. However, if we can arrive at the number of times the net operating revenue covers the fixed charges like rentals and interest payments, it might be useful. Fortunately we can have such a figure. In its simplest form:

$$\text{Fixed charges coverage ratio} = \frac{\text{Net Profit + Income Taxes + Interest Expense}}{\text{Interest Expense}}$$

We can work out this from Bharti Airtel's income statement.

$$\text{FCC ratio} = \frac{57{,}300 + 17{,}489 + 13{,}962}{13{,}962} = 6.35 \text{ times}$$

The leading telecom operator is comfortably placed with regard to the payment of its fixed interest charges, considered in isolation. Telecom operations in India are high fixed cost ventures, subject to hyper-competition in a low-priced market. If the revenues begin to erode position may turn out to be difficult for Bharti. To garner information regarding the strength of the revenue stream the reader must turn to other sources. The financial statements are by and large pictures about the past events and therefore needs to be handled as such. At the time of writing this book, reports from various quarters are emerging which show that Airtel's position is far from comfortable. The company's quarterly revenues have been falling for the 7th quarter in a row. The much hyped acquisitions have not turned out to be a gold-mine the company was hoping it would be. Noises emanating from the board room have a worried flavor to them. With a mega-scale of operations and strong brand image the company management may yet need all skills to weather the oncoming storm.

Diagnostic Ratios from the Cash Flow Statement

As a natural follow up of the above analysis one must turn to the cash flow statement for some answers which are not present in the other two statements. This statement analyses the company's sources and use of cash at the most basic level. Corporations are generally reluctant to issue new capital, for fear of diluting the existing shareholders' interest. This means that if there is a shortfall in operational cash the companies generally turn to borrowing. This reduces a company's financial flexibility and profitability in later periods. For industries such as telecommunications which are highly capital-intensive, the key ratio to look out for is the cash flow to capital expenditures.

$$\frac{\text{Cash flow from operations}}{\text{Capital Expenditures}}$$

Generally, the higher the ratio the higher is the financial flexibility. But here we must add a word of caution. The ratio for Airtel from its cash flow statement is (128,341/126,118 = 1.01) is just one. This just about explains company's eagerness to borrow heavily in the open market to maintain its future competitiveness. If a company cuts back investments this ratio will improve, but it leads ultimately to a loss of financial flexibility in subsequent periods.

Another useful ratio to predict sustainability of cash flows in future is to estimate the level of depreciation as a percentage of cash from operations. This is so because depreciation is somewhat a stable figure in the short run. A higher percentage of depreciation to operating cash flow means that the company is assured of a higher proportion of cash flow that is fixed, at least in the medium term.

Perhaps the most important of the ratios from the cash flow statement is the percentage of capital expenditures to depreciation.

$$\frac{\text{Capital Expenditures}}{\text{Depreciation}}$$

A ratio less than 1.0 over several periods, suggests that the company is consistently failing to replace its assets and is then exposing itself to competition and may face gradual liquidation. But the reader should not automatically come to the conclusion that just because the ratio looks alright, everything is fine with the company's future.

There are three reasons why this is not correct. First is inflation. This means that the same rupee amount spend while acquiring the assets will fetch lower capacities than originally obtained, even though technological advances may have completely revamped the production process. In that case, the company will need to push investments even harder to stay in the same market-space. This happened to all incumbent telecom operators during the De-monopolization of the sector in many countries during the late 1980's and 1990's. It is no surprise that many incumbent operators (*mostly government controlled*) went under during subsequent periods.

The second reason is the fundamental dichotomy between depreciation (an accounting concept, which follows the matching principle we so emphatically stated in an earlier chapter) and the actual wear and tear of the equipments in question. The danger is that a strong ratio may hide the actual worthlessness of the equipments. BSNL was the leading telecom operator in India producing annual revenues of over 350 billion up until 2007. What was not understood by the management was that more than 70% of this revenue was accruing from landline services, piggybacking on a large network of physical wires and lines that overnight suffered loss of value due to the disruption from mobile telephony. An examination of the ratios up until 2007 based on BSNL financial reports gives no inkling of this impending catastrophe.

Thirdly, capital expenditures must match competitor outlays rather than depreciation. Any company that fails to keep eye on the competitor's every move and match it or exceed it will eventually lose market share.

Putting It All Together

The Power of Combination Ratios

We have already seen some powerful combination ratios, which combine the earnings numbers with the balance sheet figures, in the form of returns ratios, relative to assets or capital investments. These measures act as a link between credit analysis as viewed by the creditors and productivity of capital as generally managed by the professional executives. We have seen the analysis of returns on assets and the DuPont approach and shall not dwell on them, therefore in this section. Instead, we shall move on to another set of measures which will point to the quality of the assets that the company's balance sheet displays. These are called turnover ratios, as a category by themselves. The two most prominent assets that the balance sheet must have apart from the fixed assets are: receivables and inventories.

Average Days of Receivables

There is a well-accepted notion that a business needs to offer a certain amount of time to customers to pay up for the products it has sold. Normally, it gets time to pay for raw materials and services purchased from suppliers. This results in a mismatch not only between income and sales but also purchases and cash outflows. This system prompted the accountants to introduce the accrual concept and is a foundational principle for the matching revenues and expenditures in the income statement.

Let us assume that a company has a stated policy of offering a 30 days' time-period for payment for goods sold. If all customers paid up for sales within the 30 days, the amounts due from customers (*also called the accounts receivable*) at any point of time will be exactly 8.2% of annual sales (*30/365 = 8.2*). Looking at the same number from the opposite direction, 8.2 represent the number of days that the sales revenue due from customers is outstanding. Day's sales outstanding (DSO) is also known as the *average collection period* or *receivable days*. It measures how fast the customers pay their bills. We have worked out the number of receivable days from the Airtel's income statement and balance sheet numbers.

Day's sales outstanding (DSO) is calculated as:

$$\text{Average days of receivables} = \frac{(\text{ARBY} + \text{AREY})/2}{(\text{Annual Sales}/365)} = \frac{(54{,}929 + 63{,}735)/2}{(416{,}038/365)} = 52.05$$

Where : ARBY = Accounts receivable at the Beginning of the Year
AREY = Accounts Receivable at the End of the Year

As long as the company continues to sell on the same terms as at present, the level of receivables will rise as sales increase, but the ratio will remain the same. If at any time, the ratio deteriorates (*meaning an increase in the number*) it would imply several factors at work. The immediate question is why it is taking longer to collect payments, is the customer unhappy with the product, or is in financial difficulties? Are sales people increasing the sales by offering more discounts, or are they dealing with less creditworthy customers? Is there a problem with the collection software of the agents involved? Is there leakage in cash collected? It takes management skills and other accompanying data to arrive at the right answer and take initiatives that focus on appropriate solutions.

The DSO number is an important criterion for judging the quality of receivables and sales. This number varies from industry to industry and like all other ratios, by region, economy and seasonality. Whatever the background, a deteriorating ratio over several periods is a red flag. Unless that company has reflected this fact by increasing the provision for doubtful debts, it may have to write off some portion of the income at some future period. Businesses looking at an acquisition proposal may be interested to know the target company's financial flexibility management practices. DSO may even reveal extreme accounting artistry with the numbers as in the case of Sunbeam, the story we have narrated earlier.

Inventory Turnover Ratio

If a company has piled up unsold inventory, the asset shown in the balance sheet under the heading current assets will show an increase. But the value of that inventory can be far less than the historical cost shown in the balance sheet. This could be the case with a fashion store that has leftover clothes from the previous season or a computer manufacturer who has a large stack of desktop computers designed around an out-of-date processor chip. A rise in the level of inventory without a corresponding sympathetic rise in sales is a precursor to inventory write-off. We can arrive at this symptom through the calculation of inventory turnover ratio.

$$\text{Inventory Turnover ratio} = \frac{\text{Annual Sales}}{(\text{IBY} + \text{IEY})/2}$$

Where: IBY = Inventory at the Beginning of the Year

IEY= Inventory at the End of the Year

Of course, it is possible that sales have fallen thereby increasing the inventory turnover ratio. However, the implications are quite different. The value of inventory may not have suffered, but drop in sales creates a glut nevertheless, prompting the management to cut back production. But this takes time. In the meantime precious cash is locked up in inventory, thereby making the company short of resources for much needed activities, net impact being loss of financial flexibility. Profitability may take a hit as price-cuts of discounts are needed to get rid of excess goods.

A possible distortion in the interpretation of this ratio is apparent. If the price of a commodity rises due to a sudden spurt in demand or a temporary shortage, the inventory turnover ratio might show a dramatic improvement. This is true for Kerala based Jewelry shops that experience increases in gold prices on a daily basis during 2011 and 2012, yet physically the quantity of goods sold or the stock of inventory remains more or less the same as before. The converse is also true in the case of a price-cut in response to poor off-take. One solution is to use 'Cost of goods sold' in the numerator instead of sales figure as both numerator and denominator then will be based on historical costs.

Debt to Cash Flow Ratio

We could look at the financial flexibility of the company from the point of view of a lender by calculating the total debt the company holds as a percentage of the cash-flow-from-operations.

The formula will then be:

$$\text{Total Debt to Cash Flow} = \frac{\text{(Short-term + Overdraft + Long-term)}}{\text{Cash Flow from Operations}}$$

The ratio looks at the business unit from the point of view of cash that is available in the bank rather than the accountants' view of earnings which is sometimes not so real. Let us consider the case of an imaginary company which has a total debt obligation of ₹100 crs and a cash flow from operations of ₹20 crs per annum. The ratio then states that the company can clear its debt in 5 years' time if it uses all its cash for debt repayment. No company can earmark all its cash for debt servicing however, but the ratio reveals that such a company is definitely in a better position than another which has ₹80 crs debt and a cash flow of ₹10 crs yearly. The later company will then be able to redeem its total debt in 8 years if all cash goes for redemption. But it will face redemption pressure if the maturity period of the debt changes or interest rates moves up due to rebalancing of debts.

The ratio then is a fairly reliable measure of the financial flexibility of the company, as it is fashioned from numbers that are hard and somewhat more realistic and therefore would reflect a more real picture of the ability to meet such obligations. We have presented this unconventional ratio at the end of this section on credit analysis because the other commonly used ratios for measuring creditworthiness suffer from definite known weaknesses which are the result of the accounting process itself. Here I invite the reader to revisit the two major ratios in vogue. The popularity of debt-equity ratio in textbooks on finance and management discussions constitutes an exalted position in business journalism. But it suffers from a major weakness. Equity value cannot be assessed realistically till the company is involved in a sale/purchase transaction. (Accountants refuse to record anything other than historical values unless a premium is realized through a sale.) Therefore the true value of the ratio is unknown even so, it will be more hazardous to compare two or more companies based on this ratio. Fixed coverage ratio also lacks conviction as it is based on earnings as the numerator and you have already learnt that earnings are subject to the accountant's opinion. This is because the accountant can and often do use the depreciation number to boost earnings. But cash flow cannot be manipulated (*except in extreme cases where the company is fraudulent*) and debt obligation is also a real number that represents real cash outflow.

Can We Predict Bankruptcy?

Any discussion on the creditworthiness of a company naturally leads to the problem of bankruptcy. The lender and the ordinary investor must be able to answer the question as to whether it is absolutely certain that the company will not go into liquidation in the near future. Many readers might imagine that the question is somewhat far-fetched and perhaps irrelevant because bankruptcy is the last resort action of the business to protect its assets, and to salvage whatever remains of the unfortunate enterprise before complete erosion of the net worth. So far in this book we have approached the issue of creditworthiness from calculating ratios from the numbers put out by the management. We have shown that a careful analysis of the ratios after eliminating the biases built into the numbers can reveal a lot about the quality of risk involved in lending to the company. We used basically two techniques. One was to compare the ratios against some well-established norms prevalent in the industry among peer-groups resulting in a ranking of those companies and the other was the trend analysis of the ratios themselves for the particular company. The later technique will be discussed in more detail in a later section on comparative ratio analysis.

This discussion is still incomplete because we have not yet answered the question as to how to rank a company if two ratios which are related are in conflict with each other. For example, how would the reader rank a company that reflects a poor debt-equity ratio but is fixed-charges coverage ratio is excellent? (*The reader may recall that Bharti Airtel exhibits this characteristic while looking at its ratios.*) In other words, is coverage more important than leverage? This requires more thought than a mere subjective opinion of the reader. Fortunately for us statistical studies have attempted to establish a relationship between ratios and default. One such model which attempted to closely establish a relationship between the financial profile and loan default, otherwise called bankruptcy, is the Edward I. Altman's Z-Score model.

Altman's Z-Score[7]

A mathematical formula developed in the 1960s by NYU Professor Edward Altman that attempts to express the chances of a public company going bankrupt within a two-year time period. The number produced by the model is referred to as the company's Z-score, which is a reasonably accurate predictor of future bankruptcy. The model is specified as:

$$Z = 1.2A + 1.4B + 3.3C + 0.6D + 1.0E$$

Where

Z = Score

A = Working Capital/Total Assets

B = Retained Earnings/Total Assets

C = Earnings before Interest & Tax/Total Assets

D = Market Value of Equity/Total Liabilities

E = Sales/Total Assets

The zeta model returns a single number, the z-score, to represent the likelihood of a company going bankrupt in the next two years. The lower the z-score, the more likely a company is to go bankrupt. A z-score lower than 1.8 indicates that bankruptcy is likely, while scores greater than 3.0 indicate bankruptcy is unlikely to occur in the next two years. Companies that have a z-score between 1.8 and 3.0 are in the gray area, bankruptcy is not easily predicted one way or the other.

We have presented this analysis primarily because; we believe that mathematical models based on actual statistical information collected from real market correlating financial variables with the propensity to default have certain distinct advantages. The foremost among them is the elimination of biased opinions of analysts which are fairly more subjective in comparison. The second aspect is that in real practice rating agencies like Moody's and Standard & Poor have arrived at their default rating evaluations through such a process. Academic studies like the Z-score have confirmed this process rather than contradict them. The rating by agencies is a probability ranking of default within next one year, next two years and next twenty years and so on. These conclusions are merely vindicated by the academic studies. The reader must remember that even though this is so, quantitative models, sometimes very elegant and sophisticated cannot substitute for human judgment in its entirety. As stated elsewhere in this book, prediction is always defective, especially if it is about the future since probabilities are most often based on past data extrapolated to represent future. It is good to remember that future is never a continuation of the past even though it might appear to be so.

One another albeit important aspect is that default and shutdowns might occur for reason other than financial. Companies are forced out of business because of environmental issues or other social factors even though they might be sound financially.

10 Brands That Will Disappear

Research In Motion may be the best example of an innovative company that lost its edge. As a result, it will disappear in 2013. Five years ago, RIM was the only smartphone company of any size, and it had almost the entire corporate market. But it made a fatal mistake in failing to adapt its technology for consumer use. In June 2007, Apple launched the iPhone, and the rest is history.

A few of the companies we said would vanish are still operating – barely. American Apparel is now a penny stock. Nokia is another company 24/7 still predicts will go away soon. The former Finnish heavyweight just fired 10,000 employees, or 20% of its workforce.

We also made a few bad calls. Sears and Sony Pictures are still operating in essentially the same form they were a year ago. Kellogg's Corn Pops and Soap Opera Digest are doing just fine.

This year we continue to take a methodical approach in deciding which brands to include on our list of brands that will disappear. The major criteria are:

1. a rapid fall-off in sales and steep losses;
2. disclosures by the parent of the brand that it might go out of business;
3. rapidly rising costs that are extremely unlikely to be recouped through higher prices;
4. companies that are sold;
5. companies that go into bankruptcy;
6. companies that have lost the great majority of their customers; or
7. operations with rapidly withering market share.

Each brand on the list suffers from one or more of these problems. Each of the 10 will be gone, based on our definitions, within 18 months.

American Airlines

US Airways already has made it clear that it wants to buy American's assets. As soon as the rumors of a potential buyout started in April, some of American's largest unions said they backed such a plan as a way to protect jobs. Earlier this month, US Airways CEO Doug Parker announced his desire to merge the two airlines. With US Airways probably willing to give AMR's creditors a good deal to get American's assets, the potential deal received tremendous support from bondholders and analysts. US Airways has much to gain from this transaction, as its position in the carrier market has been eroded by the mergers of Northwest and Delta and the later combination of United and Continental.

Current TV

Al Gore's Current TV was on life support even before it fired its only bankable star, Keith Olbermann, in March following a set of battles with the host over his perks. He was replaced by serial talk show host failure Eliot Spitzer. Compared to Olbermann's March figures, Spitzer's ratings in April were down nearly 70%, according to TV audience measurement firm Nielsen. At the time, *The Hollywood Reporter* wrote, 'Replacement Eliot Spitzer pulled an anemic 47,000 total viewers in the first outing of Viewpoint, with just 10,000 adults in the age group 25-54. The weeks since saw an early rebound, particularly in the demo, but in its four weeks on air Viewpoint has steadily declined in both respects.' Reuters recently reported that Current TV's audience had fallen enough that cable giant Time Warner Cable may have the right to discontinue carrying the channel. The closest Current TV has to a star is talk show veteran Joy Behar, a former cast member of 'The View,' who had her own show canceled by CNN's HLN in November. Gore does not have the pockets to keep a network with no future going.

Research In Motion

RIM once owned the smartphone market. Its BlackBerry products were used largely by businesses. It is hardly worth repeating the story of how RIM was late to the consumer market, where it has been pounded relentlessly by Apple and an army of Google Android phones from manufacturers as diverse as Taiwan's HTC, South Korea's Samsung and Motorola in the US. The pace at which the company fell apart once the process began was even more extraordinary than its rise. The best measurement of the swiftness of RIM's fall is the change of its share of the US smartphone market. Research group NPD recently reported that RIM's US market share was 44% in 2009 but only 10% last year. Data from research group Comscore shows that share has fallen further this year. The net effect on RIM's stock price has been devastating, taking it down from $144 four years ago to $11 recently. RIM cannot survive as a standalone operation in the face of these trends. The Wall Street Journal recently reported 'outright buyers could include Asian handset makers like HTC Corp or online retailer Amazon.com Inc. which has jumped into the tablet business.'

Suzuki

American Suzuki Motor sold 10,695 cars and light trucks in the first five months of this year. That was down 3.9% compared with the same period in 2011. The sales gave the manufacturer a US market share of just 0.2%. One reason the company has trouble moving its vehicles are the poor reputation of its cars. In the 2012 JD Power survey of US vehicle dependability, Suzuki's scores in power-trains, body and materials, and features and accessories were below those of almost every other brand. One sign Suzuki is having trouble selling its vehicles is that it currently offers a very aggressive zero-percent financing package for 72 months on all of its 2012 cars, trucks and SUVs. Even with aggressive sales tactics, Suzuki cannot improve its position in the American market. Most of its cars sell for less than $20,000 and its trucks and SUVs for under $25,000. Almost every other manufacturer with a broad range of vehicles has flooded this end of the market with cheap, fuel-efficient models. Arguably the most successful car company in the US based on growth – Hyundai – does particularly well in this segment.

Avon

It would be hard to find another large American company as bad off as Avon Products (NYSE: AVP). Avon's long time CEO, Andrea Jung, was ousted late last year after nearly wrecking the company. Avon's new CEO, Sherilyn S. McCoy, formerly of Johnson & Johnson (NYSE: JNJ), joined the company in April. She has not run a public corporation, let alone one in big trouble. The Securities and Exchange Commission's examination of Avon's communications with securities analysts already has cost CFO Charles Cramb his job. Avon is also under scrutiny for whether its Chinese operations meet compliance standards under the Foreign Corrupt Practices Act. One of Avon's core problems is that the beauty market is highly competitive, yet management has not concentrated on its core business. As Morningstar analyst Erin Lash recently wrote, 'Despite restructuring initiatives that have cost the firm nearly $800 million through fiscal 2011, it appears to us that Avon is constantly putting out fires rather than proactively moving forward.' There is much to fix. Avon announced disastrous earnings in the previous quarter, and it forecast that things will get worse. Avon, however, is fortunate that it may have a suitor. In May, perfume company Coty offered $24.75 a share for Avon, nearly 20% above Avon's stock price at the time. Coty had the financial backing of, among others, Warren Buffett. Avon dragged its feet and Coty withdrew its offer. But Coty, another consumer products firm or a private equity house will be back. Since the Coty offer was withdrawn, Avon's shares have dropped below $16. That price is down from $43 four years ago. The market has no confidence in Avon, but with its brand and revenue, it is an ideal takeover target.

Another interesting yet valid approach to the issue of default is to compare book value (*of a company's obligations*) with the market value (*unit value of a share × number of shares outstanding*) of the company. In theory, owner's equity or net worth as we have defined is the residual value of the company after it has met all its obligations to its external creditors. We then proceeded to inform that the market value of this equity is the price at which an investor is willing to buy the assets of the company, in an arm's-length transaction. Therefore if at any time, the market value of the equity falls below the total value of a company's liabilities, it means that a unit of stock of the company is worthless. In fact the company is bankrupt. Simply by watching the trend of share-price values must thereof be able to predict an oncoming bankruptcy.

As has become our habit, we end this section with a word of caution. Looking at share prices is certainly a useful way of arriving at the company's financial health, but it is not infallible. At best it is a good signal. Like most signals it has to be interpreted and decoded. Let us imagine the case of a company that borrows heavily to buy-back its own shares. The result is that its debt-to-equity ratio rises dramatically; also its share price in the market tends to rise. Larger loan boosts earnings-per-share due to tax advantages of financial leverage and reduced number of shares outstanding. Such rises in share prices does not in fact improve its default risk but considerably increases it. A further consideration while relying purely on mathematical calculations is that companies do change their capital structure in response to take-over bids or to finance an attractive acquisition. Such actions can render ratio analysis irrelevant. The second problem is that not all companies have shares which trade on the stock market. In such cases substituting the share prices of a peer group company is not a solution as this method cannot expose the specific problems and internal conditions of the company in question. The reader must dissect the financial statements through ratio analysis and turn simultaneously to other data to arrive at a definitive conclusion about the default risk of the businesses they are interested in.

The Outsider's Point of View

B. Equity Analysis

Everyone is an expert on the stock market. The number of books and write-ups on the subject on stock-picking is as numerous as the stocks themselves, perhaps only more. From the highly sophisticated models built by PhD's in mathematics to the 'panwallah' on the streets in 'Lal-Darwaza' of Ahmadabad's sprawling business community, everyone seems to know what stocks will hit the roof and what should be avoided. In the midst of all these noises and voices, why would the author of this book attempt to explore the subject of equity analysis? The answer is rather straight. This section is not about stock-picking at all. We will deal with the topic in a purely simple form, intended to introduce the concepts of equity evaluation in only so far as it throws a definite light on the aspects of valuation of that portion of shareholder's stake in the business. Its relevance is its ability to enhance the reader's financial skills. The task may look simplistic at first, but is a complex enough task to reduce its sophistication to a basic form, as we promised to keep the book free of jargons.

Two Approaches to Equity Valuation

Foremost among all keen observers of a business are the owners themselves who wish to see their original contribution into the business growing year after year. This is the true meaning of profits. Any other number does not constitute real profits. Accruing wealth and in a concrete form of annual payouts, is otherwise called dividends. He might be willing to sacrifice present dividends in the hope of greater dividend payouts sometime in the future. But dividend is the basic motivation. Analysis that attempts to reveal the true and fair value of a unit of stock in a business based on wealth creation in its real sense is known as 'fundamental analysis'. Those who adopt this method are convinced that the financial characteristics of the company in question reveal a lot about its value. They therefore believe that the market for securities and stocks take all available information about a company both as revealed in its accounting statements as well as those that fall outside the purview of accounting information. This essentially implies that the market is efficient enough to incorporate all available information about a stock before arriving at its price. (*The price is the 'fair-price' we had introduced earlier in the book as the price that two parties are willing to pay dealing at an arm's length.*)

Fundamental analysis can break-up the financial statement of companies into various ratios and attempt to eliminate biases involved in accounting process. However, there are those who argue and demonstrate that the prices of shares are, as a matter of fact, influenced by events which cannot be captured by accountants in their well constructed statements. For example, a company subject to hostile raid by a competitor, will exhibit share prices not realized by fundamental analysis. Ownership pattern perhaps is a greater influence on such matters. This is true in situations of leveraged buyouts or liquidation by court interference.

'Leveraged Buyout – LBO'

The acquisition of another company using a significant amount of borrowed money (bonds or loans, usually a ratio of 90% debt to 10% equity) to meet the cost of acquisition. Often, the assets of the company being acquired are used as collateral for the loans in addition to the assets of the acquiring company. The purpose of leveraged buyouts is to allow companies to make large acquisitions without having to commit a lot of capital. In an LBO, because of this high debt/equity ratio, the bonds usually are not investment grade and are referred to as junk bonds.

It can be considered *ironic that a company's success (in the form of high value assets on the balance sheet) can be used against it* as collateral by a hostile company that acquires it. For this reason, some regard LBOs as an especially ruthless, predatory tactic.

Then again there is the hitherto unexplained influence of 'market-sentiment' which sways prices of the shares even though such fluctuations are not warranted by fundamental factors. Such views have prompted certain section of the market-oriented analysis to abandon the concept of fundamental analysis and purely use the data of prices obtaining in the market to analyze the stock values. Past behavior of prices of shares is therefore used to predict future values. Their approach is generally referred to as 'Technical Analysis' as it relies on purely computerized data crunching to uncover patterns of behavior of such data. Sometimes this is called 'charting' as they tend to extensively rely on 'charts' of data and graphs that reveal patterns to predict future direction of the graphs themselves.

Scattered in places in this book the author has ventured to reveal his inability to subscribe to the view that the past, merely because it did occur, is a reliable basis for prediction to the future. Someone here might say: that he 'bets a million rupees that the sun will rise tomorrow!' Yes, indeed the sun will rise, but what if the person did not rise in the morning to win the bet? This book, therefore, will not criticize the practitioners or the methods of technical analysis, but suffice it to say that most data series exhibit a particular pattern because of the fundamentals driving the data to the surface and not because the data elements did occur in the past. Cyclicality and patterns are observable all over in nature, but what explains and predicts their behavior is the causality and interrelationships among variables. In this book, we will approach equity analysis from a fundamental standpoint, namely, future values of stock are driven both by the present financial situation of the business and its future earnings capability. However, we recognize simultaneously that prediction of earnings is hazardous because of the existence of '*black swan events*' which are events that cannot be predicted by anyone. Consider the events of '*September 11*' in the USA, which no one on earth could have predicted, not even the perpetrators themselves. But these events have affected the earnings of insurance companies and so on in an extraordinarily direction, hitherto unanticipated by anyone.

The Dividend Based Model

We have hinted rather emphatically that investors expect returns in the form of dividends from the business (*either distributed or accumulated*) that in effect add to the wealth of the investor over a period of time. Perhaps the most intuitive appeal of the argument is that from this concept of future dividends, we can build a discount model for the present price of a single unit of share of the company. It will then follow that the current price of a unit of stock in a business is the discounted value of all expected future dividends. Here the smart reader may point out an apparent contradiction with the statements in the previous paragraph, namely, when the future is itself uncertain how could one predict the dividends payouts? True indeed, the problem can be overcome if we vary the applicable rate of discounting to suit the expectation of future dividends. A high discount rate will then represent a more uncertain world and a lower rate reflects lot more confidence. This is entirely left to the individual as prediction is always entwined with subjective affiliations. The uncertainty premium or the risk premium that a certain level of dividend will not materialize is the mark-up that investors will demand on the risk free rate that individual can get if he invested his money elsewhere in absolutely no risk situation. As an example government treasury bonds currently fetch 8% and is assured. To motivate the investor to place a bet on a unit of stock in a business 8% + a premium (say 4%) is needed to cover uncertainty of realization. We may call this the 'required returns' for investment decision into a stock. Then the price of stock is:

$$P = D/K$$

D = current dividend rate
P = Current Stock price
K = required rate of return

Here is the critical part. If your analysis of the statements of accounts put out by the company through ratio analysis and other methods described in the book reveals that the appropriate discount rate is in fact higher than what the current price of the stock in the market implies, you will conclude that the stock is overpriced. In other words your analysis concludes that the future dividends are not so certain, you will apply a higher discount rate in the formula, making the price of stock lower as a result. The important element in this analysis of the price behavior of a stock in the market is the 'required rate of return' which is a subjective element.

What About Appreciation?

When introduced this way the intelligent reader, perhaps based on observations from real world, would turn around to pose what he would consider a legitimate question. 'People buy stocks not only for the dividends expected, but also for the appreciation in price of the stock. Should not the valuation of a stock include this aspect as well?' The concept can perhaps elegantly counter this question, in a fully convincing manner. The answer to the above poser is another equally powerful poser. Why should the price of a stock increase unless there is an expectation of future dividends to rise? In a situation where there is no growth of dividends at all the valuation of a share will be exactly the same as before assuming that the interest rate and certainty of these dividend payouts do not change. The stocks prices will raise only if the dividend-returns are expected to rise with more or less certainty, else the stock value remains or may even fall. The foundational concept of future dividends as the basis for valuation of a business is established more than before.

The Price-Earnings Ratio

The P/E ratio is a valuation ratio of a company's current share price compared to its per-share earnings. This is among the most popular ratios in investment literature. However, it is as popular as it is misunderstood. As a matter of fact, this ratio came into financial literature, not because the dividend models were defective, but because it was not easy to compare companies based on it. The difficulty arose due to two main reasons. First and foremost it required basic understanding of financial models of discounted cash flow method and related concepts. Secondly it was initially a static model that did not seem to fit in with growth companies that plowed back earnings back into the company to fire future growth prospects.

We propose to deal with issue of growth companies in this section, as we have already explained to the reader the fundamental concepts of discounting elsewhere in this book. For the present in order to fully appreciate that the valuation of growth companies can be better understood by the dividend discount models itself, we need to digress into the concept of price-earnings ratio. The reason is that the two concepts are interrelated.

P/E ratio is calculated as:

$$P/E = \frac{\text{Market Value per Share}}{\text{Earnings per Share (EPS)}}$$

For example, if a company is currently trading at ₹43 a share and earnings over the last 12 months were ₹1.95 per share, the P/E ratio for the stock would be 22.05 (₹43/₹1.95).

The most commonly heard ratio in the street is also perhaps the least understood.

In general a higher value for P/E ratio suggests that investors expect higher earnings growth in the future compared to companies with a lower P/E. This logic follows from our earlier model of dividend based valuation. Thus if we substitute the formula for price from the dividend discount model, we get:

$$\text{P/E ratio} = \frac{\text{D/K}}{\text{Earnings per Share (EPS)}}$$

The above formula suggests that, the value of P/E depends on the discounting factor applied by the investor or the required rate of return that follows directly from the certainty or uncertainty of dividends that are expected from the company in future. Let us now assume that the growth rate in dividend-payouts for a company of any size is *g* (*growth*). Our formula for the price of a share then can be recast as follows:

$$P = D/K - g$$

Let us try to understand the implications of this formula in some detail. Let us assume a company with the following numbers in their books. Total earnings ₹4,000,000, number of shares outstanding 15,000,000. The current market price of a share is ₹48.75. If dividends are expected to grow at a definite rate of say 10% per year, and the investor has already a required rate of return say 13% (*which we explained earlier as the assured rate of return in an absolutely certain investment like treasury bond, say 8% plus his subjective premium for the uncertainty of return from the dividends, say 4%*), then we substitute this numbers in like this:

$$P = \{(4{,}000{,}000/15{,}000{,}000)\}/(0.13 - 0.10)$$

$$P = 1.2/0.03$$

$$P = ₹40$$

The above illustration was brought in merely to demonstrate that an expected growth in dividends decreases the discounting factor by that much percentage (*3% in this case*) and therefore increases the price of the share in question, which otherwise would have been 9.23 (*1.2/0.13 = 9.23*). A ten percent expected growth in dividends brings in a dramatic increase in the current price of the share. This model is then valid even if the growth rates of dividends is not uniform over the future, even though the calculations become a little more involved.

Continuing with our argument we can expand the above formula to work out the P/E ratio thus:

$$P/E = \frac{D/(K-g)}{EPS} \text{ where EPS = Earnings per share}$$

This formula reveals that if the expected growth rate in earnings is high then the P/E ratio also will be a high figure, which is not a surprising result because it is intuitively true. A high EPS produces a higher multiple because it in turn reduces the uncertainty of dividends, and shows up a lower discounting factor in our formula for P.

However, the P/E ratio doesn't tell us the whole story by itself. It's usually more useful to compare the P/E ratios of one company to other companies in the same industry, to the market in general or against the company's own historical P/E. It would not be useful for investors using the P/E ratio as a basis for their investment to compare the P/E of a technology company (high P/E) to a utility company (low P/E) as each industry has much different growth prospects.

The P/E is sometimes referred to as the 'multiple', because it shows how much investors are willing to pay per rupee of earnings. If a company were currently trading at a multiple (P/E) of 20, the interpretation is that an investor is willing to pay ₹20 for ₹1 of current earnings.

It is important that investors note an important problem that arises with the P/E measure, and avoid basing a decision on this measure alone. The denominator (earnings) is based on an accounting measure of earnings that is susceptible to forms of manipulation, making the quality of the P/E only as good as the quality of the underlying earnings number. The intelligent reader perhaps spotted the full potential of such an analysis. Let us imagine that a company's management has 'creatively' used accounting skills to manipulate its earnings that show up as a higher EPS in the annual report. The analysis using techniques we have described will reveal this inconsistency and therefore he will assign a higher discounting factor to eliminate the potential distortion in pricing because of the manufactured earnings figure. Such a company cannot hope to have its shares valued at the same multiple as another peer-group company that has not indulged in such inconsistent accounting practices.

Why P/E Multiples Vary

We have listed below a random set of telcos in various countries, to show that P/E ratios can vary widely between companies even within the same industry. This will be true for companies within the same country. The issue here that we will try to answer is why P/E ratios vary.

Rank	Company Name	P/E ratio
1	Cellcom Israel	5.25
2	USA Mobility	5.80
3	Telefonica Brasil	10.99
4	Turkcell Iletisim Hizmetleri	13.68
5	TELUS Corporation	16.03
6	Bharti Airtel Ltd	16.71

7	United States Cellular Corporation	18.53
8	Telular Corporation	27.97
9	Vimpel-Communications	36.21
10	China Unicom	52.61

Large cap companies like Telecommunications operators do not show P/E multiples as uniformly as we would normally expect. The reasons could be anyone of the following:

- Managements have a reputation for erratic changes in policy, such as ill conceived acquisitions that makes prediction of earnings difficult for the investor.
- Company may be known to have manipulated earnings in the past or reported 'earnings surprises' that were not consistent with reality.
- Regulatory and governmental policy predictability in many countries is responsible for sudden earnings pressure for many telecoms in recent years.
- Falling ARPUs of Telecommunications in hyper-growth markets have placed pressure on returns on assets.

The analysis may be mistaken in these perceptions, but it is generally observed that smaller companies have lower multiples than larger competitors who are better capitalized. China Telecommunications sector is perhaps the largest in the world and has high potential for further growth because of the expanding economy and population. So is the situation in its neighboring country India, and it is not unreasonable to expect higher multiples for companies that operate in these economies as compared to a mature market like US currently in the throes of a downturn. India's leading telecom operator has been under pressure due to a spate of acquisitions in Africa and Bangladesh financed by debt. It has been facing declining earnings margin over several quarters in a row. This is perhaps reflected in lower P/E ratios.

Faced with lower multiple estimates as a signal from the market many managements attempt to defend the indefensible, namely that their share prices are undervalued. However, the arguments often revolve around forward-looking analysis of future potential. Investors would do very well to remember that it is much easier to create a positive image of the company than recast its current operations to improve all-round efficiencies. The other danger for the unwary investor lurks in the creation of 'trends' almost like fashion fads. During the late nineties, it was fashionable for all outfits, however small, to be known as software-solutions provider or as being related to internet or telecommunications industry. Unreasonable multiples were attached by the euphoric markets to such companies, and write-ups about their future potential appeared in every publication like mushrooms after the rain.

Attaching too much credibility to high multiples of P/E without the real numbers to show for it is a destructive tendency that hurts the uninformed investor. When the telecom and internet bubble burst, these companies no longer wished to be associated with it. A similar story repeated during 2003-05 when banking was considered the future success mantra. Mutual fund managers even created the concept of sector-funds that invested solely in banking companies. Then it shifted to energy and power generation companies, when RNRL (Reliance Natural Resources Ltd) a reliance owned company reached stratospheric heights in terms of P/E multiples. Such stories are examples to drag us back to the concept of fundamentals based analysis to arrive at an independent evaluation of the company numbers to assess the real risk of earnings in future and to apply a reasonable discounting factor to such earnings to estimate future potential.

How Do We Know if P/E is Realistic?

The previous paragraph may have prompted many readers to wonder, how then do we know is the P/E multiples are real or imaginary? Sustainability of growth rates as we discussed not only in connection with the calculation of P/E ratio, but also in a critical examination of growth rates in the past is to be carefully understood. How can we be sure that past growth will be maintained into the future? The answer is probably not. The answer is definitely no if the growth rates are sustained by anything other than accumulation of retained earnings per share. Here we are again emphasizing our earlier position on growth in dividends. We showed that a business is accumulating wealth when its net worth grows from year to year. Net worth makes the businessman wealthier. Dividends are nothing but portion of the net worth that is distributed to the owners. What is not distributed accumulates as retained earnings. We can then define earnings per share as:

$$\text{Asset turnover} \times \text{Return on sales} \times \text{Leverage} \times \text{Book Value per Share} = \text{Earnings per Share}$$

OR

The more familiar statement:

$$\frac{\text{Sales}}{\text{Assets}} \times \frac{\text{Net income}}{\text{Sales}} \times \frac{\text{Assets}}{\text{Net worth}} \times \frac{\text{Net worth}}{\text{Shares outstanding}} = \frac{\text{Net income}}{\text{Shares outstanding}}$$

Earnings per share will not grow merely because the sales increase, since it is cancelled out by the denominator for return on sales. Any attempt by the management to enlarge its profit margins, will attract new competitors into the market and the subsequent competitive pressures will drive down the margins. Similarly, increasing the leverage to take advantage of borrowed funds as opposed to owner's equity funds cannot go on beyond a limit. Lenders will then get alarmed at the abnormal debt-to-equity ratio of the company and will refuse to lend more money as they fear for the ability of the company to repay principal and interest. Aggressive management tactics to squeeze existing capital equipment and other assets to improve asset turnover efficiency will not succeed in the long-run because of the operation of the universal law of diminishing marginal productivity of capital. Most interesting of all is the hard truth that a company's book value per share will not raise at all if the company distributes all its net income earnings in the form of dividends to its shareholders. This is the reason why you may have seen in the real market situation that share values do not spike proportionately to increases in dividends immediately on its announcement. It also implies that the company can earn its traditional return on equity invested if it plows back profits rather than distribute it to shareholders. This leaves us with only real increases in net profits that will boost earnings per share.

One another way of course is to reduce the number of shares outstanding, by buying back a company's own shares. However, stock-buyback if resorted to against other growth opportunities will be self defeating. Between 1995 and 1999 IBM resorted to buying back its own shares by borrowing funds, and therefore exposed itself to more financial risk. Such a move has been seen through by the market and the growth story has been self-limiting. However, if a company has idle cash in the bank far more than it can deploy profitably in investment opportunities, an attempt to boost the EPS through share buyback cannot be faulted.

a good shark knows his finances... a great one takes the Auditor for his lunch

Summary of Chapter Seven

This has been a rather longish chapter, as compared to its predecessors, but with a good reason. The key message to take away from this discussion is, indeed, that a clear understanding of the financial statements is a foundational requirement for analyzing a business. The basic concepts that we have presented at the start of this book namely the concept of net worth gets clearer and more vivid with each progressive chapter. Ratio analysis is aimed at laying bare the various angles that the users of financial statements may wish to explore, confirm and satisfy about the business. We looked at the techniques of ratio analysis from an internal point of view to understand the working of the company and its consistency in reporting. We also needed the statements to break apart the creditworthiness of the company and how safe the lenders are to assume repayments periodically. Here the issue that statements are subject to manipulation, much of it perfectly legal. We warned the reader to equip himself with all the tools described, but to be wary of the games the managements may play, and not to be too complacent about them, as factors that lie outside the accounting statements do influence the net worth of a business.

Finally we came to the aspect of company's value in terms of fundamental analysis based on a clear understanding of the financial statements. Highly volatile market for securities do not represent any kind of analysis at all, but are largely based on emotional sentiment ruling at the split moment of decision-making by the players. While this indeed is a fact to be reckoned with, it rightly belongs to behavioral scientists to explore. Long term players in the market must take into account the valuation based on fundamental analysis that has its invaluable foundation in financial statements. Stock may move in frenzied reaction to events of little consequence to a company's fundamentals, however, in the long run the true value of a share depends on the ability of a business to generate sufficient earnings and cash in future. Previous performance of a stock must be seen in this light, which moves sympathetically with its earnings' potential after eliminating all sentimental short-term movements.

8
How Far Can Ratio Analysis Be Stretched?

ANALYSIS OF A COMPANY'S FINANCIAL STATEMENTS AS WE HAVE presented in the previous pages starting with chapter five through to seven may have held some surprises for many readers. At the outset let me say that that was not purely unintentional. However, as a direct follow-up of the immediately preceding chapter, you may have noticed that analysis by itself is enlightening as it throws open many grey and shadow areas within the confines of the business organization, though not perhaps illuminating enough to predict the future outcomes of the business actions. But the future outcomes of earnings and dividends determine the value of the business. The published financial statements of companies are available to all investors simultaneously. There is nothing to be gained by studying them more competitively than anybody else, because the market price for the shares of the company in question would certainly reflect the collective analytical opinion of thousands of investors.

The fundamental value of the share is reflected in its market price. It is not possible that this price is wrong because, that is the price at which knowledgeable investors dealing at arms' length have arrived at and are willing to pay. But they could be wrong about the future estimation of prices and therefore, this price could be undervalued or overvalued in relation to the actual future-earnings capacity of the company being traded. We would like to enter with some degree of boldness into the discussion of this topic, knowing fully well the hazards of predicting the future. Here again, we are not assuring the reader that after reading this section you will be able to predict the future earnings-level of a business. No technique as yet has been discovered for doing this. But what we are about to attempt is to throw some light into what could be the tools that are useable and under what circumstances to gain a fair degree of assessment about a company's performance in subsequent periods.

Financial Projection

Projection about financial performance of a business will be accurate to the extent that the assumptions on which these are based prove correct. Merely analyzing financial statements will not equip you with information to predict the future outcomes. You must voraciously pursue information about the company from its customers, suppliers, employees and above all from its competitors to gain a meaningful understanding of probable outcomes. We will demonstrate the various steps involved in the process.

Forecasting Earnings

Step 1

The first step in projecting any company's future is to estimate the future earnings. The two key elements in the forecast are the net income and the depreciation figure. These two figures then will appear in the forecast of the statement of cash flows. This will then result in the projection of a future balance sheet. Indeed if this section does not teach you how to forecast future earnings, it will certainly teach you more than any other section in this book about the interrelationship between the three statements, namely the income statement, the cash flow statement and the balance sheet. The earnings forecast significantly affect the appearance of all three statements.

Step 2

Projections for sales figure. In order to project earnings figure for any period, you must already have undertaken a keen study of previous financial statements of the company for several years. This not only gives a feel of the company's performance, but brings in lots more understanding of the market, management reactions and dynamics of the business in question. Reliance can be placed on outside sources such as trade journals, industry studies and econometric projections. Assumptions about the growth of the economy and the particular industry must be carefully evaluated for realism. While this could be easier in certain established industries, such as chemicals or paper, predicting the earnings of technology companies like telecom or computer software could be very hazardous. In such case, it is best to rely on insider sources. Geographical peculiarities, like political unrest or affiliations, must be discounted.

Step 3

Projection of other components of the income statement. Cost of goods sold is usually a historical percentage of the sales. But here again, it must be remembered that it involves the projection of gross margins automatically. That means the cost of labor and materials are to be managed depending on the intensity of competition for these factors and perhaps more importantly the ability of the brand to pass on increased costs to its customers.

In capital intensive industries like telecommunications, if there is full capacity utilization, the operators are able to spread the costs over millions of customers, and they will try all out methods to increase customer-base by any means including cutting prices. But this cannot go on forever, as regulatory and other hurdles will eventually lead to halt such expansions. We have discussed the impact of fixed vs. variable costs on margins in an earlier section. By compiling such information over several periods, the analysis can be extended to future cost of goods sold and gross margins.

Step 4

Arriving at the operating income involves the projection of three other items at least. They are Selling General and Administrative Expenses (SG&A), Depreciation and Research and Development costs if any. SG&A projection is based on the assumption that there exists a stable relationship between such costs and sales. This is to be checked by studying the percentage over several years of data. Variation of this percentage is to be built in if industry sources point to a higher or lower level. Depreciation is based on the total base of fixed assets, and tends to be a stable percentage again, but in case of software companies the period is rather short and in other cases management may vary this percentage to bring it in tune with the actual obsolescence of assets. R&D expenses are undertaken to remain competitive in the market. But it is generally a percentage of the sales-budget. Barring major acquisitions or entry into less research intensive fields, it is safe to project previous years' percentages. Now the forecaster can arrive at the operating income and if his assumptions are sound it should prove good enough.

Step 5

Calculation of net profit involves assumption regarding the key item of interest costs and income taxes. Many companies detail out the debt in their annual reports. In that case, it is easy to work out the weighted average costs of debt but if otherwise, a greater reliance on assumptions and other company sources are needed. Well managed corporations have typically a low interest burden ranging from 1% to 2% of sales; therefore a major effort to arrive at an exact figure is not warranted. But for high leverage companies this might be a key parameter to watch out for. Having arrived at these figures, one must then apply the statutory rates of income taxes to arrive at profit after tax. Effective tax rates vary widely across companies due to carry forwards of previous losses, investment rebates and such other items as tax-laws in effect would dictate.

Forecasting Cash Flows

Step 1

Operating Cash Flows

Working out the operating cash flows from the income statement we must work backwards to arrive at the cash figure. The two major lines that determine the operating cash flows is the net profit and depreciation. This has been explained in detail in the chapter on cash flow statement. The other items have marginal impact on operating cash flows, nevertheless needs to be understood. Deferred taxes depend on the gap between tax and book-depreciation and on other items like leases, instalment receivables and so on. Changes in working capital need to be worked on the basis of previous balances as it appears in the balance sheet. Even though working capital may appear to be a percentage of sales in most situations, care should be taken to watch out for sudden fluctuations in sales leading to an accumulation of inventories or even a spike in accounts receivables.

Step 2

Investing Cash Flows

Additions to fixed assets such as property, plant and equipment is the largest cash outflow in this group. The company usually provides a number in its annual report. Working out the differences in figures from the balance sheets and adjusting for depreciation is a good method but news from the company regarding last minute investments will ordinarily not be reflected therein. Company source however, will be happy to provide the actual numbers.

Step 3

Financing Cash Flows

The power to declare dividends rests solely with the board of directors, and there is no reason to assume that they will follow the previous policies in this regard. Boards are known to declare dividends even in years with earnings-losses by borrowing the funds needed, even though it invites sharp criticism from various stake holders. However projection of cash outflows for dividend payouts must be held back until the actual declaration of dividend itself as strong earnings is not a guarantee for maintaining the dividend payout ratio. Debt repayment of long term nature are shown in the current liabilities of the balance sheet. The other use of cash is the repurchase of shares could be effected by increasing borrowings. Instead the company may have a practice of financing cash needs by a combination of debt and equity through a policy of keeping the debt-equity ratio constant. In all these situations the analyst will encounter difficulties and these numbers are little more than guess work by stretching the historical ratios that are worked out for the company.

Projecting a Balance Sheet

The intelligent reader would now have surmised that projecting a balance sheet requires no further assumptions other than those which have been made in the income statement and statement of cash flows. Balance sheet merely gathers all the new figures that have been arrived at in respect of inventories, accounts receivable, accounts payable etc. The new level of fixed assets is prior years' level plus additions less depreciation. The projected cash flow statement can then be used to plug in the figures for notes payable, deferred taxes and changes in equity less of course the dividends paid. Long term debts and current maturities are also available as worked out earlier in the cash flow statement.

How far can we Rely on such Projections?

Realization of the important fact that as conditions change it would not be wise to rely on such projections in its entirety. These forecasts can be subjected to the same type of analysis that the historical data were subjected to using ratio analysis. However, as stated earlier, the assumptions form the key to the question of its reliability and accuracy. It may then be a prudent practice to have a range of projections to assess potential rewards and risks of decisions based on them. Such variations in assumptions yield a possible less optimistic view as compared to the earlier views, and therefore give the analyst a chance to compare outcomes against it. Sensitivity analysis as it is popularly known can also be used to analyze the impact of more changes within the figures themselves. For example the impact of a 1% change in taxes or the changes in earnings due to a variation in gross margins on sales, and consequently cash flows of the company.

A word of caution is in order again! Sensitivity analysis presumes that a change in one aspect does not impact other areas of the business. This is rarely true in practice. If sales fall, so do margins, and this puts pressure on prices, leading to piling up of inventory as production cannot be adjusted in the short run, locking up cash and perhaps drying up investments in other vital areas. Rise in interest rate not only impacts interest costs and incomes, but depresses the whole economy perhaps resulting in lower overall demand due to lower off-take of credit. Predicting such scenario and its impact on the individual business is a most difficult task.

Stretching financial ratio analysis to look into the future business prospects of a company requires the greatest skills and is capable of yielding the greatest rewards. Looking forward is also a riskier form of analysis. However, not to be disheartened, this method is also to be taken for its value as a probabilistic approach and you should not aim for absolute prescience. The objective would rather be to incorporate all the relevant information about the company both from within and outside, into the historical financial data to arrive at a reasonable conclusion as to whether the current valuation of the company is justified judging from its future prospects.

Pitfalls in Comparative Ratio Analysis

Comparative ratio analysis is a method companies use to assess financial performance. This is an internal management process, in an attempt at self-diagnosis. A company typically starts with a comparative ratio analysis by separating ratios into groups, such as profitability, liquidity, financial leverage, and asset turnover. The ratios test different parts of the business based on related accounting data. Information provided from each group may include the ability to meet short-term debt obligations, use of assets to generate profits, use of debt in the business, and profit earned from single or multiple product lines. Accountants prepare the ratios as they are neutral parties in the analysis. Their job is to hold the mirror. Owners and executives then take it forward for comparative review purposes.

Benchmarking is typically the most common purpose for comparative ratio analysis. For example, a company often tracks its financial leverage over several months or years to determine if it is more or less during current periods. Managers may also be subject to performance reviews based on financial ratios that explain their departments' efficiency. Herein lurks the major weakness of the method.

Inward-looking analysis often makes the plain greener than it actually is, since the interpretation of the number is what really matters. Comparing with previous ratios yields somewhat biased view, while comparison with the competitors' figure would be more educative. A 10% improvement in the DSO ratio over the previous quarter is welcome, but if the industry trend is much higher, there would be very little cause for celebration. Although the ratios carry the name *financial ratios*, they are often more of an internal accounting tool for specific stakeholders, following no standard format. Therefore, the report can have a format that best suits the owner's needs, executives, or managers and are in fact tailor made for these users, especially when performance review and bonuses depend on it. The order of importance or other ranking is purely decided by the needs or demands of the business.

Trend analysis is another major use of comparative ratio analysis. Accountants prepare data for several months and place them in order by month and year if necessary. Report users can then look at the increase or decrease in the different ratios and assess performance. For example, decreasing current and quick ratios can indicate a tougher time meeting short-term debt obligations. Weaker profitability ratios can also provide information as to why the current or quick ratios are losing ground.

Benchmarking also compares one company's performance to another business. This allows owners and executives to determine how well the company operates under the same economic conditions. When a company is significantly behind its competitors, there is typically a major issue at hand. Comparative ratio analysis tends to strip away any accounting policies that change or alter a company's earnings. This allows for a one-tone review on financial performance. As we have discussed earlier, identification of the peer group companies is a major task. Even among the peer-group variations in capital structure, strategy and product differentiation can have significant impact on performance of the ratios.

While financial statements can present a company's current financial health, stakeholders often desire more information from these reports. Ratio analysis represents a series of mathematical formulae a company can apply to financial statements. While these measurements do provide essential data, there are limitations of ratio analysis. A few of the most glaring limitations include potential flaws in accounting information, the need for a reference point, and the potential for ratios to be completely meaningless. Firms must overcome these flaws in order to prevent the limitations of ratio analysis from entering a company's decision-making process.

Accounting information and data are not always flawless. While most accountants work hard to present financial information in accordance with national accounting standards, there may be some flexibility in the guidelines. This flexibility represents the starting point for limitations of ratio analysis. For example, an aggressive income recognition process can present higher profitability ratios. A reference point is also necessary to prevent the limitations of ratio analysis. For example, a company may discover certain results when calculating asset turnover ratios, such as inventory or accounts receivable turnover. Most companies use the industry standard as a reference point to determine if they are better or worse off in terms of their operating environments. When this reference point is not available, however, the company must select another. The lack of a reference point or the selection of an inappropriate reference point can skew the ratios or the use of ratios.

Financial ratios can also be meaningless when calculated alone. These limitations of ratio analysis exist if a company asks its accountants to compute them after preparing each financial statement. The results from each ratio, however, will not hold any meaning. In short, the results are simply additional numbers. Companies must have a well-defined purpose for calculating and using financial ratios.

The purpose of ratio analysis is ultimately the comparison of more than one company's financial data for a given period. It is often difficult to make these comparisons when the financial statements are different or in alternate formats. Therefore, the ratios strip this subjectivity away and leave stakeholders with usable information so long as the limitations of ratio analysis are not present. In short, an attempt to diagnose the company through an internal analysis of ratios would present the same difficulties that face an external analyst trying to compare the performance levels of various related groups.

Trend Analysis of Ratios

When trying to assess a company's financial performance, usually there are two approaches. One method is to assess the value of a company's net worth by looking at the price of its share in the securities market. The other way is to look at the financial performance from the statements of financial position presented by the annual reports of companies. Looking at the financial ratios as extracted from the statements is the technique we have explained in the earlier sections. However, the reader might have noticed that ratios by themselves mean very little in isolation. A percentage acquires meaning when it is compared to similar figures in related fields.

A series of such percentages compiled over many years yields a somewhat clearer picture of the trend of these ratios. For example, an analyst performing a trend analysis on an income statement will express every item on the statement in terms of its percentage of net profit or loss. He will then compare these percentages for several years to look for any meaningful trends. Investors also use trend analysis on balance sheets by calculating the percentage of each line item, a technique with which the reader is already familiar. For example, on a balance sheet each asset is listed as a percentage of total assets. Ratios are important financial analysis tools that help determine profitability, liquidity, financial structure, leverage, and interest coverage. Ratios report primarily on past performances. However, ratios can be predictive as well because they can point to potential problem areas. Trend analysis is when ratios are compared over a period of time. Trend analysis is useful to determine patterns in a business. They are also used to compare one business to another business, both inside and outside of an industry sector. In comparing trend analysis keep the following four points in mind.

1. Make an allowance for changes in accounting policies that occurred during the time span being examined.
2. Take into consideration material differences in accounting policies between a company and industry norms.

3. Know the types of accounting policies used. Different accounting methods can result in a wide variety of reported figures.
4. Determine if ratios were calculated before or after adjustments were made to the balance sheet or income statement, such as non-recurring items and inventory or pro forma adjustments. Adjustments can significantly skew the ratios.

The following series of ratios compiled from the annual reports of BSNL for nine years tells its own story. We have used this example to show how a company's performance over the years either improves or deteriorates with respect to its own past performance.

Trend-Analysis of BSNL
Financial Ratios (2002-03 to 2010-11)

Year	02-03	03-04	04-05	05-06	06-07	07-08	08-09	09-10	10-11
Current Ratio	0.78	1.33	2.65	2.79	3.22	3.34	2.79	1.29	1.20
Liquidity Ratio	0.64	1.21	2.49	2.62	3.08	3.15	2.57	1.17	1.02
Net Profit Ratio	5.58	17.62	28.22	22.25	19.65	7.91	1.61	-5.69	-21.50
Operating Profit Ratio	10.27	26.52	21.95	21.02	20.53	11.70	3.55	-6.86	-22.16
Return on Investments	2.58	9.48	13.99	11.07	8.98	3.41	0.65	-2.11	-7.97
Debt-Equity Ratio	0.42	0.27	0.23	0.20	0.16	0.14	0.13	0.11	0.13
Fixed Assets to Net Worth	1.29	1.09	0.91	0.79	0.70	0.65	0.67	0.92	0.96
Current Assets to Net Worth	0.29	0.44	0.53	0.57	0.62	0.66	0.65	0.64	0.33
Fixed Assets Turnover	0.36	0.49	0.54	0.63	0.66	0.66	0.60	0.40	0.39

Year	02-03	03-04	04-05	05-06	06-07	07-08	08-09	09-10	10-11
Work Cap2 Net Worth	5.81	5.01	2.19	1.64	1.24	1.10	1.12	4.84	14.17
Debtors Turnover	8.79	8.52	5.44	6.38	6.37	6.96	7.59	6.75	4.69
Creditors Turnover	1.50	2.27	2.48	2.43	2.38	2.19	1.73	0.75	1.35

Source: 'DIAGNOSING BSNL AS A BUSINESS' by the Author, MANAGEMENT ACCOUNTANT. Mar 2012 Vol.47.No.5

The steady decline in the liquidity of the company is strikingly visible over the years. Even though the ratio has not been presented, the acid-test-ratio would have shown that the company' cash asset has sharply been eroded slowly declining into a position where it is not in a position to meet its annual commitments. From a further analysis of this condition it is obvious that the real reason for this liquidity crunch is the fast decline in profit margins, both the ratios of which have been negative in the final two years. The reader may recollect that we presented a hypothetical Biggest Telecommunication Company Ltd. (BTC) in our discussion on cash flow statements, which found itself in an almost identical situation on its transition into mobile operators from the position of an incumbent wireline company.

The most possible explanation of this decline in profitability of BSNL operations is the decline in the efficiency of assets usage. The ratios relevant to this are the assets-turnover ratio. There is a sharp decline in the ability of the assets to produce sales growth. This we know is because the company has been producing its major chunk of sales from the fixed wireline services the market for which has taken a heavy beating because of the oncoming threat of obsolescence of landline services with the entry of mobility based telecom products. It also points to the inability of the management to keep up with the changing market conditions and most importantly inability to keep up with the regulatory pressures of the sector's opening up of the telecom market to private players.

The assets-base of BSNL is wasting away and its efficiency is in decline smartly due to these factors. What is perhaps needed is to thoroughly modernize the assets-base to match the market preferences and not only match the competition but exceed it based on inherent strengths. However, at present the company does not have the financial flexibility to engage this aspect of the business. It will have to use all its managerial skills to find sources of cash to ward of liquidity problems and simultaneously enhance its assets to increase productivity. The management's upper most concern should be to actively explore the fundamental reasons for reduction in margins. All out efforts may be needed to increase optimum use of cash from operations conservatively and eliminate waste of resources in operations management.

To compare this very performance with the peers in the industry group would involve a trend analysis of BSNL's major competitors. And that would be a more revealing approach but much more difficult because of the four issues connected with the internal accounting practices of the other players, listed above. Further, even if data could be obtained for the other operators, the individual strategy followed, the management constraints of a public sector fully-government owned company as compared to that of a private corporate set-up would again be a subject for keen observation without which the conclusions arrived at may not be fully valid and substantiated. However, in contrast we present below the ratio analysis for the largest private sector telecom operator in India: Bharti Airtel.

Trend Analysis of Ratios – Bharti Airtel 2008 to 2012

	Mar'12	Mar'11	Mar'10	Mar'09	Mar'08
Liquidity ratios					
Current ratio	1.34	0.82	0.71	0.72	0.58
Current ratio (incl.st. loans)	1.01	0.70	0.68	0.69	0.56
Quick ratio	1.28	0.77	0.71	0.64	0.55
Profitability ratios					
Operating margin (%)	32.98	35.25	39.08	38.74	41.37
Gross profit margin (%)	18.76	24.22	28.15	29.33	29.08
Net profit margin (%)	13.69	20.21	26.36	22.58	23.99
Adjusted return on net worth (%)	11.39	17.43	23.27	33.74	32.04
Reported return on net worth (%)	11.60	17.60	25.79	28.13	30.94
Leverage ratios					
Long term debt/equity	0.16	0.20	0.11	0.25	0.30
Total debt/equity	0.28	0.27	0.13	0.28	0.32
Turnover ratios					
Owners fund as % of total source	77.76	78.65	87.88	78.11	75.43
Fixed assets turnover ratio	0.69	0.82	0.87	0.99	1.03

When presented this way, the contrast between the two companies emerges. The first thing that hits you is that whereas BSNL's profit margins have not only turned negative and is widening, in contrast Bharti's margins are healthy, but declining over the same period. This level of profitability has enabled the company to maintain a reasonable level of liquidity to meet current obligations, even though the position is not emphatic. Is there trouble brewing in the sector itself? This is a relevant question because, Bharti Airtel is the leader among 15 operators and its margins are under pressure. This is emphasized by the measures of return on net worth, ratios of which are declining more sharply than that of profitability.

The second aspect confirming our observation of heavy competition in the sector is the inability of fixed assets to efficiently increase sales revenue. The efficiency of assets though much better as compared to the public sector giant BSNL, nevertheless is declining fast. This sector is highly capital intensive with high propensity to obsolescence of technology. Even with a healthy profit margin, Bharti Airtel's investment in fixed assets is under pressure to perform in terms of sales revenue. The numbers can reveal they have the inherent ability to lead you on to more probing questions that point the way to a deeper analysis to understand the core issues. For example, this analysis of the ratios of the two companies (*one, a public sector giant fully owned by the government and the other a private sector company with public ownership and listed on the securities exchanges*) throws up the core issue of comparability. These two companies are operating as service providers in the telecom market. However, apart from this, the two companies are divergent in terms of ownership and control, nature of the products; the market segment they cater to and the managerial profile of the companies.

This directly brings us to the next section where we present the concept of peer-group comparison of fundamental financials.

Inter-Group Comparisons

What then constitutes a peer group? How can companies in the group be compared based on their financials? Size is indeed a good generalization as a starting point. Larger companies have better economies in scale of operations, may enjoy greater leverage with suppliers by virtue of their bigger purchasing power. Compared to a smaller operator, a large telecom operator can take more market segments and geographical areas to spread variable costs over larger customer base. Unexpected loss of production does not expose top-line to critical levels and managerial depth in a larger organization permits manpower churn without loss of productivity.

Undoubtedly larger corporations have failed miserably in the past, reason being the size itself. Bureaucratic management, lack of nimbleness in decision-making, inefficiency and wastage of resources is definitely higher in larger set-ups.

Ratios comparison across different industries is certainly not acceptable, because each industry has inherent unique characteristics, somewhat like the skills in play needed for rock-climbing and cricket for example, even though both are considered 'sporting activities'.

A comparison between Chris Sharma and Sachin Tendulkar would be meaningless.

Rock climbing is a very diverse sport. There are many different aspects to the sport of climbing - from bouldering to mountaineering. All climbing disciplines command a different skill set. Here is a list of the greatest climbers of all time.

1. **Chris Sharma,** known as the best rock climber in the United States, literally lives under a rock. He doesn't own a home, but instead travels around the world looking for the next best climb. He has completed some of the most technically difficult and dangerous climbs in the world. Sharma says climbing is 'like a dance.' in his movie, 'King Lines'.
2. **Russell Brice**, the CEO of Himalayan Experience, a mountaineering guide company is one of the best climbers and mountaineers in the world and he has scaled Mt. Everest twice. The Discovery Channel filmed a documentary on his second ascent to the top of Everest.
3. **Dean Potter** is a free climber and base-jumper. Potter is best known for his daring free climbs with no live saving gear and his controversial climb of the Delicate Arches in Utah.

4. **Tommy Caldwell** is skilled in diverse climbing disciplines and free climbed the Nose of El Capitan. He is best known for pioneering some of the most difficult routes.
5. **Josune Bereziartu** started climbing when she was 17 years old. She is from Basque country, Spain and climbs routes most accomplished male climbers won't even attempt.

Line of business is another and perhaps more justifiable basis for classification of companies into peer-groups. Even in the same line of business, the sub-grouping can make comparisons difficult. This would then imply that to make the comparisons meaningful, we should have a peer group with virtually identical product lines. Otherwise, ratio analysis would cross the boundaries of broadly defined sectors and render itself merely numbers incapable of speaking a meaningful language.

Then it would follow that BSNL with 60% of its revenues accruing from Landlines services, is not strictly comparable to Bharti Airtel that accumulates revenues from mobile services. Logically that segment of BSNL which is engaged in Mobility services would stand comparison with other mobile operators in a general way. However, there are common resources and equipment in BSNL that are deployed for both landline and Mobile segments. If the costs are perfectly allotted between these services, the comparison ratios would be comparable, otherwise it gets qualified in several ways.

Trying, on the other hand, extremely hard to obtain a homogenous group to compare with produces distortions of the other kind. Comparing with only one other company may not be very informative or necessary.

One possible way out of this problem is to define common grounds for comparison, without prejudice to some peculiarities that are seen in some sub-group or sub-segment of the market. The resultant ratios point to particular aspects or characteristics that distinguish the group of companies from other industry segments.

Publicly listed companies, operating the mobile segment in India, for example, will include a large number of players and simultaneously meet the peer-group criteria. MTNL, a publicly listed company, would need to be excluded from this list because of its government ownership and the fact that it operates in the landline segment also with sizeable revenues accruing from that segment as a proportion of its total revenues. But it would be perfectly reasonable to compare BSNL with MTNL, because of the ownership pattern of the companies and the management structure obtaining within both, even though the latter is a listed company and the former is not.

Comparative ratio analysis then is a particularly effective skill that the reader must possess. If used effectively it adds considerable value to ratio numbers, but careless usage leads to distortions that may be hidden beyond the numbers, and render such analysis a lot less effective. Stretching the ratios to accommodate preconceived notions about a business is neither informative nor praiseworthy.

What Ratios Do You Really Need?

You have by now come across several ratios in this book and elsewhere and would most probably notice that ratios can be manufactured by anyone depending on what he is looking for. You would in all probability be wondering how many of these you would really need. Each industry and sector has its own peculiarities and nuances of operations. It is important to understand not only how to analyze a business but also to understand the business itself before the analysis can actually begin. But to get to the core of a business, far more information than what the financial ratios can provide will be needed. However, to meet the specific requirements of analysis, we can categorize ratios and use only those ratios to study a particular aspect of the business, rather like a mechanic who knows whether it is the spanner or the winch that he needs when he sees the job at hand.

- **Categories of Ratios**
    - o Growth Ratios
    - o Price Ratios
    - o Profitability Ratios
    - o Ratios of Financial Condition
    - o Investment Ratios
    - o Management Efficiency Ratios

Here is a recap of all the ratios that we have discussed in previous sections, and where they could be used when looking for specific answers to questions that may arise while analyzing a business.

Growth Ratios

Growth ratios, or growth rates, tell us just how fast a company is growing, and what growth rates the annual reports are claiming. Any abnormal rates then would raise a red flag.

- **Sales (%)** - Sales growth is normally stated in terms of a percentage over previous year. '*Sales*' is another term for operating revenues. While it is important to see high sales growth rate it is prudent to check if these rates are feasible and that management is not being too optimistic.
- **Net Income (%)** - Net income or Net Profit growth is even more important than sales because net income tells how much money is left over after all of the operating costs are subtracted from sales. Here it is good to remember that '*net-profit*' like 'paternity' is a matter of opinion, and '*cash flow*' like 'maternity' is a fact, but together they make the business go round.
- **Dividends (%)** - Dividend growth is a good indicator of the financial health of a company. Some companies do not pay stock dividends at all; rather they use these excess profits to reinvest money back into the company to accelerate growth. The change in dividends (%) should not be negative. That is,

once a dividend rate is established, a company needs to have a very good reason to decrease the dividend payout. You may also recall that dividend is sometimes also used as a signaling devise to the investing public in general.

Price Ratios

Price ratios are financial ratios that normalize a stock's selling price against a measure of the profitability of the company.

- **Price/Earnings Ratio** - The price to earnings ratio, or P/E ratio is the stock's price divided by the latest 12 months of earnings per share. The P/E ratio is an indicator of the premium the investor will be paying for a stock. It is also an indicator of future growth expectations.
- **Price/Sales Ratio** - The price to sales ratio is the stock's price divided by the latest 12 months worth of sales. This measure became popular during the dot com years, when companies showed no earnings or profits. For that reason, it is not a very useful measure in today's environment.
- **Price/Book Value Ratio** - The price to book value ratio is the stock's price divided by the book value of the company. A company's book value is a measure of the amount by which assets exceed liabilities or by the now familiar concept of net worth of the business (in terms of shareholder's equity).
- **Price/Cash Flow Ratio** - The price to cash flow ratio is identical to the P/E ratio except that it removes non-cash expenses and other accounting adjustments such as depreciation from that measure.

Profitability Ratios

Profitability ratios, or profitability margins, are a good measure of whether the business is achieving what it set out to do in the first place, adding wealth to the owners in every period. These measures are normally used to compare a company to its industry (as a benchmark), since the profitability of companies can vary greatly by industry.

- **Gross Margin (%)** - The gross margin is a ratio of a company's operating revenue to sales. Operating revenue is the company's sales revenue minus the cost of goods sold. It is the broadest measure of profit performance.
- **Pretax Margin (%)** - The pretax margin is a ratio of the company's pretax profits divided by operating revenues. It is the net income left over after all claimants except the government have been satisfied.
- **Net Profit Margin (%)** - The net profit margin is the ratio of net profits to sales. This is the best indicator of the company's efficiency because net profit takes into consideration all expenses including the tax claims of the company. Investors want the net profit margin to be as high as possible.

Ratios of Financial Condition

Evaluating the financial condition of a company consists of two related, but distinct types of measures. The first has to do with how much money the company has borrowed relative to how much money is 'invested' in a company. This concept is known as leverage or the debt-to-equity position. If there were no taxes, it would not matter where a business got its money from. But since we live in a world of tax, too much equity in relation to debt deprives the business of several tax advantages. On the other hand, too much debt increases its fixed costs of servicing interest burden and robs the company of financial flexibility.

The second measure of financial condition has to do with a company's ability to pay back its creditors in terms of interest and principal payments. This is called the creditworthiness of the company. These measures indicate the overall financial flexibility of the business.

- **Debt/Equity Ratio** - The debt/equity ratio is a measure of the long-term debt divided by the common stock equity. This financial ratio is a measure of leverage. The lower the debt to equity ratio, the less likely a company will be affected by fluctuations in sales.
- **Current Ratio** - The current ratio is a measure of the company's current assets divided by current liabilities based on the most recent quarter. The current ratio is used to provide broad guidance on a company's ability to meet current obligations.
- **Quick Ratio** - The quick ratio, or acid test, is the sum of cash and receivables divided by the total current liabilities from the most recent quarter. The quick ratio is another measure of a company's latest liquidity position.
- **Leverage Ratio** - The leverage ratio is calculated by taking the total assets and dividing them by total stock equity. The leverage ratio gives us an indication of the company's leverage. For example, if the ratio is high, then assets far exceed stock equity (*meaning the company has acquired a lot of assets through borrowing relative to owners' money*), the company is considered leveraged.
- **Interest Coverage** - The interest coverage is the company's latest 12 months' earnings before interest and taxes (EBIT) divided by the latest 12 months' interest expense. Interest coverage tells us how much earnings it has relative to the interest burden, showing how easily a company can handle its debt service. The higher the interest coverage value, the easier it is for the company to pay back its debt.

Investment Ratios

This next set of financial ratios gives us a good indication of how much of a return the money invested in a company is providing.

- **Return on Equity** - A company's return on equity ratio, or ROE, is calculated by taking the latest 12 months' net income divided by common stock equity. The return on equity ratio is perhaps the most widely used, and most valuable measure of how well a company is performing for its shareholders. The higher the return on equity, the better.
- **Return on Capital** - The return on capital, or ROC, is calculated by taking the latest 12-months' net income divided by invested capital. Invested capital is defined as long term debt plus common stock and preferred equity.
- **Return on Assets** - The return on assets ratio, or ROA, is determined by taking net income and dividing it by total assets. The measure is used to get a feel for how well a company is using their assets to generate earnings.

Management Efficiency Ratios

This last category of financial ratios is unique in that we would not consider any of these ratios as a primary driver of the value of a company. That being said, it is important to understand exactly what these ratios are telling. These are the ratios the managers should be using to look inside their businesses and come up with solution to correct the course on which the business is heading.

- **Revenue per Employee** - The revenue per employee ratio is calculated by taking 'defined revenues' and dividing them by the total employees of a company. The revenue per employee ratio gives us a feel for the labor intensity of a business and the productivity of labor. Thus a manager could focus clearly on the HR department of the marketing wing to analyze the labor productivity.
- **Receivables Turnover Ratio** - The receivables turnover ratio tells us how many times 'accounts receivable' have been collected in a given accounting period. Receivables turnover

is calculated by taking the last 12 months of sales and dividing by the average receivables from the latest two quarters.

- **Inventory Turnover Ratio** - The inventory turnover ratio is determined by taking the cost of sales for the latest 12 months and dividing by the company's average inventory. The resulting inventory turnover ratio tells us how fast the company's products are moving on the marketplace. For the inventory turnover ratio, a higher number is better.
- **Assets Turnover** - The ratio of sales to assets, or asset turnover ratio, tells us about the capital-intensity of a business, and how well it uses assets to produce revenue. Companies that require a large infrastructure in order to produce, or deliver their product, such as electric utilities and telecommunications require a large asset base to generate sales.

Summary of Chapter Eight

We have entitled this chapter with a straightforward question. It was intentional. The reader must realize that though the analytical methods elaborated in this book have validity in so far as practitioners have relied on them and obtained satisfactory results, it also has several pitfalls that must be understood before they can be used effectively. Among the issues we tried to answer first was the question of future predictability of ratio analysis as a method. We found that stretching financial ratio-analysis to look in to the future business prospects of a company requires the greatest skills and is capable of yielding the greatest rewards. Looking forward is also a less certain form of analysis. The results obtained are only as good as the assumptions made to predict the outcomes.

Using financial information to compare performances over a period of time, both internally by the management and externally by the analysts and investors, is a practical method of using the financial theory in practice. However, one must be extremely careful while using data for intercompany comparisons; we listed possible differences in accounting policy and accounting practices as a major cause for exercising caution. A different set of cautionary principles will apply while attempting to compare trends in ratios for companies within the same industry. It is essential to identify the peer-group companies based on valid and scientific criteria before the comparisons can begin. Finally we probed the practical question of how many ratios are really essential to a good analysis, and how many of these are really helpful in reaching satisfactory answers. The reality is that ratio analysis or any other technique is just a tool in the hands of the financially skilled. How it is to be effectively used will depend on the financial intelligence of the user and the nature of the analytical questions that need answers.

Find the Needle in the Haystack

Issues Based on Concepts in Part Two

Making the numbers speak is a skill that can be acquired with sufficient practice. You need to attempt reading the annual reports of companies. Warren Buffet reportedly reads thousands of annual reports of companies operating in hundreds of countries. He knows where the needles are and therefore finds them quite easily. You need to get a feel for it. That's all. There are a few important steps.

1. You must have a clear idea of what you are looking for.
2. You must know where to find those numbers and whether they are reliable.
3. Draw your own conclusions from what they are telling you

Let us look at some practical issues while looking at financial figures of companies to find out what they are really worth for.

1. Can you identify the company's revenue model? Put simply how is it making money?
2. Can you identify its main competitors? Don't be fooled by the products themselves, because it is possible that the company is turning out the wrong product.
3. Is the company putting its money where it fetches maximum returns? Are they missing something?
4. What demands on cash can come from environmental and external factors that the company needs to manage to stay in business?
5. Are these ratios the result of managerial action or managerial response to internal processes? What internal processes can sabotage managerial effectiveness?
6. Even if you have calculated all possible ratios you can still reach the wrong conclusions. Do you think the statement is true?

7. Will the borrower always pay back the debt? Is it possible that even if a company has the ability to pay back borrowings they still refuse? Can credit analysis deal with such situations?
8. Return on Capital Invested (ROCI) is perhaps the best measure of company's performance. Are there any excuses for poor ROCI in public sector companies?

PART THREE

FINANCIAL SKILLS AT WORK

9
Building On Return Concepts

DESPITE ITS MAJOR ADVANCES, FINANCE THEORY HAS HAD SCANT impact on actual day-to-day managerial practices at the business level operations. The decisions taken by most businessmen are actually 'an act of faith' based on intuition or other several considerations based on experiences of the past. Nevertheless, finance being an integral part of managerial structure, executives everywhere must learn to apply finance theory correctly. Simultaneously, finance theory must be extended in order to reconcile theoretical concepts with practical applications. One of the first things that finance executives deal with is deciding how to commit the firm's resources across lines of business. The financial side of the job is to allocate a particular resource, capital.

In this chapter we try to present some well established financial tools derived from finance theory, like discounted cash flow analysis, and return concepts for allocation of capital. Yet, it is true that many of these concepts are used in day-to-day business implicitly by managers that may not have been exposed to financial theory in any formal manner. These are the effective tools that need to be understood by the executive who despite having exposure to financial analysis would not be conversant in applying them in practical life either for his own benefit or for the improvement of performance at his workplace.

The Discounted Cash Flow Method

There are many uses of cash. These alternatives of the use of cash are not all equally attractive. Some uses would fetch more return in future than others. Then again the length of time involved in realizing these returns also may differ from one use to another. How then can we decide which usage is a better choice than another? There are much formalized arithmetical calculations of how this can be done. But despite the complexity of the calculations involved, the purpose of Discounted Cash Flow (DCF) analysis is just to estimate the money you'd receive from an investment after adjusting for the time value of money. This is known as the Net Present Value (NPV) which is obtained after appropriately discounting the Future Value (FV).

A business organization is a collection of projects. Each project, no matter how big or small, is a small company. The project must generate wealth for the investor in order to be justified. The adding to wealth or the net worth of the project is the extra return that the project has made during its period of execution and existence. We can estimate whether a project is making money and adding to the net worth of the business (*in this case the project itself*) by estimating the amount of cash flow that it generates over its life time. In other words the expected future cash flow must be greater than the present total cost of the project, in order to be able to create a surplus.

But the future cash flows are not known with any amount of certainty. (*Please read the sections on forecasting future earnings in chapter eight and how risky it is to forecast unless completely accurate assumptions about the future can be made.*) Therefore, the future being uncertain and risky, the expectation of cash flow must be discounted by a factor which explains the amount of risk involved. This means that while the outflow of cash for the project is certain, the inflow is uncertain. This risk of loss is what the businessman must take a call on. The intelligent reader has immediately sensed that it is a purely subjective estimation that we are talking about here. The expected returns from a project therefore are always subjective, even though with experience and information about competitors, and state of the market and economy in future are all estimable by the businessman, whereby he might achieve a certain degree of accuracy. Nevertheless the process and the results are inevitably subjective.

The DCF method is in effect and practices a subjective exercise, undertaken by the businessman in order to decide whether he must throw good money to get more but risky money in future. Those managers who hold MBA degrees would calculate the DCF figure by arithmetically discounting the estimated cash flow from a project and advise the owner to go ahead, provided the future discounted value is greater than present outflows. The MBA-manager can go wrong in calculating the future cash, because it is merely an estimate and there are uncertainties lurking along the way. It becomes increasingly more difficult to predict cash flows over longer periods of time. He has but a fizzy idea about the future levels of inflation, and how it will affect the economic activities, or whether rising interest rates will lower the demand for this product and so on. The manager, nevertheless, applies a discounting factor, which is the interest rate of a 10-year-government bond plus a margin for risk, (*The higher the risk the greater is the margin*) to arrive at the net present value.

No businessman in real life takes these figures produced by the MBA-manager quite seriously. He will approve a project if he inherently believes that the opportunity is good enough as compared to his core-strength vis-à-vis the competitors and therefore has potential for producing a higher return than the cash involved in the project. The actual numbers are not important for him but the inherent strength of the future opportunity is. The future is full of intangible opportunities that cannot be reduced to numbers on an excel-sheet. Projects bringing intangible assets or growth opportunities to the firm have correspondingly higher NPVs. He knows well in advance that such projects have positive NPVs. This business ability is what creates wealth.

For you as a reader, the DCF holds great value if you can master the concept for practical applications. If the company is a collection of projects and each project has a discounted NPV then the company as a whole must be the sum total of all the NPVs of all the projects that the company has. In simple terms, discounted cash flow tries to work out the value of a company today, based on projections of how much money it's going to make in the future. DCF analysis says that a company is worth all of the cash that it could make available to investors in the future after adjusting for the time value of money.

What is Time Value?

At the most basic level, the time value of money demonstrates that, all things being equal, it is better to have money now rather than later. This means that time literally is money - the value of the money you have now is not the same as it will be in the future and vice versa. You can then distinguish between the worth of investments that offer you returns at different times.

There are several tried and true approaches to discounted cash flow analysis, including the dividend discount model (DDM) approach which we have discussed in detail in chapter seven.

As an investor, you have a lot to gain from mastering DCF analysis. For starters, it can serve as a reality check to the fair value prices found in brokers' reports. DCF analysis requires you to think through the factors that affect a company, such as future sales growth and profit margins. It also makes you consider the discount rate, which, as already explained, is the estimation of risk that the promised returns will not in fact materialize. All of this will give you an appreciation of what drives share value, enabling you to put a realistic price tag on the company's stock.

Investors will put cash on a share of a business only if they think that the business can do better, after the risks are considered, than the investors can do on their own. They should not generally go by the accounting earnings of the firms as reported in the financial statements. Not only because accounting earnings are subject to the whims of the management, but also because accounting figures do not reflect the future earnings capacity of the business in any manner. For example telecommunications industry by definition is highly capital intensive. To obtain the license from the respective governments to start operations huge cash outlay is required. If investors merely look at the accounting earnings of a start-up telecom operator, the valuations would not be correct. However, the market prices of these companies will have high multiples to their EPS not justified unless we factor in the future earnings opportunities involved in such venture. Fundamentals drive the pricing of a stock, not hype or the declared EPS figure.

The DCF Method in Action

If you are an executive reading this book, you might worry that investment decisions taken will have an adverse impact on the accounting figures of earnings per share or net profits during a particular period. If EPS were the only criterion for the price of a share, all shares in the market should have the same P/E ratio. But that is not the case. This is to be categorically understood that if you as an executive is convinced that the project adds to the wealth of the company in the specified period, it will be better to forget accounting rate of return and proceed to add to the real wealth. Some managers worry about risk to the project, and diversify into second or third level projects with lesser NPVs. Such diversification in fact reduces net worth of the company over time.

DCF approach is a valuable tool for taking practical decisions in real life. But there are pitfalls to be wary of. Where the income and cash streams are steady, certain and foreseeable into the future, DCF works well as for example in the case of a bond or preference shares or bank deposits. You might even use it for blue chip shares that regularly fetch a fixed dividend annually. But be very careful in arriving at the value of a company that has future growth opportunities and current earnings are low.

If you are a top-level manager in a corporate environment or a CEO, you can spot opportunities to use DCF methods. Financial leases is one area where the cash-flow is steady and certain. The 'cash-cows' in your portfolio of products are there because of their ability to generate cash which can be used to make investments. Engineers in various fields can use this concept to decide about replacement of equipments where the costs and benefits are clearly visible. But it will not come to your help while deciding about R&D projects that are highly uncertain in their promise of returns.

DCF analysis has been installed in the highest sanctuaries of financial theory. The fundamental principles on which it rests, namely the time value of money and risk factors connected to the future cash flows, are true and unchallenged contribution of finance theory. However, practicing the DCF method to invest hard earned cash is hazardous, because beyond the fundamental theory lay the subjectivity of estimations with regard to risk and returns in an uncertain future.

Before anyone even dreamed of 'Googling' for information, Yahoo! was the king of the Internet. In the late 1990s, Yahoo! decided to put good money into buying up smaller companies to grow faster than its competitors and also reap the benefits of future revenue flows due to the addition of fresh visitors to the site. In May 1999, Yahoo! acquired GeoCities, which reported a GAAP loss of $19.7 million on revenues of $18.4 million in 1998. Yahoo! paid up $2.9 billion in stock for the company. In July 1999, Yahoo! purchased Broadcast.com which had the then revolutionary idea of broadcasting of audio and video content across the Internet. Yahoo! paid up $5 billion for this company, which had reported a $16.4 million loss on revenues of $22 million in the year just before its sale.

Since then, 'Google' the search engine has emerged as the biggest challenger and eclipsed Yahoo!. Yahoo is currently being run by its founder members Jerry Yang who is a co-founder and the chief executive officer, Roy J. Bostock who is the current chairman, David Filo, co-founder, and Susan Decker who is the current president. These business-persons, brilliant as they are, have used the wrong number to discount the future cash flows from acquisitions of companies. These subjective estimations of risk and certainty have resulted in loss of value for themselves and other shareholders. The Yahoo! stock is still down about 80% from the peak reached in the late 1990s.

Amp'd Mobile was a mobile content provider that leased spectrum from Verizon and other wireless operators, targeting the 18- to 35-year-old segment for its revenues. The company raised $350 million of funding from venture capital firms and other investors through March 2007 and set out to conquer the wireless world, offering services in the United States and Canada. The estimations of future cash flows didn't quite turn out as expected for these investors, as Amp'd Mobile filed for Chapter 11 bankruptcy in June 2007, citing the inability of the company's back end infrastructure to keep up with rapid growth. The real cause of the bankruptcy was the company's decision to lower credit standards to boost subscriber growth. This strategy led to 45% of the company's subscriber base defaulting payment of their monthly phone bills.

The business-landscape is littered with the corpses of promising investments made by some of the smartest people in the room, based on carefully analyzed future cash flows. The subjective element of discounting for the risks and the extreme nature of difficulties that will be encountered in forecasting cash flows will ensure that we have not seen the last of these high-risk and high-return decisions.

The Payback Period

The definition of payback period is simple. It is the number of years it takes to payback the initial investment of a capital project from the cash flows that the project produces.

Calculated as:

$$= \frac{\text{Cost of Project}}{\text{Net Annual Cash Inflows*}}$$

The capital project is any outflow of cash with a view to generating higher cash flows in future. It could be buying a new plant or building or buying a new or replacement piece of equipment. Most people have a cut-off payback period, (say 3 years) depending on their business. In other words, if the actual payback is 2.5 years, the firm would purchase the asset or invest in the project. If the payback were 4 years, it would not.

Payback period, simple as it may appear and intuitive as it seems, can be misleading at the same time. Imagine that you are purchasing a machine to manufacture envelopes. Machine A is preferred because it gives the investment back in 3 years over B which gives in 5 years. But if you consider the economic lives of the two machines, you could get a very different answer, because the first machine being ultra high speed wears out mechanical parts faster. Perhaps an even more distorting aspect of payback period is that it does not consider time value of money. Cash inflows from the project due in future years are weighted exactly the same as the cash flow expected to be received in year one. That is not good finance. The situation is

* The net annual cash inflow is what the investment generates in cash each year. However, if this investment was a replacement investment; for example, a machine replaced an obsolete machine, then the net annual cash inflow becomes the incremental net annual cash flow from the investment.

worse compounded with even greater problems if the cash flows are uneven over the subsequent years. The method then becomes not only faulty but reliance on it as a thumb rule distorts the investment decision, making it a fairly useless tool for capital budgeting.

The one reason why people still discuss the payback period is that it is 'quick and easy'. In top level meetings the initial reaction to a new idea or project is always based on a mental calculation of the time taken to get back the money. It is a sort of reality check against all the confusion of the data available. It gives the big-boss an idea as to whether to look at the project and explore the real numbers later to study it in detail.

However, business is not just about getting the money back, after all. It is more about creating wealth for itself by investing in schemes that yield real return over several years. The payback period estimation is just another term for breakeven analysis, where there is neither loss nor gain in a venture. Cash beyond the breakeven is the profit and net addition to net worth. Payback period is not finance at all. It is a rule of the thumb that contains an element of truth, but one which needs to be tested against other more valid criterion, such as net present value of the cash flows and discounted value of intangibles that cannot be quantified, including the risk of such benefit-inflows. We then move on to a more scientific and financially more satisfactory method of estimating the returns from investments.

The Internal Rate of Return

We have stated at the start of this chapter that investment decisions are based on the future cash accumulations that flow from the project periodically. These cash flows are then discounted by a rate that will represent the investor's assessment of risk of not getting these cash flows as expected. The present values of all such discounted cash flows then represent subjective estimation of the likelihood of adding to wealth from that project. Even if the cash flows are known with some confidence the risk is not known clearly. Therefore, the estimation of risk is the real issue involved. To eliminate this problem, imagine that you could arrive at *a discount rate that equates* the *future inflow* of cash with *the actual outflow* needed to finance that project. This rate is then called the internal rate of return. In other words, this discount rate is independent of the expectations of risk, but merely equalizes the cost of the project with the expected future cash inflows. Generally speaking, the higher a project's internal rate of return, the more desirable it is to undertake the project. As such, IRR can be used to rank several prospective projects a business is considering. Assuming all other factors are equal among the various projects, the project with the highest IRR would probably be considered the best and undertaken first.

IRR is sometimes referred to as 'economic rate of return (ERR)', because it achieves equilibrium of costs and benefits in the true economic sense. IRR can be viewed as the rate of growth a project is expected to generate. Even though the actual rate of return that a given project will generate may differ from its estimated IRR rate, a project with a substantially higher IRR value than other available options would still provide a much better probability of stronger growth.

The concept of IRR becomes a criterion for investment decisions when it is matched to the cost of resources and against prevailing alternatives to the use of cash including the rates of return in the securities market. If all the proposed projects have an IRR less than the returns available in the stock market, it would make sense to invest the retained earnings in cash equivalents in the securities market, or distribute the surplus as dividend to the shareholders.

Net Present Value and IRR – What is the Difference?

In the DCF method, we arrive at the net present value of the future stream of cash flows by using a discount rate that matches the risks associated with the future cash flows. The discount rate is actually *a risk free rate plus the premium which is a subjective assessment of the amount of return that is needed to motivate the investor over and above the risk free rate.* Sometimes it is referred to as the 'hurdle-rate' since it is the fence beyond which the investor will not step out. It is also the cost of capital for the investor, the cost which includes a psychological appetite for risk, or what economists would call the 'investor's surplus'. The business needs to decide whether undertaking the investment will generate *net economic profits or losses* for the company.

Economic Profit Vs Accounting Profit

Economic profit is revenues earned less opportunity costs. Opportunity costs are the alternative returns foregone. As a result, you may have a significant *Accounting profit* with little to no economic profit.

Let us imagine that you invest ₹100,000 to start a business, and in that year you earn ₹120,000 in sales revenues. Your *accounting profit* would be ₹20,000. Now imagine, that same year you could have earned a net income of ₹45,000 as a salaried employee. Therefore, you have an economic loss of ₹25,000 (120,000 – 100,000 – 45,000). *Most people are fooled into thinking that accounting profits are real additions to wealth!*

To do this, the firm estimates the future cash flows of the project and discounts them into present value amounts using the 'hurdle rate'. All future positive cash flows are reduced into single number. Subtracting from this number initial cash outlay provides the net present value (NPV) of the investment. This is what we have described as the DCF method.

If the resultant number is positive, then the firm is likely to make an economic profit from the project. So if the project has a positive

NPV, we know that there is an addition to wealth in the real sense. But how much is this addition to wealth? Is it possible to get higher increases in wealth from some other projects with similar investments? In other words, what is the opportunity cost of this investment? Since business is all about making more real wealth, the businessman needs to know what rate of return will be generated by this investment.

To find out, the business can simply recalculate the NPV, this time setting the NPV *minus* cost equal to zero. Solving for the now unknown discount rate, we can arrive at the project's internal rate of return (IRR). If there were projects that a business can undertake with higher IRRs, it should pursue the higher-yielding project instead. Thus, you can see that the usefulness of the IRR measurement lies in its ability to represent any investment opportunity's return and to compare it with other possible investments. The example in the definition box can be translated as: salaried employment has a higher IRR than starting your own business. Therefore you might eventually destroy your net worth if you insist on going into the proposed business on your own.

What is CAGR?

A business must grow in real terms in order to be able to increase its net worth. To measure this growth rate we come to the concept of Compounded Annual Growth Rate. CAGR is an average year-over-year growth rate of an investment over a specified period of time. The compound annual growth rate is calculated by taking the nth root of the total percentage growth rate, where n is the number of years in the period being considered.

This can be written as follows:

$$CAGR = \left[(EV / BV)^{1/n}\right] - 1$$

Where:

EV = Investment's ending value

BV = Investment's beginning value

n = Number of periods (months, years, etc.)

CAGR is an imaginary number that describes the rate at which an investment would have grown if it grew at a steady rate. It is not the actual growth rate. You can think of CAGR as a way to smoothen out the returns over several years.

CAGR is one of those terms best defined by an example.

CAGR – an Example

Suppose you invested ₹10,000 in a portfolio on Jan. 1, 2005. Let's say by Jan. 1, 2006, your portfolio had grown to ₹13,000, then ₹14,000 by 2007, and finally ended up at ₹19,500 by 2008.

Your CAGR would be the ratio of your ending value to beginning value (19,500/10,000 = 1.95) raised to the power of 1/3 (since 1/# of years = 1/3), then subtracting 1 from the resulting number:

$1.95^{1/3} = 1.2493$.

$1.2493 - 1 = 0.2493$.

Thus, CAGR for three-year investment is equal to 24.93%, representing the smoothed annualized gain you earned over your investment time horizon.

Why It Matters:

The compound annual growth rate (CAGR) is a useful measure of growth over multiple time periods. It can be thought of as the growth rate that gets you from the initial investment value to the ending investment value if you assume that the investment has been compounding over the time period. Although average annual return is a common measure for mutual funds, CAGR is a better measure of an investment's return over time.

For example, consider Year 1 and Year 2 of a hypothetical investment in Fund XYZ. (NAVs Y0 = 1000, Y1 = 750, Y2 = 1000) At the end of Year 1, the Net Asset Value (NAV) has fallen from ₹1,000 to ₹750 for a return of -25% [(750 – 1,000)/1,000]. By the end of Year 2, the portfolio value had grown by +33% [(1,000 – 750)/750]. Averaging the Year 1 and Year 2 returns over two years gives us an average return of 4% [(–25 + 33)/2], but that doesn't accurately reflect what has happened. We began with ₹1,000 and ended with ₹1, 000, which is a return of 0%.

While appreciating the growth of a company over the years, it is essential understanding to see how its net-worth has grown over the period. Managements may tout the average growth rates in their enthusiasm to present a positive number. However, the intelligent reader must see through the game to understand the reality of wealth creation by looking for the CAGR over several years from the balance sheet.

Financial Facts

(A comment by the author is related to the chapters in the book so far)

1. Warren Buffett bought a 40-acre farm at age 14 with $1,200 in savings from delivering newspapers. (*What was the opportunity cost to the boy Warren when he decided to invest in Land?*)
2. Warren Buffett claims the worst investment he ever made was in 1993 when he bought Dexter Shoes. The loss to Berkshire shareholders was $3.5 billion. In his letter to shareholders he quoted a line from country singer Bobby

Bare to explain his feelings on the failed acquisition: 'I've never gone to bed with an ugly woman, but I've sure woke up with a few.' (*Optimistic estimations of returns makes the IRR of investment opportunities look higher than they really are.*)

3. Herbert Hoover infamously declared in March 1930 that the US had 'passed the worst.' The worst, however, had just begun. From 1929 to 1932, more than 100,000 businesses failed, banks collapsed at a staggering rate of 200+ per month and GDP fell from $81 billion to $49 billion. (*No one can predict future situations. Not even if you are the president of the United States of America.*)
4. The main article in *The Economist* in March 1999 was famously titled, 'Cheap Oil: The Next Shock?' The article surmised that oil prices could be headed to $5 a barrel and prices might hover in a 'normal' range of $5 to $10. (*Highly informed editors too can make mistakes in interpretation of data, which common man may find amusing. Relying on ones' own judgment in such circumstances needs courage.*)
5. The four countries with the fastest GDP growth in 2011, according to CIA estimates: Mongolia (17.3%), Turkmenistan (14.7%), Ghana (13.6%) and Timor-Leste (10.6%). (*Looking at percentages alone without additional facts can be misleading. These countries have some of the lowest standard-of-living in the world.*)
6. The average American family's net worth plunged by nearly 40% between 2007 and 2010, according to the Federal Reserve. Net worth fell from $126,000 to $77,000. In 2011, according to the World Bank, 33% of people in India live in poverty. About 70% of people in India live on less than $2 per day. (*Comparison such as these do not yield any valid conclusions.*)

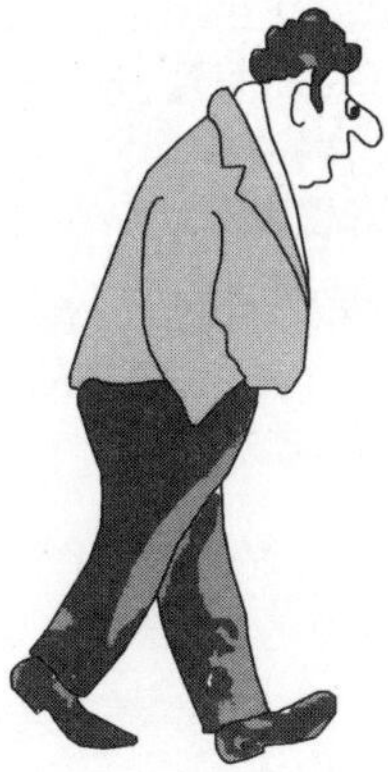

....even my casual morning walk is fraught with uncertainty and discounting problems... dogs, potholes, acquaintances...

Summary of Chapter Nine

Understanding the basic concept of returns is an essential financial skill. In this chapter we have stressed the view that an estimate of returns always involves the use of time value of money. Estimations of future incomes are what drive value to the business. The ability to make this estimate accurately is true business acumen. However, it is easier said than done. Even highly sophisticated models with lots of data cannot accurately predict future cash flows with any degree of accuracy. Therefore it is only natural that business decisions can occasionally go the wrong way and end-up destroying net worth rather than create it.

But the saving grace is that a business is for the long term. Any estimation of the worth of a business should be based on a long term perspective. Here the concept of compounded annual growth comes in handy. Difficult years where losses have occurred are often interspersed with good years. To smoothen out such performances CAGR needs to be looked at. Even though there are other methods of evaluating investment decisions like pay-back period, their utility is limited. The fundamental concept of DCF holds value even if the calculations do not yield actual number-results for managers to use. The twin concept of DCF and IRR complement each other and the skills that need to be applied relates to the particular circumstances where they can be used rather than the question of their use itself. Financial theory has yielded satisfactory foundations on which these concepts are used today and continues to enjoy practical applications in business.

10
Cash Inside Your Own Business

TO HAVE ACCESS TO CHEAP CAPITAL IS ONE OF THE REASONS WHY companies publish their annual reports, apart from the compulsion of meeting regulatory guidelines. But sourcing capital from the market is not easy as investors are prone to considerations of returns, creditworthiness and even sentiments prevailing in the financial markets. This is often a difficult task even during normal times. During times of credit squeeze companies slow down expansion and even day-to-day operations. But all this may not be necessary if the business can manage its cash flows a little more intelligently. In this chapter we explore the possible ways in which a business can generate cash from its own operations, by intelligently managing the balance sheet.

Where is the Cash in the Balance Sheet?

When attempting to understand a company's financial situation, what section of the annual report does the financially skilled reader see first? Most people will look at the profit and loss account. There is nothing abnormal about this; top managers too focus mainly on P&L account, when the company performance is an issue. They cut costs. When the pressure builds to improve performance, most business leaders adopt measures that affect the income statement. They cut discretionary spending. They centralize support functions. They lop off layers of management, refuse to promote executives, abandon low-value projects, all with an eye to 'rationalize' the cost structure. They may try to increase sales without any clear strategy of how to do that.

Our aim is not to belittle these efforts which can genuinely boost results. But these actions tend to by pass the hidden value of managing the balance sheet. The anxiety of the managerial efforts when concentrated only on the profit and loss account often misses out on those issues that hide inefficiencies in the system. Many companies have far more working capital than they need. We have seen in the previous chapter that even in the best managed corporation's decision-making with regard to capital investments may sometimes be ill-timed or ill-advised. They own large quantities of unproductive fixed assets. The focus on P&L account has another hidden danger. Efforts to boost revenues and profitability and some of those actions to manage costs can actually inflate the balance sheet, consuming cash and destroying value.

True Financial Management is to assiduously handle issues in a much more sophisticated manner. The trick is to manage the balance sheet as tightly as you would manage your profit and loss account in order to be able to obtain the desired objectives. The results that follow could be very satisfying. We have explained the mechanics of the balance sheet in chapter two. We will briefly recapitulate what we learned there. This will lead us to a better understanding of the sections that follow here.

The balance sheet is a statement as on a particular date of what a business owns and what it owes. Every line item in the balance sheet is either an asset or a liability. Liability of the business represents what it owes to outsiders. It is also the source by which the capital that has been deployed in the business has been obtained. The assets represent the uses of this capital. The preference of the management for a particular type of asset is displayed by the deployment of resources into assets. These assets manifest their value in turn, through their ability to generate products and services that convert into sales revenues.

We have dealt with the value problem in our chapter on the balance sheet. We also realize now that there is no proven method by which the entire value of the firm can be manifested in the balance sheet, precisely because all items of value are not displayed in the balance sheet. Human resources, for example, are among the most valuable resources that run the company and produce value, and are obtained by the company by paying cash for it, but get no mention on the balance sheet. A software company has very little real assets other than software engineers. Yet can command high valuation levels in the market. However, if the company pays more cash than the true revenue earning capacity of the assets, then it would represent a less than efficient use of cash resources.

Looking for cash in your own business implies freeing up those inefficient uses of capital resources which lock up cash. Increasing the efficiency of the use of cash as a resource in the business can be achieved in several ways by examining critically the following aspects of the balance sheet.

1. Identifying Use of Capital
2. The Burden of Fixed Assets
3. Is Asset Ownership Vital to Business?
4. Budgeting for a Fresh Start
5. Dissecting Working Capital
6. Internal Processes and Cash Consciousness

Measures listed free up amounts of cash, which can then be redeployed. The real value addition comes from increased net worth at a lower cost than would have been possible by focusing on the income statement. There is no magic here, just a different frame of reference and a series of practical, well-honed disciplines that any executive can use to improve workplace performance.

We deal with each of these concepts in the ensuing sections.

1. Identifying Use of Capital

Capital decision making in organizations generally is usurped by the central company leadership, often located at headquarters level. Few boards have a routine visibility to the true nature of the deployment of the capital at the field level on a regular basis. Even if they do, they do not care to look below the large circle or geographical area level formations such as a division. Majority of the directors in boards have no understanding of where the capital is actually invested and how much.

The managers below at the field level have consequently neither interest nor information about the profitability or cost structure of their areas, or products that they are responsible for. Few operational level executives understand the concept of the cost of capital they are dealing with. They neither have exposure to the budgeting process nor need to concern themselves with the sources of funds or how they are managed in the organization.

On a similar level, operational managers are generally confined to specialized areas of duties and they seldom have an overall perspective about the kind of revenues they are directly or indirectly contributing. They do not know the value of the assets they manage and very often are merely interested in following the company procedure written down as 'operational manuals' without ever innovating in the area in tune with changing market conditions. In very large organizations this problem can turn out to be the cause of downfall in times of a financial crunch. Managers at all levels begin to ask questions at cross-purposes achieving very little understanding of the situation, but instead contributing to the general deterioration of services.

But imagine a situation where the balance sheet in its true form is prepared for each circle, division, product or service, plant by plant. Every manager in the system gets to know what assets he is managing, how much it costs, what its returns are and how he compares with similarly placed managers within the same company. The natural corollary is that he begins to take up the business of managing actively for return and profitability. He then begins to eliminate low return activities for higher yielding deployment. He will escalate problems in his area of management actively suggesting solutions that really work. Mapping capital to each business, product, customer, geography and activity enhances financial skills and leads to a boosting of enterprise value. A spin-off from putting into practice the idea of '*granularity of financial statements*' is that the management can then devise measures of efficiency at the bottom most rung in the enterprise to monitor key parameters.

Once capital use is measured at that level, executives will be compelled to manage it closely. It is not enough to set the parameters, what is needed is to assess actual performance at individual manager's level by a system of rewards and punishment. Consider an annual target for operating return on assets. Managers will then have to quickly learn what actions are required to hit their targets.

We display the annual operating return on capital invested in BSNL for a period of ten years.

Annual Operating Return on Capital in BSNL

	2003	**2004**	**2005**	**2006**	**2007**	**2008**	**2009**	**2010**	**2011**	**2012**
Return on Capital Invested (ROCI)%	2.58	9.48	13.99	11.07	8.98	3.41	0.65	–2.11	–7.97	–12.3
Assets Turnover Ratio (ATR)	0.36	0.49	0.54	0.63	0.66	0.66	0.60	0.40	0.39	0.27

Without a visible balance sheet, operating managers play the game of making the best case for their business's allocation of capital. Once the allocation is made, the resources will carry no costs.

Companies with granular balance sheet information, in contrast, can assign appropriate capital costs to each unit and product, assess true performance and take appropriate action.

At the apex level balance sheet information in BSNL becomes available well into the middle of the financial year. These then have mere academic value, perhaps to be discussed in official meetings with ministry level bureaucrats, with no actionable impact on the management. If this very information were to be compiled at the operational circle domain, it will be apparent that several of the operational areas are 'capital hogs' with even lower return on capital invested. Senior executives perhaps can attempt to reduce capital use, drive profit improvements and de-emphasize units that weren't able to generate adequate return on capital.

2. The Burden of Fixed Assets

Large corporations with many segments of businesses and products have a major problem. They have too much capital locked away in their fixed assets. Even the more efficiently managed companies have a fair share of unprofitable products, customers paying below breakeven point and business segments that are loss making. The issue is typically not that. What matters is the amount of precious capital locked up in those areas, which are unproductive. Managements seldom pay attention to this aspect of their balance sheet so much so they may have as little as 20% of the fixed assets contributing to 100% of the total company value. Liberating these fixed assets from under-productivity and low profitability can release a significant amount of cash into the business, leading to better valuation of the business. The value of this key principle in freeing up cash from fixed assets that are no longer yielding value to the company is best demonstrated by the IBM Turnaround story. Few people then realized how perilously the company was running out of cash.

After he decided to save IBM, L. Gerstner hired Jerry York, a former Chrysler CFO known for wearing Harley-Davidson tee shirts with a cigarette pack rolled up in a sleeve. York, whom employees called a 'pit bull,' was charged with getting costs under control. York launched a benchmarking study to determine how IBM's costs in each of its businesses compared with those of competitors. The results were daunting: the ratio of expense to revenue (42% in 1993) needed to be reduced by 9%. Overall, the company was too expensive by at least $7 billion. Opting for the single swing of the scythe rather than the slow and traumatic reductions of the previous few years, York and Gerstner approved layoffs of over 75,000 employees in early 1993. Business unit managers were charged with '*fixing, closing, or selling*' underperforming parts of the business.[1]

The actions that Gerstner took in the PC division represent the fundamental principle we are trying to explain here. Almost all of the PC company brands were killed except ThinkPad brand for the laptop computer business. PC manufacturing was not a core competency in IBM and the PC factories had high fixed costs. It was cheaper to outsource PC manufacturing. The other products moved under ThinkPad brand and there was one marketing team, one development team, shared synergies, and an executive team slimmed by 25%.

The number of data centres were reduced from 155 to 3 regional 'mega centres' fed by 11 'server farms,' Chief Information Officers (CIOs) were reduced to 1 from 128. Networks were converted to one common protocol (TCP/IP), internal applications decreased from 16,000 to 5,200, and component reuse increased by 34%. By the fourth quarter of 1993, IBM posted a small profit of $382 million. A similarly sized profit followed in the first quarter of 1994 ($392 million). By the third quarter of 1993, the company's stock price had doubled. By year-end 1994, profits had risen to $5 billion on revenues of $64 billion.

IBM Turnaround

Freeing up fixed capital	Cash released
1. Decreased data centres from 155 to 11	1. 50% reduction in total cost of ownership for data centre and network operations and internal enterprise application development and maintenance
2. Developed single global Internet network	2. Direct cost savings in internal IT expenses of over $2 billion per year beginning in 1997
3. Shifted to 'open source,' (Linux) and enterprise applications (SAP, PeopleSoft, Siebel)	3. Return on invested capital $100 million between 1994 and 1996.
4. Redesigned system development process to modular design	
5. Decreased number of global applications from 16,000 to 5,200	
6. 60% reduction in IT professional headcount	

Companies facing a cash crunch need not go far to identify 'liquidity', underutilized capital can be converted into cash. The incumbents in high technology areas are especially vulnerable to downturn in revenues and piling up of inefficiencies with the passing of old technology products. New entrants into the industry quickly establish a superior product that customers prefer, and consequently leave the hapless industry leader facing an acute cash problem for daily operations. Since the tech segment is generally high capital intensive, fixed assets in the erstwhile leader start wasting away, while it struggles to maintain and finance new projects. Managements then need to concern itself with future liquidity squeezes and launch a balance sheet review to find 'trapped' capital.

In companies such as BSNL, that have never managed capital, executives may be unfamiliar with the balance sheet or the cost of holding unnecessary assets. Freeing up capital can entail a substantial change in mindset. Executives must rethink the way they run their business. Assets that previously were considered essential for the company to own, such as data centers, can be outsourced, liberating significant amounts of cash and reducing long-term costs. Sometimes entire segments of the business can be outsourced. That can simultaneously reduce future capital investments and provide customers with a more appealing offer. A word of abundant caution in this section is considered appropriate, as freeing up fixed assets may not turn out to the panacea for cash flow problems in all environments.

Executives sometimes believe that fixed assets consist of mainly building, equipments and intangibles like software. They tend to overlook the fact that the pool of employees is in fact the largest fixed assets that many organizations have. This is a fixed asset so long as the company does not have the freedom to expand or shrink its volumes according to business needs. Attempts of the management to downsize employee volumes in response to changes in sales revenues or profitability may fail due to cultural factors and unionization of the workplace. This is an established convention in government sector and public sector organizations and in countries where cultural and traditional pressures hold job-security an entrenched act of faith. Attempts by the Jet Airways management to retrench part of the operating crew due to falling profits and cash flow pressures failed due to the above environment prevalent in India.

These assets are to be deployed along with the physical assets like equipments and software to produce the goods and services that will result in revenue accumulations. But in environments such as the one alluded to, the division of cash expenditure in an organization into operating expenses (OPEX) and capital expenses (CAPEX) will appear to be somewhat artificial. The Accountant's view is not generally endorsed by the businessman, who is more concerned with the cash outflow that must be compensated by cash inflow to make the business viable. The highly instructive story of BSNL, a giant in Telecommunications sector in India is worth recounting. Financial figures of revenues and expenditure for this incumbent Telecom operator is presented in a table below. What needs to be carefully looked at consists of expenditures flowing into fixed assets.

The company deploys less than a quarter of its revenues into the two vital segments for growth, mainly because of its burden of the largest 'fixed assets' component, employee base. The obvious solution lies in downsizing this volume and has been suggested vehemently by a highly respected telecom professional to the government during 2009. However attractive and in tune with business logic, the proposal refuses to take off the ground because of the cultural and environmental factors that prevails.

The returns on capital invested in the mobile business is at par with industry standards, the segment contributing nearly 40% of the total revenues from a capital investment base of around 10% of the total expenditure in the business. The total returns percentage in BSNL is negative (–12%) at the time of writing.

Segment-Wise Deployment of Capital in BSNL (Figures in Rs. Crores)*

	2005	2006	2007	2008	2009	2010	2011
Landline Segment (Ll)							
Revenues	29,607	29,672	24,972	21,016	19,081	17,216	16,349
Net Profit	3,642	3,754	–179	–4,728	–4,963	–7,401	–7,605
Assets	70,419	74,583	71,875	65,117	72,235	85,291	103,541
Captial Expenditure	4,812	4,536	3,555	4,343	5,546	5,061	–2,322
Mobile Segment (Mob)							
Revenues	3,842	6,466	9,643	11,342	11,183	10,697	10,695
Net Profit	785	3,880	5,631	6,006	5,302	3,739	1,204

	2005	2006	2007	2008	2009	2010	2011
Assets	4,979	9,357	13,044	14,355	22,819	28,071	7,213
Captial Expenditure	2,759	2,281	2,163	16,72	4,466	24,231	8,138
Total Assets	75,398	83,940	84,919	79,472	95,054	113,362	110,754
Mobile Assets %	7%	11%	15%	18%	24%	25%	7%
Total Revenues	33,449	36,138	34,615	32,358	30,264	27,913	27,044
Mobile Revenues %	11%	18%	28%	35%	37%	38%	40%
Mobile Asset Turnover	0.77	0.69	0.74	0.79	0.49	0.38	1.48
Landline Asset Turnover	0.42	0.40	0.35	0.32	0.26	0.20	0.16
Capex-Revenue Ratio(Ll)	0.16	0.15	0.14	0.21	0.29	0.29	–0.14
Capex-Revenue Ratio(Mob)	0.72	0.35	0.22	0.15	0.40	2.27	0.76
Total (Opex)	19,777	22,531	22,316	23,940	25,831	29,292	5,816
Total Capex	7,571	6,817	5,718	6,015	10,012	29,292	111,679
Total Expenditure	27,348	29,348	28,034	29,955	3,5843	58,584	117,495
Capex % (For Landline)	72%	77%	80%	80%	72%	50%	5%
Capex % (Mobile)	28%	23%	20%	20%	28%	50%	95%
Return on Capital Invested (Mob)	28%	170%	260%	359%	119%	15%	15%
Return on Capital Invested (LL)	76%	83%	–5%	–109%	–89%	–146%	–328%

	2005	2006	2007	2008	2009	2010	2011
Return on Capital Invested (Total)	16%	26%	19%	4%	1%	–6%	–5%

***Source:* Compiled by the author from BSNL annual reports 2005 to 2011**
**** The percentages shown will not tally with figures in other sections of the book, since unallocated expenses have been ignored here.***

3. Is Asset Ownership Vital to Business?

Liberating fixed capital and identifying the deployment of scarce resources are just two of the steps superior capital managers use to streamline the balance sheet. Over time, the obsession with a lean and efficient balance sheet encourages many executives to explore entirely new approaches to their business. They explore new ownership patterns essentially creating a new business model shifting fixed capital from their own balance sheet to those of more advantaged owners.

The classic example is Marriott, which recognized in the mid-1980s that its core business was managing hotels, not owning real estate. As a result, it began divesting its hotel properties, creating limited partnership arrangements and selling them to tax-advantaged investors. In more recent times Bharti Airtel Ltd became India's leader in the telecommunications industry by using such a model. It entered into simultaneous agreements with leading telecom equipments supplier Erickson of Sweden and IBM, the former for switching capacity as the customer base increased and the later for complete management solutions for its back office operations. In this way it ensured adequate supply of mobile switching systems as its customers and usage traffic grew during the explosive phase in the market. The billing systems and service delivery being a major capital expense for any telecom operator worked seamlessly under expertise from IBM. Companies in semiconductors, transportation and other industries have taken similar measures more recently. A logistics company today, for example, may own few warehouses or trucks, and instead contract with companies or individuals who do. Such tactics enable businesses that would otherwise be capital-intensive to generate higher returns and grow more profitably.

Businesses must learn to concentrate on core revenue earning investments, rather than try to manage the entire service delivery chain through creation of assets. This involves excessive capital outlay that leaves very little financial flexibility in terms of free cash flows.

4. Budgeting for a Fresh Start

At most companies, of course, working capital represents a relatively small percentage of total capital requirements. But setting an implicit (or explicit) limit on capital expenditures based on the performance of the business is the key to cash management within the company. Capital purchases of fixed assets account for a large percentage of the total expenses in a business. Therefore, it is necessary to rationalize this portion of the business. Conventional approaches to capital investments and assumptions about the continuance of the projects that were taken up in previous periods needs to be challenged.

Conventional methods of capital allocation in very large organizations generally follow the percentage rule: find out the outlay during the previous year, add a percentage over the figure and presto, you have the budget for the next year. This is a 'sure-fire' method to squander capital, simultaneously spreading resources thin like butter on toast. Jack Welch in his somewhat self-laudatory book 'Winning' has called this type of budgeting 'an annual ritual' designed to fool everyone involved.

Instead a serious attempt to generate maximum returns from scarce resources should analyze the strategic position of each business-project and its market attractiveness and ability to win.

The business then applies differential targets for investment. Thus highly advantaged businesses, those with high ROIC and good growth prospects, might receive investment at 90 percent or more of depreciation while disadvantaged businesses might get only 50 percent. A complete review of each business vis-à-vis the competitive scene is undertaken each year. The process allows the company to fuel its growth without overinvesting in unattractive businesses.

It also stretches out its capital plan when appropriate. During a downturn, the company can ask its businesses to reschedule their facilities and slow down orders to prevent the buildup of excess inventory. Corporate management can then hold back the capital it had budgeted in order to ensure sufficient liquidity, pay down debt and reduce borrowing costs. Effective capital budgeting is to set targets for asset productivity. Like individuals, capital should become more productive over time. Yet many companies don't have explicit capital productivity targets, and so they spend on more capital without requiring more output.

5. Dissecting Working Capital

Working capital is a concept not generally understood outside the pure financial management theory, and is opaque to a large number of executives who may perhaps be able to define it in the classic textbook style. Here we propose to take the concept beyond the textbook into the practical business world of managing it properly for results. We begin with the definition:

$$\text{Working capital} = \text{Current assets} - \text{Current liabilities}$$

What is generally missed out in this equation is the fact that it is cash that is involved in each of these elements of working capital. Current assets consisting of cash, inventory and receivables of course, are but different forms of the same thing: namely cash.

Current liabilities, on the other hand, are payables and short-term obligations. A little reflection reveals that these too represent cash outflow incurred during the production of the company's services. We promise to have a full chapter on working capital and its levers, but for the present, we need to understand that the larger the working capital requirement of the business the more cash is locked up in its elements.

The chain of cash conversion (*that should result in more cash at the end of the chain*) needs to be efficiently managed to achieve optimum usage of cash within the production cycle. In very large organizations, purchase of raw materials is a large department by itself. The managers involved in purchase act on inputs from a purchase controller, who watches the sales figure closely. However, the information flow between sales department and purchase department can be seriously out of sync lagging in real-time business intelligence. It is therefore not infrequent that purchased inventory of raw-materials can pile up, while production has been slowed down due to slower off-take. Sales people on the other hand may push sales through without a care about the possibility of the customer paying up. Again the result is cash getting blocked into the form of receivables.

Managing working capital is to mount a multipronged attack on its various elements after carefully gathering information. Perhaps the first step is to polish up a business's information technology systems, to the point where it had good, easily accessible data on each department that is involved in the process of production. This allows for reliable data on how much cash is held up where and perhaps suggests solutions that are not easily visible without such information systems. The next step is to manage the assembly line. Even in a service oriented company like telecommunications or Airport-ground-handling system there is sufficient scope to eliminate wastages and delay. An inventory turnover-time (*a ratio we have discussed in chapter seven*) in tune with the industry standards needs to be aimed at. This will reduce the work-in-progress locking of real cash in these assembly lines drastically. Walmart, the famous retail store, is known to have achieved remarkable results in this area by careful management of its stores reducing the time a product sits on its shelf. Such savings in cash-lock up enables the company to offer everyday low prices to its customers.

The third and perhaps the most visible stage of cash locked up are in receivables. A business that manages its receivables effectively enjoys operational freedom beyond the normal levels. Cisco Systems focused intensely on working capital, trying to improve days-sales-outstanding every year for three years. They were almost maniacal about collections receivables from its customers. Cisco even began examining its customers' working capital levels. Bottlenecks in a customer's operations, the company found, often led to slow collections on the customer's part and slow receivables for Cisco. Helping customers fix their problems benefited both parties.

6. Internal Processes and Cash Consciousness

Ultimately, of course, managing the balance sheet is all about freeing up cash and redeploying it in the best way possible. Most companies that successfully manage their assets find themselves developing cultures that emphasize not just the balance sheet but cash as well. That kind of culture is typically reinforced by a host of policies and systems that encourage managers to continue taking the balance sheet into account in their day-to-day running of the business. One such policy – a powerful one – is to reward managers for hitting balance sheet targets, just as most are already rewarded for hitting income statement targets. The company must create well tried out performance matrices to not only measure managerial effectiveness but also to add in flexibility to working capital and cash management.

Some astute balance sheet managers, such as Dow Chemical, create two-way performance contracts. The corporate center agrees to provide a certain level of resources to the businesses; and business-unit leaders commit to a certain level of performance. That is an essential policy for any investment requiring a long-time horizon. Most balance sheet investments represent multi-year commitments – the corporation invests now and may not see a return until much later. Without some form of contract, good money can be poured after bad and losing projects will never be cut short.

People begin to understand the 'physicals' of cash and what concrete actions on a daily basis result in cash conservation.

- They come up with new and better ideas for running the business, greater focus on the fastest-selling products, enabling dealers to reduce inventories without hurting sales.
- The company can communicate regularly about cash levels, reassure investors and help ensure that the stock is fairly valued.
- Executives approach the capital budget differently. Instead of cutting capital expenditures, the company must emphasize efficiencies in the way it spends capital, thus doing more with less.

In contrast, large public sector undertakings and governments generally make the right noises about cash conservation by issuing circulars to field formations on the importance of economy in spending. These pious intentions sometimes are carried a step further by actively cutting the budget allocations. Companies faced with falling revenues control cash disbursements through their banking channels, which result in accumulation of payables, carry forward of liabilities to subsequent periods and other undesirable consequences, like unrest within the staff unions and vendors resorting to 'speed money' payments. These are just peripheral symptoms of failure to manage cash through deeper understanding of how the organization functions at the resources and returns level.

Leading companies have overcome such issues through a systematic training of their executives about balance sheet concepts and what they can do to contribute. Such organizations generally have a spread of executives who exercise administrative and financial powers and get attached to such authority unwilling to let go even if extreme situations warrant it. Reorganization and right-sizing becomes then a more complex issue for the top management, often frustrating any attempt in that direction. Finance is largely about the culture within the business. Great business leaders have always emphasized that without a conscientious culture that treats cash flow as of vital importance within a business, finding cash within your own company will be contentious and sometimes unsuccessful.

....it does not really matter whether you win or lose...
what really matters is whether I win or lose....

Summary of Chapter Ten

A business in difficulty usually gets there because it is short of cash. When such a situation arises managers take the short-cut to cash management by introducing control over expenditure aimed at reducing costs in the profit and loss account, since that is the obvious route. However, there is a better and perhaps more efficient way to managing cash. True finance management skills emerge when cash is controlled through the balance sheet. This is because the balance sheet displays the cash position more accurately than the income statement. It is a photo shot of the sources and uses of cash at any particular moment in the business. This is valuable information that does not emanate from the other statements as clearly and therefore needs to be focused on more emphatically.

Unlocking cash from the places where they have been temporarily trapped needs careful observation, granular breakdown of the balance sheet into not only its component elements but also into division-wise and project wise information. Efficiency of cash usage needs to be measured in terms of returns on cash invested into various businesses and the proportion of returns that each project brings into the company as a whole. Thereafter a careful pruning of the projects, no matter at what stage they actually are, depending on a fresh look at its viability and returns in relation to the competitive environment is called for. Looking at the balance sheet further reveals invaluable information about company practices related to purchases of raw materials, the time delays and efficiencies in the system of production and policies of the sales-persons that ultimately reward the company through receivables.

Finally, the culture of cash-awareness that is built into the company management practices and everyday language of operations matter immensely in helping the business stay afloat during the bad times. A comprehensive approach to the issue of managing resources, inbuilt awareness of costly delays and time overruns enables a company to emerge successful during periods of cash squeeze.

11

Adding Financial Skills to Working Capital

A BRILLIANT IDEA THAT ADDS VALUE TO HUMAN EXPERIENCE IS the foundation of a business venture. But it will remain an idea without cash to back it up. To understand this, let us imagine a small manufacturing outfit about to start converting this wonderful idea into a product. It begins with cash, which it uses to buy materials needed. These materials are then subjected to processes which turn it into finished goods, ready for sale. Once sold, the seller collects cash as a reward. This cycle from cash to cash with varying degrees of discrete stages involved is the universal operating cycle, and is the same for all business units. Throughout this operating cycle, cash remains the common link, and though it changes form from raw materials-inventory to work-in-progress-inventory and finished goods-inventory turning into receivables on sale. The quantity of cash trapped inside the cycle remains the same from start to finish, until it is liberated in the form of collections from customers who purchased the goods. The longer the cycle-time involved, the greater the quantity of cash that will be locked up in the process. The actual amount of cash needed to cover the operating cycle from start to finish is the working capital needed. All businesses, big or small, need a large proportion of cash to manage this operating cycle. Better working capital management makes a company more efficient at converting inputs to outputs and ultimately into cash. Businesses that can generate more cash in less time enjoy greater financial flexibility and may not need to depend on outsiders to employ cash through borrowings or investor funds.

The Cash-Flow Time-Line

The production cycle or the cash conversion cycle as it is sometimes called is essentially a timeline that traces the initial investments of working capital and relates it to the stages involved in production. Part of our quest for financial skills is met when we understand the mechanics of this timeline. It has explicitly distinguishable levels. They are explained by the following diagram:

The Business Cash-Flow Cycle

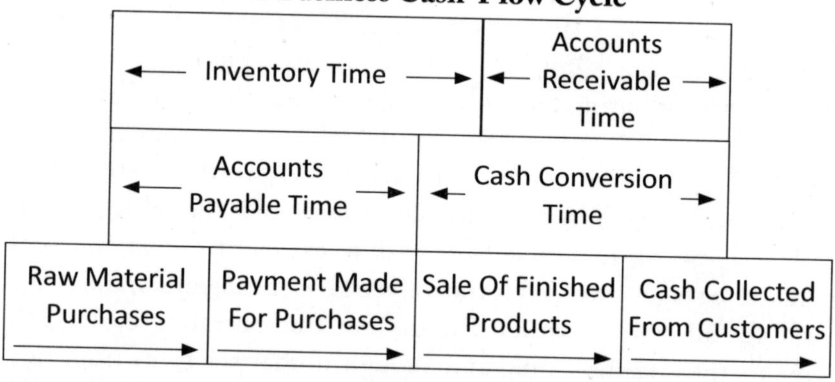

When the materials are purchased, the inventory time and the accounts payable time starts ticking. Since there is a time-gap between materials receipts and the processing time, inventory time is inevitable, either as raw form materials or semi-finished goods. There has been an outflow of cash for purchases as well as processes. Since no goods are as yet available for sale, the business still gets no money from the activities. Eventually when sales do take place, the company just enters the accounts receivable period, as most sales are not necessarily for immediate cash. The actual conversion of goods into cash takes place when it does collects money from its customers.

This might indeed appear simple and elementary to most readers, but it is important to notice that the time cash is trapped in this cycle matter a lot to the business, in terms of liquidity and flexibility of operations. All the materials purchased represent current commitments that the business has made to the process, and is the current assets that it has exchanged its cash for. The ability to meet its obligations in terms of payments to be made to suppliers and labor that are engaged depends on the conversion of goods into cash at the end of the cycle. If it cannot meet its current obligations and payables, it will need to find external sources of cash to fill in the gap. This means putting in good cash after the bad or doubtful. Intelligent financial management involves the speeding up of the time-lines at every stage. A common fallacy of managers everywhere is to concentrate on the last phase of the business cycle, namely the cash conversion cycle. The strenuous efforts they make to chase receivables, no doubt praiseworthy may sometimes miss the real point of managing cash long before it is due from customers.

Managing the Cash-Flow Time-Line

It is valuable information for the managers to know the total time it takes from materials purchase to cash collections. They must determine how many days it takes for each stage to complete because that is the number of days that cash is locked up in the process. Fortunately for us there is a method of doing this. We can use this simple formula:

$$\text{Cash conversion time-line} = \text{DSO} + \text{DII} - \text{DPO}$$

Where:

DSO = days in sales outstanding

DII = days in inventory

DPO = days of payables outstanding

The cash conversion time-line gives the managers an idea of the quantity cash needed to finance the business. This can be easily found by multiplying the average sales per day by the number of days in the cash conversion time-line.

Cash Requirement in BSNL for a Year		
Figures From Balance Sheet 2012	**₹ in Crores**	**Average Days**
Receivables	4,200	58.96
Inventory	3,800	52.96
Current Liabilities	9,800	26.97
Sales	26,000	71.23
Cash Conversion Time-Line		
58.96 + 52.96 – 26.97 = 84.95		
Cash Needed To Finance Operations		
85 × 71 = 6035 Crores Per Year		

Source: figures compiled from BSNL annual report 2012: by the author

BSNL has very large operations across the Indian sub-continent. But it has machinery in place to collect its receivables fast, and its inventory lock up period is also short. Because of its mammoth size it is able to obtain credit easily from its suppliers. The cash flow from its operations is generally adequate to keep operations running smoothly. However, in recent years the scene has dramatically shifted to a more precarious state. This is not unusual for very large corporations to have a large proportion of cash for its operations support, faced with stiff competition from the market players. In the case of BSNL, the problem is falling sales against fixed payables commitments in the form of huge wage bill for its employees.

The cash conversion time-line can be shortened by active management of the elements that constitute working capital namely, receivables, inventory and payables.

Working Capital Components

How much working capital does a company really need? Every company no matter what its nature of operations needs enough cash and inventory to carry out its job. If the company's sales are growing, or its operations are spread over a large geographical area, it will need more of it. But the real issue is to use capital efficiently and here the managerial skills both financial and otherwise play important roles. Managing the numbers through accounting tricks can impact these elements, in somewhat oblique way. Inventory valuation policies of the company will show numbers in the balance sheet which might represent a value off the real market valuations. Again revenue recognition issues we have met earlier can put out numbers that are wholly out of tune with actual receivables of cash. Higher receivables and higher inventories constitute a healthy outlook when viewed by outside creditors who ought to receive cash from the company.

In reality however, suppliers prefer to understand the payment policies of the company before entering into commitments. Delaying payments is not good business and certainly not part of financial management, even though businessmen do resort to such tactics in times of squeeze. In general therefore it would not be far-fetched to assume that payables as shown by the company do represent real cash outflow especially where convention requires written acknowledgment from the payee. Creative accounting practices when related to current assets can be somewhat ineffective in face of inquisitive analysis. However there are authentic actions that can manage receivables and inventory to release cash into the system if managers are willing to explore the possibilities. We examine some of them.

Working Capital Levers

Many businessmen knowingly finance other people's purchases. The amount of cash owed to the company, shown as accounts receivable in the balance sheet under current assets, constitute the amount advanced to customers in order to enable them to buy the company's products. We have examined the ratio dealing with the average number of days a company takes to collect these receivables, in chapter seven. We called this the 'day's sales outstanding or DSO'. The longer it takes the customers to pay up, the more working capital the company needs to keep its operations going normally. In other words, if customers keep the company's cash, it will need to find more of it to keep producing the services and goods.

Managing the Receivables

It would be logical to conclude that faster payments are indeed a better way to run the business. And it is true. The telecommunications industry is among the most innovative service providers in the modern era of business. This industry was also among those that extended maximum advances to its customers by raising invoices for telephone services 60 days after the services have been provided. Further, as a convention customers were allowed an average of 30 days to make payment before services were disconnected. However, in a brilliant stroke of financial and operations management, telecom companies no longer need to carry fresh receivables in their books on account of voice call services. They asked the customers to pay in advance in a complete reversal of conventions. *The pre-paid card* or *the calling card* first conceived and introduced by mobile operator *Mobile Italia* has eliminated the receivables problem for most mobile operators.

It may not be technologically possible for most businesses to emulate mobile operators. Some headway has been achieved by banking sector through the use of debit-cards and petroleum companies who have attempted to issue co-branded debit-cards to sell-off their products, bulk of transaction even today are through post-paid systems. As long as a company continues to sell on such terms, the level of receivables will rise as sales increase. But alarm bells should start ringing the moment the DSO-ratio deteriorates (*meaning an increase in the number*). The ratio is then the mirror to inefficiencies in the internal systems related to quality, credit policies, and sales practices of the company. The management needs to arrive at the right answers.

Ageing Receivables

The DSO number that we discussed earlier is just an average. Like all averages, it fails to reflect the distribution within it. For example if a company had ₹1,000 crs outstanding as receivables that are about 10 days and ₹4,000 crs that are 90 days, the average is ₹50 crores/day which looks innocent enough. But the bulk of the receivables are outstanding for a long period and the company could be in substantial trouble because 80% of its customers don't seem to be interested in paying their bills. Ageing analysis of total receivables segregates the customers into prompt payers, laggards and defaulters. Most companies have a policy of disclosing the numbers about accounts receivable by the period of time they are actually pending for payment from customers.

Customer Acquisition Process

Marketing systems today concentrate on the quality of customers they are willing to acquire. Receivables management therefore must begin with customer profiles and their creditworthiness. Databases that reveal not only the income and family status, but also usage patterns for services online are available to businesses to decide whether to sell or not. Internet based systems that tract the financial health, regional and cultural attitudes towards settlement of obligations etc are essential tools to manage bad debts. Large customers are tracked by groups of dedicated teams who visit customer's facilities and monitor activities not only for cross-selling opportunities, but also for gathering information regarding possible financial difficulties that may endanger the quality of a sale.

These are not merely the signs of the emerging times or symptoms of sophisticated use of technology, but essential finance management tools for ensuring smooth cash flow within a business. The reader would have noticed that reducing the DSO figure by even one day makes a large difference to the amount of cash flowing into the company. Let us take the example of BSNL given above. Reducing the cash conversion cycle time by a single day brings in additional cash resources to the tune of ₹72 crores.

The Inventory Problem

The costs of inventories are generally hidden from managers' view. Studies have shown that inventory costs sometimes do account for nearly 15% of the total costs, even though this might vary from product to product. A multi-product company that tries to be 'all things to everyone' by having a wide range of products in its portfolio may not be able to reap the advantages as costs of the inventories that are slow moving outweighs the advantages of having a full range of product-variants.

Inventory costs flow from the various elements of the nature of the product itself and the management of stocks:

Cost Implications of Inventory

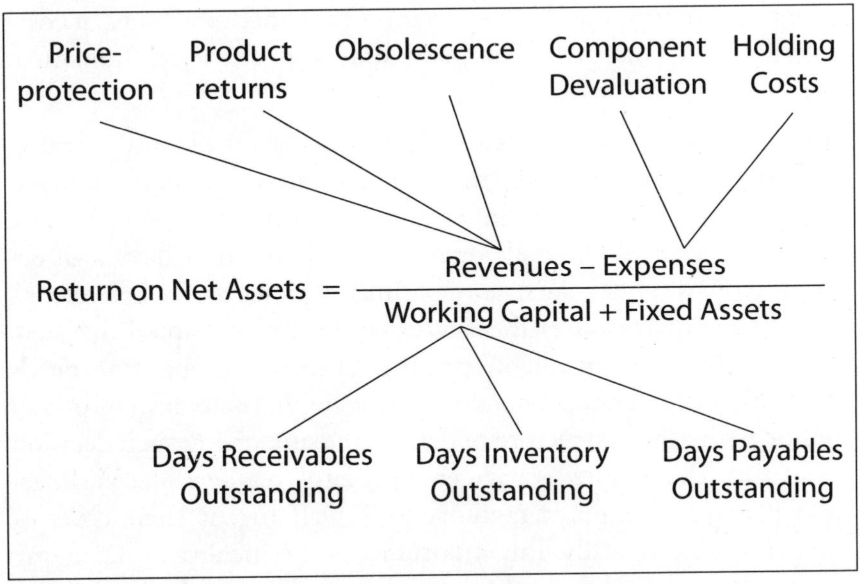

The above diagram is a complete overview of the various elements of costs associated with the inventory problem in a typical business concern. Let us examine the elements in some detail. Component devaluation occurs when the product loses its price realization potential over time either due to the perishable nature of the goods themselves or some of its components have been outdated by availability of better parts. Further, if a company has already shipped the goods to dealers and to enhance sales, it offers discounts on pricing the company is under obligation to protect the price already given to the franchisee. In other words it has to reimburse the discounts to the franchisee and dealers. If, on the other hand, a customer returns the product for unsatisfactory performance or whatever reason, the company has to affect a full refund. Obsolescence as universally understood can take place in several ways; disruptive technology and change of fashion (in readymade clothing industry and other consumer items) are only the most visible of them. Holding costs impact several points in the system, for example, storage at multiple locations, warehousing charges, demurrage and transportation could become issues of costs management both at the company level and the dealer/franchisee premises.

The managerial perspective on inventory control and working capital in general have to be therefore mounted on a multi-pronged level based on accurate information systems that supply data regarding each of these elements. Those items that have a direct impact on revenues such as discounts policies and sales-returns are to be understood in the context of return on capital invested. Goods which are perishable or open to heavy competition needs to move faster and production processes have to be controlled online with a superstructure of data-bases supporting such decision processes. These systems have enabled large retailers like Walmart and personal computer manufacturer Dell to cut their costs of inventory dramatically. The importance and criticality of managing the working capital through a careful monitoring of the three ratios related to its control cannot be overemphasized.

....oh well...I think I should enjoy being the CFO of this Company...
You see, being cruel and rather incompetent comes naturally to me....

Summary of Chapter Eleven

True skills of financial management and practical application of financial intelligence is visible in a business through its levels of working capital management. The aim of controlling working capital is to reduce the operations cycle time. This simultaneously reduces the total cash requirement of the business and introduces an element of financial flexibility into the financial management of the business. There is a tendency to focus on receivables alone in attempting to control cash-flow. However, the entire cash time-line is important as cash gets locked up in various forms of inventory during the production process. The financial impact of inventory can be substantial. The overall measure of managerial efficiency namely return on assets is influenced by the levels of inventory which has direct implications on revenue and expenses.

Find the Needle in the Haystack

Issues Based on Concepts in Part Three

1. The line between operating expense and capital expenditure is sometimes not clear. How can you tell?
2. What are the effective actions to turn around a loss-making Government company? Are they all equally desirable?
3. What are the practical implications between managing the income statement and managing the balance sheet?
4. Do you think managing a business is really all about allocating resources optimally?
5. So 'Cash only matters in business', do you agree?
6. Family-owned business tends to have near relatives occupying top-managerial positions. Is it a professional method of doing business? Do they harm the companies they manage in this way? Why do shareholders accept it?

PART FOUR

CONNECTING THE INSIDE AND THE OUTSIDE

12

Finance and Financial Skills

THE MOST IMPORTANT JOB OF A MANAGER IS THE CREATION OF value for the firm. Every executive and employee is charged with the task of contributing towards this goal. Each person has to contribute in his own way. Owner value in a business is enhanced when the claims of all stakeholders such as bondholders, suppliers, employees and governments on the surpluses generated have been satisfied. The residual equals the reserves and surpluses accumulated over the years over and above owners' capital. The nature of job of the finance manager is primarily to ensure optimum use of financial resources in this process of value creation. So what does a Finance Manager do?

What Does the Finance Manager Do?

Finance function essentially involves the achievement of three basic objectives. More than just a glorified bookkeeper (or someone whose long service to the company has been rewarded with a fancy title) an effective finance manager plays a number of important roles within the entrepreneurial company that are essential in providing a strong financial foundation for a growing business.

1. Holding the Mirror

The preparation and presentation of financial statements is the overall reflection of the financial situation of the company. The Chief Financial Officer holds the mirror to the top-most company management, of which he is an integral part. He is confident in the knowledge that the financial numbers reflect the true state of affairs within the company. These numbers are what serve as basic inputs to the system of decision making within the company. The integrity of these numbers, their availability at the right time to the right people and confidentiality of the information are vital to the competitiveness and future of the business. The more you know about your business, the better its chances of success. Noticing potential problem areas before they mature into full-grown crises can save a business from ultimate failure. Planning and allowing for growth before it kicks in helps your company expand in the most profitable ways. The financial statements presented by the CFO reflect all this information just as a mirror would but financial skills will reveal the full picture through a detailed analysis of this information.

2. Connecting the Inside and the Outside

A business exists because of a customer. The outside of the business drives its actions and growth. The processes are designed as a meeting point between the outside and the inside. If there is a mismatch between the two it shows up as inefficiencies of functions within the organization. All inefficiencies cost money. If products don't sell to the desired level or if customer service fails to meet expectations, the root cause is the inability to connect the inside processes with the outside environment. Finance management exists to identify these all important gaps in operational efficiency and rectify them with tools of the trade that is available. Exploring the contours of the business, probing the dark corners of operations with ratio analysis and tools of financial management is only the first step of analysis. The concrete actions that are needed to rectify the distortions within the internal managerial systems are the true level of skilled-financial management expected.

3. Advisor of the Last Resort

Finance is an integral part of management. It will act as the advisor of the last resort to the Board of Directors on all matters that have a financial implication. Through this function the CFO brings in silently and subtly cash flow controls, establishing credit policies for customers, achieving favorable payment terms, implementing procedures for measuring and evaluating optimal inventory levels and so on. An effective CFO is expected to play an important role in addressing major strategic issues that can have an impact on the company's long-term future. Such issues might include the development of company acquisition strategy to help fuel additional growth, or the divestiture of particular product lines or business activities that no longer match the company's business objectives. He will play a key role in any effort to seek investment from the public financial markets or to launch an initial public offering, making a tangible connection between a company's operations and its financial performance.

All other functions of the finance executive can be herded under these three objectives.

Looking Beyond the Financial Statements

Reader of this book, since you have persevered up until these pages you know now that accounting is the language of business. Just as you'd have trouble understanding the complexities of Japanese culture on a visit to Osaka without the ability to speak and understand the Japanese language, you cannot hope to really *know* a business venture until you can deconstruct the balance sheet, the income statement and the statement of cash flows. That's why I spent so much time explaining the mechanics of the accounting process, complexities of diagnosing a business through ratio analysis and topics such as credit analysis and financial flexibility. These topics aren't that difficult to understand but they are vital to achieving what I called the basic financial skills.

But it is important to realize that the financial world is far bigger and much more complex than what is presented here. I must urge the reader, no matter how tempting and comfortable it might appear, not to take in the statistics of the past since they are merely guideposts, subject to competitive forces and becoming obsolete as a result of technological advancement and other changes that render them and the analysis based on them rather tasteless. In other words, you have to know what information is worth knowing and whether it is relevant for the future. We have subtitled this section deliberately to focus on this aspect of finance, that there is a world beyond the numbers that do make a difference to the business activities.

Demographic Trends

Demographic trends bode well or poorly for the company depending on the characteristics of the population growth and composition. Retirement homes and health care services may experience a substantial increase in revenue in a country with ageing of baby boomers. Health care services and dentistry may flourish in a country with rapidly rising incomes. But, of course, a demographic advantage isn't going to make a business successful in and of itself – that requires a good revenue model, intelligent management, and ethical board of directors, and a product or service that customers do love.

Technological Trends

The tragedy with technological change is not the change itself but the failure to notice that a change is on. Companies that are capable of looking beyond the present numbers into the future and adapt successfully to new requirements and technology will survive as a business and others will fail. There are companies that are doomed with their business model regardless of the current financial results – no matter how cheap the stock may appear or how impressive its past record has been. Those companies that are inward-looking, forever improving on products based on current technology relegate investing for future, thereby forsaking its fruits. For example, the automobile industry based on gasoline and fossil fuels is bound to lose out in the near future, no matter how efficient the internal combustion engine may become. Investing continuously larger sums of money into engine improvement thus may not produce the required returns. Financial results of the industry will not point straightaway to these aspects.

Management's Integrity and Disposition

At the risk of sounding somewhat old-fashioned, an important and key element of success in business is ethical behaviour. The managerial attitudes towards debt, compliances and legality of operations is sometimes reflected in the accounting numbers themselves, but not necessarily visible as such. However, fraudulent practices in business with the sole aim of accumulation at the cost of society or human life-experiences are more of a criminal activity rather than business practice, since it affects the investor's faith in the system and cause losses to them on putting faith in such management. Financial skills on a basic level enable them to be on guard against such managerial propensities.

Governance is the Ability to Look Beyond the Numbers

Financial statements are an attempt to reflect the results of a business; they are not the business itself. It might surprise the reader to learn that the 'bottom line' presented to directors is sometimes not real bottom line. To accomplish this, managements filter the information flow to the top by carefully stage-managed actions behind the scenes. In companies where the majority of board members consist of functional directors, such an exercise amounts to self deception. Board of directors should look beyond financial statements and take much broader views of their businesses. Although many governance practices are already in place at some leading companies, they need much broader acceptance.

Even though board members might imagine that they have policies in place that require full disclosure and transparency and managers assert that they use the best financial systems and advisors available, the sad reality is that several companies have adjusted-numbers at the end of every quarter. Misstatements not amounting to criminal activity have been routinely made, and there are gaps in information flow to the public from year to year, conveniently forgetting that continuity in data is essential to complete the picture. Independent directors are truly 'outsiders' in many companies, since agendas for meetings filled with carefully scripted presentations are generally beyond their control.

Some of the blame falls squarely on the directors themselves as many of them do not have essential understanding of the businesses they are supposed to govern. Experienced directors then view the financial results with amazement even as the physical conditions and external observable information about the business continue to deteriorate. They are 'caught' when newspaper reports damn the company, while inside managers continue to appear positive about future prospects, despite unanswered symptoms and non-financial early warning signs of deterioration— autocratic management, new competitors, excess capacity, quality problems, and steady decline in customer base.

Financial Skills at the Governance Level

In India the new regulations for corporate governance issued in November 2010 stipulate among other things, that there should be a charter laying down clearly the role, direction and responsibilities of the board and management and the duties of independent directors. These guidelines for the first time stipulates that independent directors appointed to boards, must be imparted training in the company's revenue model in addition to subjects related to their duties and responsibilities. The chairman of the audit committee must be an expert on finance and accounting matters. Among the powers of the audit committee is their ability to make comments on the '*Management Discussion and Analysis*' in relation to the results of the operations presented to the stakeholders. In particular they are to examine all the related party transactions entered into by the company. Above all, the audit committee must thoroughly question the management regarding the internal control weaknesses pointed out by the statutory auditor.

The directors have to be true and impartial in assessing the reports presented by the management to them. They are to be extremely vigilant in the case of disclosures and compliance with the legal framework in the country. Any deviation from the accounting standards are to be explained to the satisfaction of the board as it is their bounden duty to ensure that statements reflect the 'true and fair' view of the company's financial situation. Employees also must be able to report alleged fraudulent activities directly to the board, and so-called whistle blowers must be protected against reprisals for speaking out. Segment reporting is now made compulsory.

Good governance requires directors to look beyond the numbers and consider the fundamental practices and processes of the business. An effective board must consider the environment in which a business operates and the actions and strategies that management proposes and implements, in addition to results reflected in the financial statements. This calls for financial skills of a higher order, enabling the directors set their own agenda and determines the information they want to see. Directors can hold closed executive sessions to discuss company policies, strategy, current practices, and results outside the presence of management, rather than merely rely on the skewed, upbeat information they have historically received.

The ability to evaluate businesses and management groups beyond financial statements prepared according to generally accepted accounting principles (GAAP) is what is meant by financial intelligence at the board-level.

Why Companies Must Look Outside

Rating agencies evaluate corporations on their financial capabilities. Bond ratings for corporations with public debt are published which gives a fair idea about the creditworthiness and of overall corporate financial health. Corporations with AA or AAA ratings are usually financially healthy, while those with B or C ratings are considered to be financially distressed. These agencies attempt to continuously improve their methods by incorporating more forward-looking outside data, such as investor expectations and stock prices. By lowering a rating one or two grades, a rating agency sends a powerful signal to management, directors, and the public that something is wrong. These types of signaling from the 'Outside' are valuable information in addition to the stock-market reaction to company proposals. But not all companies have traded debt in their capital structure. Further there is a lag between the information as reflected from the market and the actual situation inside the company. Such companies need to devise their own metrics for self assessment and boards are in the ideal position to request managements to call for such data. Tools such as the balanced scorecard, ratio analysis, Altman's Z-score etc. combined with banker's reactions to company credit requests are vital signs that give directors much broader and more insightful and meaningful methods for setting corporate strategy and measuring performance.

Every industry has operating benchmarks that can be used to evaluate performance. In the retail industry, for example, sales per square foot provide a sense of a retail outlet's productivity. In the steel industry, labor cost per ton is a key indicator. In the telecommunications sector Average Revenue Per Subscriber

(ARPU) is a key driver. Boards must look at estimates of these parameters whenever possible. These statistics are often tracked daily, weekly, or monthly and are used to predict future financial performance. Tracking such metrics from the 'inside' alone while necessary, can be wholly misleading unless the 'outside' view is also presented meticulously. For example, a 10 percent reduction in labor cost per ton of steel produced may seem to be a significant improvement. But if a competitor posts a 15 percent improvement from a lower cost base, the competitive position of the first company will deteriorate. More comprehensive models, exception reporting, and frameworks that include information about competitors are needed to put operating statistics into proper perspective for corporate directors and shareholders. A corporate that merely looks inside will eventually fail to be competitive in the market space.

Every business, especially those that are subject to volatile dynamics, such as weather, high growth, or high technologies will face crises at some point in its life cycle. Financial skill involves identification of the most significant business risks the companies face. Quantitative and statistical methods are available to estimate and rank those risks. Looking at the outside significantly enables boards and management to take pre-emptive actions to mitigate these risks, by working out different scenarios and help management identify the best long-term strategies for dealing with them. Allocating sufficient time to these critical activities is essential for the long-term survival and growth of the business.

Value Creation Begins By Looking Outside

Creating value for the company was understood to mean boosting of EBITDA translated to mean higher EPS in every quarter. 'Shareholder value' was the mantra for many corporations in the 1990s. Though the concept still has considerable merit, yet, it was frequently misapplied by the management focusing solely on current earnings. Current stock market pricing of its shares was the only criterion for value. The long term future valuation of the business was relegated to the backyard, in exchange for the only visible, if imperfect, driver of short-term stock prices. This concept never gained full acceptance as realization slowly dawned on the fact that a corporate body has several stakeholders that together co-operate to create value and therefore demand a share in its performance results. The importance of categories of critical stakeholders like employees, suppliers and government in the value creation process came to be recognized. The new mantra of sharing the bounty from the success of the business spawned concepts such as 'employee-stock options' and incentive plans.

When results fell short of financial goals, some of these management groups became overly 'creative,' to the point of inflating earnings through accounting tricks. Tinkering with accounting numbers cannot produce value. It is like trying to drive a car by looking at the rear-view mirror. The ultimate outcome is the destruction of the car itself. True businessmen everywhere understand the concept of cost of capital to the company. Businesses that earn more than their cost of capital generally create wealth when they grow. Companies that earn less than their cost of capital, on projects that may not cover the cost of capital, are likely to destroy value if the businesses grow. Cost of capital concept is the most important outward-looking parameter that all managers need to grasp fully in order to create value within an organization. Businesses that are not likely to earn their costs of capital must shrink to create value. However, shrinking a business may create value for the shareholders; it is not likely to do the same for employees or entrenched stakeholders. Financially savvy managers understand when and how businesses should grow and when and how they should be pruned.

Advisor for the Inside and the Outside

This is perhaps the hardest and the most challenging part of the financially intelligent manager. In *Great by Choice*, Jim Collins, the best selling management author, provides a simple framework for transforming good companies into great ones. He seems to have unearthed data from studying hundreds of great companies that discipline and focus on goals are among the most important characteristics for meeting the challenges of a modern corporation. Internal processes must have mechanisms to ensure that the right people get to leadership positions within the companies. The CFO must have clear focus on the external environment of the business and have the determined discipline to take those needed steps one by one at a predetermined pace, no matter what.

Disciplined thinking is of little value unless it is followed up by disciplined action. What worked in the past does not guarantee future success. A continual process of re-working the strategy, testing it against reality, modifying it for better results, testing it again only can guarantee results over long periods of time. Those executives no matter where they are deployed, who do not meet the exacting standards are actually pulling down the organization value. To implement such an internal process calls for extreme courage and fortitude, but it will enable the company to have the strongest group contributing to the value creation effort.

What Can Financial Intelligence Teach You?

At face value, your financial statements tell you a lot about your company's performance. The statement of profit and loss lets you know how much the company sold, and whether those sales resulted in overall profitability. The balance sheet tells you where the company stands right now, and gives you a look at the overall financial position. The statement of cash flows informs you how cash moves through your business and whether operations are supplying or draining cash. All this data is critical to your future plans, but it's really just a small part of the total knowledge you can gain from these exceptionally enlightening reports.

When you delve deeper into these statements, and add a little math to the mix, it will open up a whole new world of information that you can use to make your business a better one. With critical analysis, the relationships among the numbers become clearer, as does the impact they can have on one another. Alternate ways of measuring the same numbers offer new perspectives and insights, those dull numbers begin to speak to you and then can spark innovative and profitable ideas.

Find the Needle in the Haystack

Issues Based on Concepts in Part Four

1. Who are the key players in finance and what do they do? Are they effective in holding the mirror, changing internal processes to meet outside challenges?
2. How do businessmen evaluate other companies? Look at any recent deal; did you think the price was correct?
3. How far can you stretch accounting standards?
4. Why does stock market fluctuate? Should we react?
5. 'Employees are our most valuable assets.' Are they really?
6. Do public sector companies really care about profits? Do loss making companies like Air India and BSNL have any economic value?
7. What do you think about your company's budgeting process? Is it backward-looking? Forward looking? Inward-looking or outward-looking? What changes would you like to suggest?
8. When was the last time you made an 'arms-length deal'. What factors influenced your decision to pay 'the fair price'?
9. Do you think the price for gold reflects its true value?

A List of Definitions as Used in the Book

1. **Accounting Standards**. 'Generally Accepted Accounting Principles' (GAAP) in India, called the Indian GAAP refers to the set of standards approved by National Advisory Council on Accounting Standards (NACAS) for recording of transactions in the company's books of accounts. Indian Company's Act 1956 makes it mandatory for all registered companies to comply with GAAP. The Auditor certifies this fact.
2. **Accounting Period and Fiscal Year**. More than 87% of the companies listed in the National Stock Exchange in India use the fiscal year for their accounting year. But some companies do use other periods. Sugar companies like to coincide their accounting period with the crushing season. Hindu businessmen use the 'Diwali' festival as the beginning of their accounting year. Some Indian companies owned by foreign companies must follow the accounting year of their parent.
3. **Accruals**. The purpose of accruals is to count the chickens before they hatch. In other words, to calculate a payment obligation, before it becomes payable. Good examples are

interest payments due by the year end, or rent for premises that is already paid up in for the full year. By using accruals, a company can measure what it owes looking forward and what cash revenue it expects to receive.

4. **Allocations**. Allocations are apportionments of overhead costs to different departments or products or geographical areas within the company. This is mainly used for reporting of segmental results.
5. **Amortization**. In financial literature you might find the words amortization and depreciation being used interchangeably. This is not correct. Depreciation refers to the expensing of physical assets like buildings, machinery. Amortization is the expensing of intangible assets like patents, and copyright.
6. **Angel Investors**. Angel investors are from friends and family, give more favorable terms than other lenders, as they are usually investing in the person rather than the viability of the business. They are focused on helping the business succeed, rather than reaping a huge profit from their investment. Angel investors are essentially the exact opposite of a venture capitalist.
7. **Annualization**. It is the process of converting a rate of any length into a rate that reflects the rate on an annual (yearly) basis. This is most often done on rates of less than one year, and usually does not take into account the effects of compounding. The annualized rate is not a guarantee but only an estimate, and its accuracy depends on the variance of the rate. This rate is also known as 'annualized return' and is similar to 'run rate' calculated by statisticians during a cricket match. For example, an investment that returns 1% a month returns 12% on an annualized basis. If, however, the value was computed after only one month, it is not certain that the 12% returns will be achieved.
8. **Bad Debts Provision**. When a business provides a service in good-faith to a customer on the promise of future payment, it

is considered income of the business. The amount receivable from such customers is kept in the balance sheet as something which the company owns. However, some customers fail to keep their promise and default. These amounts are deducted from revenue in the profit and loss account. It is called provision for bad debts.

9. **The Balance Sheet**. The balance sheet of a company is like your wedding photograph taken on a particular day. It shows what the company looks like on that day. It lists all that the company owns and all that it owes, and what it is worth on that day. It is called NET WORTH. Yes, you will try to put in your best appearance on your wedding day!

10. **Capital Expenditure**. Capital expenditure is the purchase of equipment or assets that last more than a year. Since equipments work only with human supervision, part of the salary of the personnel managing it also constitutes capital expenditure. These items appear on the balance sheet. Only a portion of these expenditures (depreciation) appear in the income statement, thus affecting profits.

11. **Channel Stuffing**. A deceptive business practice used by a company to inflate its sales and earnings figures by deliberately sending to dealers more products than they are able to sell to the public. By channel stuffing, distributors temporarily beef up their accounts receivables. However, unable to sell the excess products, retailers will send the excess items instead of cash back to the distributor, who must readjust its accounts receivable and ultimately its bottom line. In other words, stuffing always catches up with the company, because it cannot maintain sales at the rate it is stuffing. This is usually done fraudulently to raise the value of the stock.

12. **Depreciation**. It is a method used by accountants to match revenues of a period with its costs. Since the capital assets and other machinery used for producing the goods and services can be used for more than one year (*a typical accounting*

period) only a part of the cost of equipments used during the year is considered as cost of production for that year. That portion of the cost of the equipment is called depreciation.

13. **Discretionary Items**. There are some items in the profit and loss account, which is purely based on the discretionary judgment of the accountant. Provisions, contingent liabilities, contingent incomes, which become cost or income depending on events that are likely to happen or not happen. The accountant is expected to be conservative in estimating these. That means: hesitate to show it as income, but be eager to show it as a loss if there is any doubt.

14. **Earnings Multiple**. It is the price in the stock market for a company's share expressed as times the net profit of the company. Another form of the multiple is the ratio of price to the earnings of the company called P/E ratio. Some analysts consider this multiple as the expectation investors have on the company's future performance.

15. **Economic Profit Vs Accounting Profit**. Economic profit is revenues earned less opportunity costs. Opportunity costs are the alternative returns foregone. As a result, you may have a significant Accounting profit with little to no economic profit.

    Let us imagine that you invest ₹100,000 to start a business, and in that year you earn ₹120,000 in sales revenues. Your accounting profit would be ₹20,000. Now imagine, that same year you could have earned a net income of ₹45,000 as a salaried employee. Therefore, you have an economic loss of ₹–25,000 (120,000 – 100,000 – 45,000). *Most people are fooled into thinking that accounting profits are real additions to wealth*! The concept is also called 'Economic Value Added' (EVA).

16. **Financing A Company**. A company gets money for its various activities only from two sources. First, from its owners. This is variously called as 'owner's capital', 'share-

capital' or 'equity'. Second, from lenders. This is 'borrowings' by the company or is a 'debt' in the books. All other forms of financing the company are categorized under either 'Equity' or 'Debt'.

17. **Fixed Costs**. Fixed costs are costs that will continue whether or not any units are produced. These costs are 'fixed' over a specified period of time or range of production.

18. **Goodwill**. Goodwill comes into play when one company buys another company. It is the difference between net assets bought and the price actually paid. The buying company pays a premium over the stated net worth because it sees values in intangibles like brand-image, human talents, customer base and so on.

19. **Investment Gain or Capital Gain**. A profit results when the price of a marketable security held by a company rises above its purchase price. If the security is sold it is realized gain, if not it is unrealized gain. In both cases the accountant can show the profits in the income statement. A capital loss would occur when the opposite takes place. Many companies hold excess cash in the form of capital assets that can easily be converted into cash when needed.

20. **The Income Statement**. Also called the profit and loss account, or statement of earnings, or consolidated statement of operations. By whatever name, it is still an income statement, *for a period* showing total income, total expenses, and gross profit. The bottom line is net profit, after all other expenses and taxes are deducted. Some people talk about the top-line (sales/revenue), bottom-line (net result of operations) and middle-line (expenses). After all we need some journalese in the dry world of accounting too.

21. **Leveraged Buyout (LBO)**. The acquisition of another company using a significant amount of borrowed money (bonds or loans, usually a ratio of 90% debt to 10% equity) to meet the cost of acquisition. Often, the assets of the

company being acquired are used as collateral for the loans in addition to the assets of the acquiring company. The purpose of leveraged buyouts is to allow companies to make large acquisitions without having to commit a lot of capital. In an LBO, because of high debt/equity ratio, the bonds usually are not investment grade and are referred to as junk bonds. It can be considered ironic that a company's success (in the form of high value assets on the balance sheet) can be used against it as collateral by a hostile company that acquires it. For this reason, some regard LBOs as an especially ruthless, predatory tactic.

22. **Non-Cash Expense**. A non-cash expense is an item shown as cost in the income statement for which no cash has been paid out. This is merely an accounting practice to spread out the cost that is already incurred in some earlier occasion. Depreciation is a portion of the total cost shown this year; similarly provision is an anticipated cost for which no cash is paid now.

23. **Operating Expenses**. Operating expenses are needed to run the business day-to-day. These items like wages, salaries appear on the income statement, as deductions from total revenues, fully impacting profits.

24. **Owner's Equity**. Equity is the shareholder's present stake in the company. It is represented by the book-value as in the balance sheet. It is calculated by deducting all outside payments from what is owned by the company. Another way to see it is, to think of it as the cumulative impact of the results of doing business over several accounting periods. (*The share capital initially given to the company and its accumulations through profits (or deductions through losses) over several years*). This is the best measure of the financial performance of a business.

25. **Preferred Stock**. Preferred stock generally has a fixed rate of dividend that must be paid out before dividends to common

stockholders, if dividends are declared. Each company may have different terms and conditions for issue of such share. The best way to think of preference shares is to see it as having characteristics of both debt (fixed dividends) and equity (potential appreciation). There are pros and cons when looking at preferred shares. Preferred shareholders have priority over common stockholder in the event of liquidation and they have a fixed dividend (paid before common stockholders), but they have no voting rights and less potential for appreciation, in comparison.

26. **Present Value and Future Value**. In its most basic form present value principle states that a rupee *now* is worth more than a rupee *tomorrow*. That is because today is real and tomorrow is uncertain. The future is both uncertain and risky[7]. Finance people, therefore, *disallow a portion* of the future cash to make it worth as much as today. This portion that remains after disallowing is called discounted cash flow or the present value of future cash flows.

27. **Real Cash Transactions**. We stated that cash is real. Well, almost. Ramalinga Raju, chairman of Satyam Computers, shocked the world by revealing that he had overstated cash balances in the company accounts. He claimed that there was ₹53.61 billion in the bank when actually he had none. (*Although he was not the first businessman to do this!*). He did this by issuing fictitious invoices, which were paid for in fictitious cash and then making fictitious documents to show that these were deposited into the bank.

28. **Share Price**. The price of a share is arrived at by two unrelated parties willingly transacting. This price is therefore considered the 'fair-value' of the share. The value of a company is the total price of all its shares put together. It is called the 'market capitalization' of the company or its 'market value'.

29. **The Stock Market**. Also known as the equity market, in which shares are issued and traded. A SHARE is a slice/unit of ownership in a company. This market has two main

sections: the primary and secondary market. The primary market is where new issues called Initial Public Offering (IPO) are made. These shares are subsequently traded in the secondary market.

30. **Time Value of Money**. At the most basic level, the time value of money demonstrates that, all things being equal, it is better to have money now rather than later. This means that time literally is money - the value of the money you have now is not the same as it will be in the future and vice versa. You can then distinguish between the worth of investments that offer you returns at different times.

31. **Variable Costs**. Variable costs are costs that vary directly with the number of products produced. It is clear then that the higher the proportion of fixed costs, the more number of units must be produced and sold to reduce the average costs of each unit.

32. **Venture Capitalists**. Venture capital may include money, managerial and technical expertise. This form of raising capital is popular among new companies or ventures with limited operating history, which cannot raise funds by borrowing. The venture capitalists usually get a say in company decisions, and are partial owners in the business.

33. **Working Capital and Efficiency**. Working capital gives an idea of the company's underlying operational efficiency. Money that is tied up in inventory or money that customers still owe to the company cannot be used to pay off any of the company's obligations. So, if a company is not operating in the most efficient manner (*slow collection*), it will show up as an increase in the working capital. This can be seen by comparing the working capital from one period to another; slow collection may signal an underlying problem in the company's operations.

    If a company's current assets do not exceed its current liabilities, then it may run into trouble paying back creditors in the short term. The worst-case scenario is bankruptcy. A declining working capital ratio over a longer time period could also be a red flag that warrants further analysis. For example, it could be that the company's sales volumes are decreasing and, as a result, money due from customers (*accounts receivables number*) continues to get smaller and smaller.

Notes and References

Chapter One

1. The Satyam Scandal Sudhakar V. Balachandran, '*Corporate governance goes kaput—again.*' Forbes.com 01.07.09
2. http://www.mca.gov.in/Ministry/notification/pdf/AS_7.pdf '*Accounting Standard No.7. Construction Contracts*'.
3. '*Significant Accounting Policies of Major Telecom Operators in India - A Comparative Study*' A. John Thomas (June 2012 2081695 :Distributed in : Applied Accounting - Practitioner e-Journal) Vol.4, Issue 30, June 21, 2012
4. *Guideline for System on Accounting Separation* http://www.trai.gov.in/WriteReadData/Recommendation/Documents/rm.pdf
5. *Who Says Elephants Can't Dance*? : Leading a Great Enterprise through Dramatic Change. Louis V. Gerstner, Jr. Harper Business, 2002ISBN: 0-06-052379-4Cover price: US$27.95 372 pages
6. '*Reality Check at the Bottom of the Pyramid*' (HBR. June 2012) Erik Simanis

Chapter Two

1. Chapter seven: '*Predictive Nature of Ratios*'
2. International Accounting Standards Board:

About the IASB:

In March 2001, the International Accounting Standards Committee (IASC) Foundation was formed as a not-for-profit corporation incorporated in the State of Delaware, US. The IASC Foundation is the parent entity of the International Accounting Standards Board, an independent accounting standard-setter based in London, UK. On April 1, 2001, the International Accounting Standards Board (IASB) assumed accounting standard-setting responsibilities from its predecessor body, the International Accounting Standards Committee. This was the culmination of a restructuring based on the recommendations of the report *Recommendations on Shaping IASC for the Future*.

The IASB structure has the following main features:

- The IASC Foundation is an independent organization having two main bodies, the Trustees and the IASB, as well as a Standards Advisory Council and the International Financial Reporting Interpretations Committee.
- The IASC Foundation Trustees appoint the IASB members, exercise oversight and raise the funds needed, but the IASB has sole responsibility for setting accounting standards.

3. Chapter Eight: '*Comparative Ratio Analysis*'

Chapter Three

1. See Chapter One: '*Assumptions and Estimates and Biases*' (pp.4 onwards)
2. See Chapter Three: '*The Correct Definition of Profit*' (pp.43 onwards)

3. *Countries where the standard monetary unit of the US and its dependencies, divided into 100 cents.* (The standard monetary unit, comprising 100 cents, of the following countries or territories: Antigua and Barbuda, Australia, the Bahamas, Barbados, Belize, Bermuda, the British Virgin Islands, Brunei, Canada, the Cayman Islands, Dominica, East Timor, Ecuador, El Salvador, Fiji, Grenada, Guatemala, Guyana, Hong Kong, Jamaica, Kiribati, Liberia, Malaysia, the Marshall Islands, Micronesia, Namibia, Nauru, New Zealand, Saint Kitts and Nevis, Saint Lucia, Saint Vincent and the Grenadines, Singapore, Solomon Islands, Taiwan, Trinidad and Tobago, Tuvalu, and Zimbabwe.) Here we have used the term mainly to denote the business done by Indian IT companies in the USA
4. Richard Zeckhauser, Jayendu Patel: Project for David Dreman Foundation (1994)

Chapter Four

1. '*The Warren Buffett Way*': Investment Strategies of the World's Greatest Investor Robert G. Hagstrom
2. '*The Quest for Value*'. Stewart, G. Bennett, III (1991). New York: Harper Business. ISBN 0-88730-418-4

Chapter Five

1. References:
   (i) '*Credit Analysis : A Complete Guide*' Roger H. Hale, John Wiley and Sons.1983
   (ii) '*Readings in Financial Statement Analysis*' ICFA, 1985, White, Gerald I., A.C. Sondhi (Editors)
   (iii) 1997-2012 Topend Sports Network : http://www.topendsports.com/world/lists/greatest-all-time/cricket.htm, Last Modified: 11/22/2012

2. '*How Albert Dunlap Self-destructed*' - Business week July 6th 1998

Chapter Six

1. '*Putting on a Happier Profit face*': New York Times, May 16 1999: Edward Wyatt
2. Prof. Messod Daniel Beneish ('*The Detection of Earnings Manipulation*': Financial Analysts Journal 1999) finds by statistical evidence that presence of the following five factors increase the probability of fraud or earnings manipulation:

   a) Increasing days sales in receivable, b) Deteriorating gross margins c) Decreasing rates of depreciation d) Decreasing asset quality e) Growing sales
3. Prof. Messod Daniel Beneish ('*The Detection of Earnings Manipulation*': Financial Analysts Journal 1999)

Chapter Seven

1. '*The Black Swan*' : Nassim Nicholas Taleb, April 17, 2007, ISBN 978-1400063512 (U.S.), ISBN 978-0713999952 (U.K.). The Nobel winning psychologist Daniel Kahneman wrote 'The Black Swan changed my view of how the world works' and explains the 'influence' in his 2011 book : '*Thinking, Fast and Slow*'
2. Published annual Report of Idea Cellular, Suman Towers, Bombay: 2011
3. Published annual reports of Idea Cellular (2011), Reliance Communications (2011)
4. See for example: '*Managerial Efficiency, Organizational Capital and Productivity*'. Author Info: Michael Gort, Seong-Hoon Lee

5. References: (1) Groppelli, Angelico A.; Ehsan Nikbakht (2000). '*Finance*', *4th ed.* Barron's Educational Series, Inc... p. 444. ISBN 0-7641-1275-9. (2) Bodie, Zane; Alex Kane and Alan J. Marcus (2004). '*Essentials of Investments*', *5th ed.* McGraw-Hill Irwin. pp. 458–459. ISBN 0-07-251077-3.
6. '*The Ascent of Money*' Niall Ferguson: Paperback: 448 pages
   Publisher: Penguin Books; 1st edition (October 27, 2009) ISBN-10: 9861735844
   ISBN-13: 978-0143116172
7. '*Zeta Analysis: A New Model to Identify Bankruptcy Risk of Corporations*' Edward I. Altman, Rober G. Haldeman and Paul Narayanan. Journal of Banking and Finance, June 1997.

Chapter Ten

1. '*Saving Big Blue: Leadership Lessons and Turnaround Tactics of IBM's Lou Gerstner*' Robert Slater, Author McGraw-Hill Companies $24.95 (309p) ISBN 978-0-07-134211

Appendix I

Sample Financial Statements

The following is a sample set of financial statements for an imaginary company.

Dream Dolls International Ltd

The Balance Sheet (in Millions) as on 31-12-2012

	31-12-2012	31-12-2011
Assets		
Cash and Cash equivalents	83	72
Accounts Receivable	1,312	1,204
Inventory	1,270	1,514
Other Current Assets	85	67
Total Current Assets	2,750	2,857
Property plant and equipment	2,230	2,264
Other long term assets	213	233
Total Assets	**5,193**	**5,354**

Liabilities		
Accounts Payable	1,022	1,129
Credit	100	150
Current portion of long term debt	52	51
Total Current Liabilities	1,174	1,330
Long term debt	1,037	1,158
Other Long term liabilities	525	491
Total Liabilities	**2,736**	**2,979**
Shareholder's Equity Common stock, ₹1 par value (100,000,000 authorized, 74,000,000 outstanding in 2011 and 2012)	74	74
Additional Paid in capital	1,110	1,110
Retained Earnings	1,273	1,191
Total Shareholder's Equity	**2,457**	**2,375**
Total Liabilities and Shareholder's equity	**5,193**	**5,354**
Notes: (2010) *Depreciation : 239* *Number of shares : 74,000,000* *EPS : 3.35* *Dividend : 2.24*		

Dream Dolls International Ltd

Income Statement (in Millions) Year Ended 31-12-2012

	Year Ended 31-12-2012
Sales	8,689
Cost of Goods Sold	6,756
Gross Profit	1,933
Selling, General, and Admin Expenses (SG&A)	1,061
Depreciation	239
Other Income	19

Earnings Before Interest And Taxes (EBIT)	652
Interest Expense	191
Taxes	213
Net Profit	248

Dream Dolls International Ltd
Cash Flow Statement (in Millions) Year Ended 31-12-2012

	Year Ended 31-12-2012
Cash From Operating Activities	
Net Profit	248
Depreciation	239
Accounts Receivable	(108)
Inventory	244
Other Current Assets	(18)
Accounts Payable	(107)
Cash From Operations	498
Cash From Investing Activities	
PPE	(205)
Other Long Term Assets	20
Cash From Investing Activities	(185)
Cash From Financing Activities	
Credit	(50)
Current Portion of Long term Debt	1
Long-Term Debt	(121)
Other Long Term Liabilities	34
Dividends	(166)
Cash From Financing Activities	(302)
Change in Cash	11
Cash at the Beginning	72
Cash at the End	83

Appendix II

How to Derive the Cash Flow Statement from Two Balance Sheets and the Income Statement

We have stated in the text that the reader can derive the cash flow statement if he has two balance sheets and the income statement for the current year. We now demonstrate how this can be achieved. Please refer to Appendix I for the financial statements of Dream Dolls International Ltd.

The logic of the cash flow is as follows:

1. We start with the net profit and work backwards to reach the cash figure
2. Remember that all non cash expenses are added to net profit
3. Find out whether the changes in the balance sheet for all line items have either increased or decreased the cash flow of the business
4. All increases are added to net income and all decreases are subtracted
5. The key to this exercise is to determine whether changes have affected inflow/outflow of cash

We now demonstrate from our imaginary company figures:

Dream Dolls International Ltd
Cash Flow Statement (in Millions) Year Ended 31-12-2012

Company Activity	Impact on Cash	Changes in Net Cash Flow
We start with net profit		**248**
Depreciation of ₹239	Non-cash expense (add+)	239
Accounts receivable net increase ₹108	Customers keeping your cash (subtract–)	(108)
Inventory reduced ₹244	Sold inventory cash came in (add+)	244
Other current assets +18	Cash goes out to buy assets (subtract–)	(18)
PPE increases +205	Cash goes out (subtract–)	(205)
Other LT assets reduction –20	Assets sold off for cash (add +)	20
Accounts payable reduces –107	More payments to suppliers (subtract–)	(107)
Credit decreased –50	Less cash came in creditors (subtract–)	(50)
Current debt rise +1	More cash came in (add+)	1
LT debt reduction –121	Creditors given less (subtract–)	(121)
Other LT liabilities rose +34	Non-cash item (add+)	34
Dividends paid out ₹166	Direct Cash outflow (subtract–)	(166)
Net cash at end	Net off all (pluses and minuses)	**11**

In order to make the statement more sophisticated and suitable for further analysis we can rearrange all the above figures into three main activities:

1. Operating activities
2. Investing activities
3. Financing activities

We can now calculate the cash from each of the above activities as follows:

Company's Activities During the Year and Cash Inflow/Outflow from Each Activity	Year Ended 31-12-2012
Cash From Operating Activities	
Net Profit	248
Depreciation	239
Accounts Receivable	(108)
Inventory	244
Other Current Assets	(18)
Accounts Payable	(107)
Cash From Operations	**498**
Cash From Investing Activities	
PPE	(205)
Other Long Term Assets	20
Cash From Investing Activities	**(185)**
Cash From Financing Activities	
Credit	(50)
Current Portion of Long term Debt	1
Long-Term Debt	(121)
Other Long Term Liabilities	34
Dividends	(166)
Cash From Financing Activities	**(302)**
Change in Cash	11
Cash at the Beginning	72
Cash at the End	83

Author's Notes:

1. If you follow the simple rule of trying to discover the actual impact of every activity on cash in your company, you tend to make better decisions as a manager.
2. The above process looks simple enough in a simple imaginary model like this. But in real life accountants have to make several assumptions to arrive at the actual cash balance in the bank. For an illustration of this point see the appendix iii, the cash flow statement for BSNL, the telecom giant in India.

Appendix III

Bharat Sanchar Nigam Ltd.
The Complete Set of Financial Statements
Balance Sheet as at 31st March 2011

	As at 31st March 2011 (₹ in Lakh)	**As at 31st March 2010 (₹ in Lakh)**
Sources of Funds Shareholder's Funds		
Capital	1,250,000	1,250,000
Reserves and Surplus	6,756,875	7,397,566
Loan Funds		
Unsecured Loans	184,574	153,370
Deferred Tax-Liability Net	-	12,384
	8,191,449	**8,813,320**
Applications of Funds Fixed Assets		
Gross Block	16,704,374	16,046,962
Less Depreciation	9,544,982	8,658,930
Net Block	7,159,392	7,388,032
	7,688,828	**7,992,452**

Investments	**550,141**	**20,000**
Deferred Tax Asset-Net	9,215	-
Current Assets, Loans and Advances		
Inventories	394,824	505,833
Sundry Debtors	632,782	474,457
Cash and Bank Balances	250,008	3,034,340
Other Current Assets	292	85,521
Loans and Advances	1,351,882	1,397,028
	2,629,788	**5,497,179**
Less Current Liabilities and Provisions		
Current Liabilities	2,200,029	4,277,642
Provisions	639,243	557,602
	2,839,272	**4,835,244**
Net Current Assets	**(209,484)**	**661,935**
Inter/Intra Circle Remittance	152,749	138,933
Total	**8,191,449**	**8,813,320**
Accounting Policies		
Notes to Accounts		

Schedules referred to above form an integral part of the Balance Sheet

Author's Notes:

1. Accounting Policies, Schedules and Notes to Accounts are not printed for the sake of brevity.
2. For a complete annual report refer to: www.bsnl.co.in.
3. A full and complete reading of the report, including the Auditor's comments is necessary to form an opinion on some of the numbers presented in these statements, especially the policy on revenue recognition, depreciation and remittances and is a must to understand the financial situation.

Bharat Sanchar Nigam Ltd.
Profit and Loss Account for the Year Ended 31st March 2011

	For the Year Ended 31st March 2011 (₹ in Lakh)	**For the Year Ended 31st March 2010 (₹ in Lakh)**
Income		
Service Revenue and Other Operating Income	2,704,471	2,791,344
Other Income	264,291	413,197
	2,968,762	**3,204,541**
Expenditure		
Employees's Remuneration and Benefits	1,379,095	1,345,504
Licence Fee and Spectrum Fee	197,172	87,555
Administrative Operating and Other Expenses	1,012,368	1,019,905
Financial Expenses	38,986	35,161
Depreciation	972,543	919,679
	3,600,164	**3,407,804**
Profit Before Prior Period Items	–631,402	–203,263
Prior Period Items (Net)	–26,479	–16,485
Profit Before Taxation	–657,881	–219,748
Current Tax	0	0
Tax For Earlier Years	2,046	14,501
Deferred Tax	–21,599	–52,100
Fringe Benefit Tax	0	0
Wealth Tax	98	116
Profit For The Year After Taxation	–638,426	–182,265
Appropriation		
Proposed Dividends		
On Equity Share Capital	0	0
On Preference Share Capital	0	0
Tax On Dividends	0	0

Transfer to General Reserves	0	0
Surplus/Loss Carried to Balance Sheet	**–638,426**	**–182,265**
Earnings Per Share		
Basic Earnings Per Equity Share	–12.77	–3.65
Accounting Policies		
Notes to Accounts		

Author's Notes:

1. For a comparison of the nomenclatures used by telecommunications operators in their income statements see '*Significant Accounting Policies of Telecommunications Operators In India- A Comparative Study*' by the author published in SSRN.com June 2012.
2. Segment-wise P&L is given below and is important to note that comparison of BSNL with other operators may have many pitfalls.

Bharat Sanchar Nigam Ltd.

The Cash Flow Statement

(In Lakhs for the Year Ended 31-03-2011)

Particulars	**Year Ended 31st March 2011**		**Year Ended 31st March 2010**	
A. Cash Flow from Operating Activities				
Net Profit/Loss Before Tax But After Prior Period and Extraordinary Items		(657,881)		(219,748)
Adjustments for:				
Depreciation	972,543		919,679	
Prior Period Depreciation	9,259		10,464	
Utilization of General Reserve for Leave Encashment Provision for Earlier Period			(33,186)	

Particulars	Year Ended 31st March 2011		Year Ended 31st March 2010	
Utilization of Capital Reserve	(2,265)		(341)	
Provision for Impairment in CWIP	1,268		558	
Provision for Decommissioned Assets	6,638		(1,905)	
Interest/Finance Charges	38,986		35,161	
Interest Income	(74,519)		(245,699)	
Loss/Profit on Fixed Assets Sold	(4,545)		(2,468)	
Capitalization of Overheads	58,555	888,810	(63,428)	618,835
Operating Profit Before Working Capital Changes		**230,929**		**399,087**
Adjustment For Changes In Working Capital				
Change in Inventories	111,009		(48,575)	
Sundry Debtors	(158,325)		(2,403)	
Loans and Advances	130,636		(305,762)	
Current Liabilities	(2,077,214)		2,205,854	
Change in Provisions	81,653		63,727	
Change in Remittances	(13,816)		(27,584)	
Cash from Operations Before Taxes		**(1,926,057)**		**1,885,257**
Payment of Wealth Tax	(110)		(119)	
Payment of Income Tax	(87,537)		(159,886)	
Payment of FBT		**(87,647)**	(1,000)	**(161,005)**
Net Cash Generated from Operative Activities After Taxes		**(1,782,775)**		**2,123,339**
B. Cash Flow from Investing Activities				
Sale of Assets	159,504		128,798	
Purchase of Fixed Assets	(858,291)		(2,950,337)	

Capital Work in Progress	75,804		(104,217)	
Investment in Retirement Benefits	(530,141)			
Interest Received	159,748	**(993,376)**	247,417	**(2,678,339)**
C. Cash Flow from Financing Activities				
Unsecured Loan Adjustments	18,868		(189,934)	
Interest on Govt. Loan	(18,868)		(32,551)	
Interest on Deposits and Others	(8,181)	(8,181)	(1,605)	(224,090)
Net Cash Used in Financing Activities				
Net Increase/(Decrease) in Cash and Cash Equivalents		**(2,784,332)**		**(779,090)**
Opening Cash and Cash Equivalents		**3,034,340**		**3,813,430**
Cash and Cash Equivalents As at 31.03.2011		**250,008**		**3,034,340**
Cash and Cash Equivalents Comprise Cash, Cheques and Drafts (in Hand)	**1,987**		**2,257**	
Balance with Banks	**248,021**	**250,008**	**3,032,083**	**3,034,340**

Notes:

1. In the absence of adequate data regarding assets appearing in the deletion/adjustments column of the fixed assets schedule all deletions have been assumed to be cash sales.
2. In the absence of adequate details regarding unreconciled inter-circle remittances with the subsidiary records, all the inter-circle remittances have been treated as part of the working capital changes.
3. Figures in bracket show outflows.

Bharat Sanchar Nigam Ltd.
Segment Reporting
(For the Year Ended 31st March 2011 ₹ in Lac)

Particulars Revenue	For the Year Ended 31st March 2011				For the Year Ended 31st March 2010			
	Business Segments				Business Segments			
	Other Than Cellular	Cellular	Unallocable	Total	Other Than Cellular	Cellular	Unallocable	Total
Income from Services	1,634,911	1,069,560		27,04,471	1,721,600	1,069,744		2,791,344
Inter-Segment Revenue	119,436	4,3010		162,446	105,126	43,472		148,598
Other Income	146,241	41,677	1,854	189,772	133,200	32,674	1,624	167,498
Net Segment Revenue	1,900,588	1,154,247	1,854	3,056,689	1,959,926	114,890	1,624	3,107,440
Segment Results								
Operating Profit Before Interest and Taxes	(771,410)	125,895	(21,420)	(666,935)	(736,787)	381,711	58,724	(413,801)
Interest Income	33,036	221	41,262	74,519	5,562	319	239,818	245,699
Interest Expenses	(765)	(629)	(37,592)	(38,986)	(596)	0	(34,656)	(35,161)
Profit Before Prior Period and Extraordinary Items	(739,139)	125,487	(17,750)	(631,402)	(731,821)	382,029	146,529	(203,263)
Change in Accounting Policy								
Prior Period Adjustments	(21,403)	(5,076)	(17,750)	(26,479)	(8,357)	(8,128)		(164,85)
Profit Before Extra-ordinary Items	(760,542)	120,411		(657,881)	(740,178)	373,901	146,529	(219,748)
Extraordinary Items								
Profit Before Tax	(760,542)	120,411	(17,750)	(657,881)	(740,178)	373,901	146,529	(219,748)
Provision Ofr Current Tax								

Particulars Revenue	For the Year Ended 31st March 2011				For the Year Ended 31st March 2010			
Provision for Wealth Tax			(98)	(98)			(116)	(116)
Provision for Fringe Benefit Tax								
Mat Credit								52,100
Provision for Deferred Tax			21,599	21,599			52,100	
Provision for Earlier Years' Tax			(2,046)	(2,046)			(14,501)	(14,501)
Profit After Tax	(760,542)	120,411	1,705	(638,426)	(740,178)	373,901	184,012	(182,265)
Other Information								
Segment Assets	10,354,140	72,139	777,690	11,853,219	8,529,182	2,807,182	3,115,427	1,445,1791
Segment Liabilities	1,705,399	605,832	1,481,241	3,792,445	1,994,197	2,400,477	1,469,911	5,864,585
Capital Expenditure	(232,281)	813,876	(3,391)	578,204	506,133	2,423,137	(6,077)	293,193
Depreciation	610,444	361,698	401	972,543	683,147	236,076	456	919,679
Non Cash Expense Other than Depreciation	91,332	18,137		109,468	104,822	16,459		121,281

Author's Notes:

1. The presence of un-allocable amounts makes the BSNL's claim to have a profitable cellular segment look somewhat unconvincing.
2. This issue might be a pointer to the internal accounting process and maintenance of records on revenues and costs.